Middle School 2-2

기말고사 완벽대비

KB084520

적중 100

영어 기출 문제집

중 **2**

시사 | 박준언

Best Collection

구성과 특징

교과서의 주요 학습 내용을 중심으로 학습 영역별 특성에 맞춰 단계별로 다양한 학습 기회를 제공하여 단원별 학습능력 평가는 물론 중간 및 기말고사 시험 등에 완벽하게 대비할 수 있도록 내용을 구성

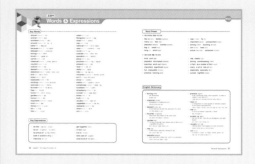

Words & Expressions

Step1   Key Words 단원별 핵심 단어 설명 및 풀이
         Key Expression 단원별 핵심 숙어 및 관용어 설명
         Word Power 반대 또는 비슷한 뜻 단어 배우기
         English Dictionary 영어로 배우는 영어 단어

Step2   실력평가 단원별 수시평가 대비 주관식, 객관식 문제풀이

Step3   서술형 대비 학업성취도 및 수행능력평가 대비 서술형 문제풀이

Conversation

Step1   핵심 의사소통 의사소통에 필요한 주요 표현 방법 요약
         핵심 Check 기본적인 표현 방법 및 활용능력 확인

Step2   대화문 익히기 상황에 따른 대화문 활용 및 연습

Step3   기본평가 시험대비 기초 학습 능력 평가

Step4   실력평가 단원별 수시평가 대비 주관식, 객관식 문제풀이

Step5   서술형 대비 학업성취도 및 수행능력평가 대비 서술형 문제풀이

Grammar

Step1   주요 문법 단원별 주요 문법 사항과 예문을 알기 쉽게 설명
         핵심 Check 기본 문법사항에 대한 이해 여부 확인

Step2   기본평가 시험대비 기초 학습 능력 평가

Step3   실력평가 단원별 수시평가 대비 주관식, 객관식 문제풀이

Step4   서술형 대비 학업성취도 및 수행능력평가 대비 서술형 문제풀이

Reading

Step1   구문 분석 단원별로 제시된 문장에 대한 구문별 분석과 내용 설명
         확인문제 문장에 대한 기본적인 이해와 인지능력 확인

Step2   확인학습A 빈칸 채우기를 통한 문장 완성 능력 확인

Step3   확인학습B 제시된 우리말을 영어로 완성하여 작문 능력 키우기

Step4   실력평가 단원별 수시평가 대비 주관식, 객관식 문제풀이

Step5   서술형 대비 학업성취도 및 수행능력평가 대비 서술형 문제풀이
         교과서 구석구석 교과서에 나오는 기타 문장까지 완벽 학습

Composition

|영역별 핵심문제|

단어 및 어휘, 대화문, 문법, 독해 등 각 영역별 기출문제의 출제 유형을 분석하여 실전에 대비하고 연습할 수 있도록 문제를 배열

|서술형 실전 및 창의사고력 문제|

학교 시험에서 점차 늘어나는 서술형 시험에 집중 대비하고 고득점을 취득하는데 만전을 기하기 위한 학습 코너

|단원별 예상문제|

기출문제를 분석한 후 새로운 시험 출제 경향을 더하여 새롭게 출제될 수 있는 문제를 포함하여 시험에 완벽하게 대비할 수 있도록 준비

|단원별 모의고사|

영역별, 단계별 학습을 모두 마친 후 실전 연습을 위한 모의고사

INSIGHT
on the textbook

교과서 파헤치기

- 단어Test1~2 영어 단어 우리말 쓰기와 우리말을 영어 단어로 쓰기
- 대화문Test1~2 대화문 빈칸 완성 및 전체 대화문 쓰기
- 본문Test1~5 빈칸 완성, 우리말 쓰기, 문장 배열연습, 영어 작문하기 복습 등 단계별 반복 학습을 통해 교과서 지문에 대한 완벽한 습득
- 구석구석지문Test1~2 지문 빈칸 완성 및 전문 영어로 쓰기

Contents

Lesson 7

Work on Your Dreams

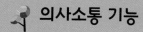 **의사소통 기능**

- 강조하기
  It's important that you never give up.

- 설명 요청하기
  What do you mean by that?

언어 형식

- 'ask/want+A+to부정사 구문
  Other teams **asked** African American players **to join** them.

- 목적격 관계대명사
  I will become a player **who** people like.

Words & Expressions

Key Words

- **achieve** [ətʃíːv] 동 이루다, 달성하다
- **although** [ɔːlðóu] 접 비록 ~일지라도
- **American** [əmérikən] 명 미국인 형 미국의
- **as** [əz] 전 ~로(자격)
- **award** [əwɔ́ːrd] 명 상
- **base** [beis] 명 야구의 루
- **baseman** [béismən] 명 (1·2·3) 루수
- **bat** [bæt] 동 (공을) 치다
- **calm** [kɑːm] 형 침착한
- **classical** [klǽsikəl] 형 (음악이) 클래식의
- **color line** 인종 차별
- **difficulty** [dífikʌlti] 명 어려움, 곤경, 장애
- **earn** [əːrn] 동 얻다, 획득하다
- **effort** [éfərt] 명 노력
- **ever** [évər] 부 언젠가 한 번이라도
- **excellence** [éksələns] 명 우수, 탁월, 뛰어남
- **excellent** [éksələnt] 형 뛰어난
- **face** [feis] 동 직면하다, 직시하다
- **fail** [feil] 동 실패하다, ~하지 못하다
- **finally** [fáinəli] 부 마침내
- **gentle** [dʒéntl] 형 점잖은
- **high five** 하이파이브(기쁨의 표시로 두 사람이 팔을 들어 서로 손바닥을 마주치는 것)
- **honor** [ánər] 동 예우하다, ~을 공경하다
- **lend** [lend] 동 빌려주다
- **major** [méidʒər] 형 주요한
- **Nobel Prize** 명 노벨상
- **overcome** [óuvərkəm] 동 극복하다
- **pain** [pein] 명 아픔, 고통
- **perfect** [pə́ːrfikt] 형 완벽한
- **phrase** [freiz] 명 구, 구절
- **plus** [plʌs] 전 게다가, 덧붙여
- **positive** [pázətiv] 형 긍정적인
- **present** [prizént] 동 주다, 수여하다, 증정하다
- **recognize** [rékəgnàiz] 동 인정하다, 알아보다
- **recycle** [riːsáikl] 동 재활용하다
- **respect** [rispékt] 명 존경
- **rudely** [rúːdli] 부 무례하게
- **sentence** [séntəns] 명 문장
- **skater** [skéitər] 명 스케이트 선수
- **solve** [sɑlv] 동 풀다, 해결하다
- **stadium** [stéidiəm] 명 경기장, 스타디움
- **support** [səpɔ́ːrt] 명 지지
- **talented** [tǽləntid] 형 재능이 있는
- **team** [tiːm] 명 (경기 등의) 팀
- **teammate** [tímeit] 명 팀 동료
- **terrible** [térəbl] 형 무서운
- **wish** [wiʃ] 동 바라다, 원하다
- **with** [wið] 전 ~와 함께, ~함에 따라

Key Expressions

- **achieve a goal** 목표를 달성하다
- **at bat** 타석에서
- **be good at** ~을 잘하다
- **by 동사ing** ~함으로써
- **cannot believe one's eyes** 눈을 의심하다(놀람)
- **earn the respect** 존경을 얻다
- **give up** 포기하다
- **help+목적어+(to) 동사원형** (목적어)가 ~하는 것을 돕다
- **keep calm** 평온을 유지하다
- **keep 동명사** ~하는 것을 계속하다
- **more than** ~보다 많이
- **no longer** 더 이상 ~ 아닌
- **one of 복수명사** ~중의 하나
- **over and over** 반복해서
- **present A with B** A에게 B를 수여하다, 증정하다
- **shout at** ~을 향해 외치다
- **take a class** 수업을 듣다
- **thanks to** ~ 덕분에
- **think to oneself** 마음속으로 생각하다
- **turn down** ~을 거절하다, 거부하다, 소리를 줄이다
- **win first place** 1등을 하다, 우승하다

Word Power

※ 형용사 – 명사

- □ **different**(다른) – **difference**(다름, 차이)
- □ **important**(중요한) – **importance**(중요성)
- □ **silent**(조용한) – **silence**(침묵)

- □ **excellent**(우수한) – **excellence**(우수, 장점)
- □ **significant**(중요한) – **significance**(중요성)

※ 비슷한 의미를 가진 어휘들

- □ **gentle**(점잖은) : **kind**(친절한)
- □ **respect**(존경) : **admiration**(존경)

- □ **finally**(마침내) : **in the end**(결국, 마침내)

English Dictionary

- □ **award** 상
  → a prize or other reward that is given to someone who has achieved something
  어떤 것을 달성한 사람에게 주어지는 상이나 다른 보상
- □ **baseman** (1·2·3) 루수
  → a player stationed at a base 베이스에 배치된 선수
- □ **bat** (공을) 치다
  → to hit the ball with a bat in a game such as baseball or cricket
  야구나 크리켓 경기에서 방망이로 공을 치다
- □ **calm** 침착한
  → not affected by strong emotions such as excitement, anger, shock, or fear
  흥분, 화, 충격 또는 공포 같은 강한 감정에 의해 영향을 받지 않은
- □ **classical** (음악이) 클래식의
  → relating to classical music 클래식 음악과 관련이 있는
- □ **earn** 얻다, 획득하다
  → to get something as a result of your efforts or your behavior 노력이나 행동의 결과로 어떤 것을 얻다
- □ **excellent** 뛰어난
  → unusually or extremely good 대단히, 심히 좋은
- □ **fail** 실패하다, ~하지 못하다
  → to be unable to do something 어떤 것을 할 수 없다
- □ **honor** 예우하다, ~을 공경하다
  → to show your respect or admiration for someone, especially by giving them a prize or title, or by praising them publicly
  특히 상이나 타이틀을 주거나, 공적으로 칭찬함으로써 어떤 사람에게 존경이나 칭찬을 보여주다
- □ **lend** 빌려주다
  → to give someone the use of something for a limited time 어떤 것을 제한된 시간 동안 사용하게 주다

- □ **major** 주요한
  → greater or more important than other people or things in a group
  한 그룹 안에서 다른 사람이나 사물보다 더 중요한
- □ **overcome** 극복하다
  → to succeed in dealing with or controlling a problem
  문제를 다루거나 통제하는 데 성공하다
- □ **pain** 아픔, 고통
  → a feeling that you have in a part of your body when you are hurt or ill 아프거나 다쳤을 때 몸의 일부에서 갖는 느낌
- □ **positive** 긍정적인
  → believing that good things will happen rather than bad ones 나쁜 일보다 좋은 일이 발생하리라 믿는
- □ **recognize** 인정하다, 알아보다
  → to see and know what someone or something is
  사람이나 사물이 무엇인지 알다
- □ **rudely** 무례하게
  → in a way that shows no respect for others
  다른 사람에 대한 존중을 보이지 않는 방식으로
- □ **sentence** 문장
  → a sequence of words forming a meaningful grammatical structure
  의미 있는 문법의 구조를 형성하는 일련의 단어들
- □ **support** 지지
  → help and kindness that you give to someone who is having a difficult time
  어려움을 겪고 있는 사람에게 주는 도움과 친절
- □ **team** (경기 등의) 팀
  → a group of people who work together or play a game or sport together
  같이 일하거나 게임이나 운동을 함께 하는 한 무리의 사람들
- □ **teammate** 팀 동료
  → a person who is in the same team 같은 팀에 있는 사람

[01~02] 다음 빈칸에 들어갈 말로 적절한 것은?

01

> He will _____ many difficulties in his life.

① celebrate   ② achieve
③ increase   ④ encourage
⑤ overcome

02 중요

> She doesn't _____ much money, but she enjoys the work.

① earn   ② effort
③ experience   ④ respect
⑤ turn

[03~04] 다음 빈칸에 공통으로 들어갈 말로 알맞은 것은?

03

> • She wanted to _____ his proposal, so she said 'no' to him.
> • Could you _____ the volume? I can't concentrate on my study.

① calm down   ② break down
③ turn down   ④ pick up
⑤ take up

04 중요

> • He took a deep breath and tried to _____ calm.
> • I don't know what I'll do if gas prices _____ going up.

① take   ② keep   ③ get
④ hold   ⑤ have

05 중요 두 문장이 같은 의미가 되도록 빈칸에 알맞은 것을 고르시오.

> • _____ he has financial problems, he has bought a new car.
> = In spite of his financial problems, he has bought a new car.

① However   ② Although
③ When   ④ Therefore
⑤ Unless

[06~07] 다음 영영풀이에 해당하는 단어를 고르시오.

06

> not affected by strong emotions such as excitement, anger, shock, or fear

① calm   ② nervous
③ serious   ④ comfortable
⑤ quiet

07

> to show your respect or admiration for someone, especially by giving them a prize or title, or by praising them publicly

① award   ② honor
③ solution   ④ effort
⑤ contest

01 다음 밑줄 친 부분과 의미가 가장 가까운 것을 주어진 철자로 시작하여 쓰시오.

> The little boy was so <u>scared</u> that he made a lot of mistakes.

➡ a_____

02 두 문장에 공통으로 들어갈 수 있는 단어를 〈보기〉에서 골라 쓰시오.

┌─── 보기 ───┐
as   at   for   from   in   to
└────────────┘

- Who is the player _____ bat now?
- I'm really poor _____ math and I want to become good _____ it.

03 괄호 안에 주어진 단어를 알맞게 배열하시오.

(1) 그들은 연습을 통해 더 빨라졌다.
(practice, they, faster, with, became)
➡ _____

(2) 난 여름방학 계획을 따르는 데 실패했다.
(to, vacation, I, plan, the, failed, follow, summer)
➡ _____

(3) 내가 그걸 처음 봤을 때, 내 눈을 믿을 수 없었다.
(couldn't, when, I, my, I, that, first, believe, eyes, saw)
➡ _____

04 다음 빈칸에 알맞은 단어를 〈보기〉에서 골라 쓰시오. (한 단어는 한 번 밖에 사용할 수 없음)

┌─── 보기 ───┐
excellent   major   positive   talented
└────────────┘

(1) He also spends a lot of time finding _____ artists.
(2) This is a _____ cause for concern.
(3) It's an _____ place to relax.
(4) Are you a _____ person or a negative person?

05 다음 우리말에 맞게 빈칸을 채우시오. (철자가 주어진 경우 그 철자로 시작할 것)

(1) 우리는 인종 차별을 하지 않는다.
➡ We do not draw the _____.

(2) Tony는 팀에서 1루수를 맡고 있다.
➡ Tony is the first _____ for the team.

(3) 비록 그들은 가난할지라도 행복하다.
➡ A_____ they are poor, they are happy.

(4) 그 프로젝트를 끝내는 데 많은 노력이 들었다.
➡ It took a lot of _____ to finish the project.

(5) 언젠가 우리 도움이 필요하면, 나한테 전화해.
➡ If you _____ need our help, just call me.

Conversation

① 강조하기

> **It's important that you never give up.** 절대 포기하지 않는 것이 중요해.

- 'It's important ~.'는 '~가 중요해'의 의미이다. important 다음에는 to부정사나 that절이 올 수 있다. 여기서 it은 가주어이며, to부정사나 that절은 진주어이다.

- important와 비슷한 뜻인 essential, critical, significant 등을 대신 사용할 수 있다.

강조하기

- It's important that 주어 동사 ~. (~하는 것이 중요해.)
- It's important to 동사원형 ~. (~하는 것이 중요해.)
- I want to stress ~. (~을 강조하고 싶어.)

- 'It's important to 동사원형 ~.'에서 '~하지 않는 것이 중요하다.'의 의미이면 to부정사 앞에 not을 붙여 'It's important not to 동사원형 ~.'으로 문장을 만들 수 있다.

핵심 Check

1. 다음 우리말과 일치하도록 빈칸에 알맞은 말을 쓰시오.

   A: I'm sorry, Ms. Song. (송 선생님, 죄송해요.)

   B: You're late again.＿＿＿＿＿＿＿ on time. (또 늦었구나. 시간 약속을 지키는 것이 중요하단다.)

2. 다음 대화의 순서를 바르게 배열하시오.

   (A) It's important to stay healthy.

   (B) But I have a big test tomorrow.

   (C) You need to rest.

   ➡ ＿＿＿＿＿＿＿＿＿＿＿＿

3. 괄호 안의 단어를 순서대로 배열하여 대화를 완성하시오.

   A: What is important when I play soccer?

   B: ＿＿＿＿＿＿＿＿＿＿＿ (is, a, to, it, lot, practice, important)

   (연습을 많이 하는 것이 중요해.)

2 설명 요청하기

What do you mean by that? (그게 무슨 뜻이니?)

■ 'What do you mean by that?'은 '그게 무슨 뜻이니?'라는 뜻으로 상대방과의 대화에서 이해하지 못한 부분이 있거나, 의도를 파악하지 못했을 때 부연 설명을 요청하는 의미로 쓰는 표현이다. that은 상대방이 말한 내용을 언급하는 대명사이고 by that은 '그 말로써, 그것으로'라는 뜻으로, 직역하면 '그 말로써 너는 무엇을 의미하니?'라는 뜻이다.

설명 요청하기

- What do you mean (by that)? (그게 무슨 뜻이니?)
- What is that exactly? (그게 정확히 뭐니?)
- What exactly do you mean? (정확하게 무슨 뜻이니?)
- Could you explain about that in detail? (그것을 자세히 설명해 줄 수 있나요?)

■ 설명을 할 때는 '~을 의미하다'의 뜻을 가진 'mean'을 사용해 'It means ~. (그것은 ~ 뜻이야.)'로 대답할 수 있다.

설명하기

- It means ~. (~라는 뜻이야.) • I mean ~. (~라는 뜻이야.)

핵심 Check

4. 다음 대화의 순서를 바르게 배열하시오.

   (A) She's a busy worker.

   (B) She's a busy bee.

   (C) What do you mean by that?

   ➡ _____

5. 괄호 안의 단어를 순서대로 배열하여 대화를 완성하시오.

   A: When it rains, it pours.

   B: _____ (that, could, about, you, explain)
   (그것이 무슨 뜻인지 설명해 줄래?)

   A: It means "When problems come, they come together."

Listen & Speak 1 A-1

G: Hey, Minho. Did you find the answer to the math problem?

B: No. ❶It's too hard for me. ❷I'm not good at math.

G: ❸Let me see. ❹It's important that you use this math rule ❺to solve the problem.

B: Oh, I see. I'll use ❻it.

G: 이봐, 민호야. 이 수학 문제의 정답을 찾았니?

B: 아니. 그건 나에게 너무 어려워. 나는 수학을 잘하지 못 해.

G: 내가 한 번 볼게. 네가 그 문제를 풀기 위해선 이 수학 공식을 이용하는 것이 중요해.

B: 오, 알겠어. 그걸 사용해 볼게.

---

❶ It = The math problem, too: 너무, hard: 어려운

❷ be good at: ～을 잘하다

❸ 대화중에 질문을 받았을 때나 생각할 시간이 필요하면 'Let me think.'나 'Let me see.'라고 말할 수 있다

❹ that 이하의 내용을 강조할 때 'It's important that 주어 동사 ～.'를 사용하며, '～하는 것이 중요해.'의 의미이다.

❺ to부정사의 부사적 용법으로 '～하기 위해서'의 의미이다.

❻ it = this math rule

Check(√) True or False

(1) The math problem was too hard, so the boy didn't find the answer.　　T ☐ F ☐

(2) The girl is better at math than the boy.　　T ☐ F ☐

Listen & Speak 2 A-1

G: Oh, this is hard to do.

B: ❶What's the matter?

G: Can you ❷teach me how to make cookies?

B: Sure. It's a walk in the park.

G: ❸What do you mean by that?

B: ❹I mean it's easy to do.

G: 오, 이것은 하기 어렵구나.

B: 무슨 일이야?

G: 쿠키를 만드는 방법을 나에게 가르쳐 줄 수 있니?

B: 물론이지. 그건 'a walk in the park'야.

G: 그게 무슨 뜻이니?

B: 하기 쉽다는 뜻이야.

---

❶ 상대방의 슬픔이나 불만족, 실망의 원인에 대해 물을 때 사용되는 표현으로 What's the matter?가 쓰이며 '무슨 일[문제] 있니?'라는 뜻이다 (= What's wrong? = What's the problem? = What happened?)

❷ teach(4형식동사)+me(간접목적어,～에게)+how to make cookies(직접목적어,～을, 를), how to 동사원형: ～하는 방법

❸ 상대방에게 설명을 요청할 때 'What do you mean by that?'이라고 말한다.

❹ 설명을 요청하는 질문에 대한 대답으로 'It means ～.'나 'I mean ～.'으로 대답할 수 있다.

Check(√) True or False

(3) The boy doesn't know how to make cookies.　　T ☐ F ☐

(4) "It's a walk in the park" means that it's easy to do.　　T ☐ F ☐

Listen & Speak 1 A-2

G: Your poster looks great.

B: Thanks, Kate. Did you finish ❶yours?

G: Not yet. ❷I can't draw well. How can I become good at drawing?

B: It ❸takes time. ❹It's important that you draw as often as you can.

G: ❺You mean I should keep practicing?

B: That's right.

❶ yours = your poster
❷ draw: (그림을) 그리다 well은 부사로 동사인 draw를 수식하고 있다.
❸ take: (얼마의 시간이) 걸리다
❹ 강조할 때는 'It's important that 주어 동사 ~.(~가 중요해.)'를 사용한다.
❺ You mean ~?: ~라는 뜻이니? keep 동명사: ~하는 것을 계속하다

Listen & Speak 2 A-2

B: I have a singing contest tomorrow. I really ❶ want to win first place.

G: I'll keep my fingers crossed for you.

B: ❷What do you mean by "keep my fingers crossed"?

G: ❸It means I wish you good luck.

B: Thank you.

❶ want는 to부정사를 목적어로 취한다. win first place: 1등을 하다, 우승하다
❷ 'What do you mean by ~?(~가 무슨 뜻이니?)'는 상대방이 말한 것을 제대로 이해하지 못하여 설명을 요청할 때 사용하는 표현이다.
❸ means와 I 사이에 접속사 that이 생략되어 있다.

Conversation A

M: ❶To achieve my dream, I went to many auditions, but I often failed. ❷However, I never gave up. I ❸took acting and dancing classes. ❹Finally, I achieved my goal. ❺It's important that you never give up.

❶ to부정사의 부사적 용법(목적)을 사용하여 '~하기 위해서'로 해석한다. achieve: 이루다, 달성하다
❷ however: 하지만 give up: 포기하다
❸ take a class: 수업을 듣다
❹ finally: 마침내 achieve a goal: 목표를 달성하다
❺ It's important that 주어 동사 ~: ~하는 것이 중요하다

Conversation B

Hana: You ❶look sad, Jiho. What's wrong?

Jiho: ❷I don't think I can achieve my dream.

Amy: ❸What do you mean by that?

Jiho: I want to be an actor, but I ❹always fail auditions. Maybe I have to give up.

Amy: Do you know this actor?

Jiho: Sure. He's a famous movie star.

Amy: He failed ❺more than 100 auditions.

Jiho: Really? Maybe I ❻should keep trying. I will practice more for my next audition.

Hana: That's right! ❼It's important that you never give up.

❶ look+형용사: ~해 보이다
❷ think와 I 사이에 접속사 that이 생략되어 있다. think의 목적어는 'I can achieve my dream'이다.
❸ What do you mean by that?: 그게 무슨 뜻이니? (= What is that exactly? = What exactly do you mean? = Could you explain about that in detail?)
❹ always(항상)는 빈도부사로 be동사나 조동사 뒤에, 일반동사 앞에 위치한다. fail: 실패하다, ~하지 못하다
❺ more than: ~ 이상
❻ should+동사원형: ~해야 한다 keep 동명사: ~하는 것을 계속하다
❼ never: 결코 ~하지 않다 give up: 포기하다

Communication Task Step 2

A: Please ❶call me "Speedy Feet."

B: ❷What do you mean by "Speedy Feet"?

A: I mean I want to be a runner.

B: What is important to do to become a runner?

A: ❸It's important that I practice running every day.

B: I'm sure you'll ❹make it.

❶ call+목적어+목적격보어: ~을 …라고 부르다
❷ What do you mean by ~?: ~가 무슨 뜻이니?
❸ It's important that 주어 동사 ~: ~하는 것이 중요하다
❹ make it: 성공하다, 해내다

● 다음 우리말과 일치하도록 빈칸에 알맞은 말을 쓰시오.

Listen & Speak 1 A

1. **G:** Hey, Minho. Did you _____ the answer to the math _____?

   B: No. It's _____ _____ for me. _____ _____ _____

   _____ _____.

   G: Let me see. _____ _____ _____ you use this math rule

   to _____ the problem.

   B: Oh, I see. I'll use it.

2. **G:** Your poster _____ great.

   B: Thanks, Kate. Did you _____ yours?

   G: Not yet. I can't _____ well. _____ can I become _____

   at drawing?

   B: It _____ time. It's _____ that you draw _____ _____

   _____ you can.

   G: You mean I should _____ _____?

   B: That's right.

Listen & Speak 1 B

1. **A:** It's _____ _____ _____ a good dancer. _____ should

   I do?

   B: It's _____ that you _____ give up.

   A: Okay. I will _____ _____ that.

2. **A:** It's _____ _____ write a good story. What should I do?

   B: _____ _____ _____ you read many books.

   A: Okay. I _____ _____ forget that.

Listen & Talk 2 A

1. **G:** Oh, this is _____ _____ _____ _____.

   B: What's the matter?

   G: Can you teach me _____ _____ make cookies?

   B: Sure. It's a walk in the park.

   G: _____ _____ _____ _____ _____ _____ that?

   B: I _____ it's easy to do.

2. **B:** I _____ a singing contest tomorrow. I really _____ _____ _____ first place.

   G: I'll keep my fingers _____ for you.

   B: _____ _____ _____ _____ _____ "keep my fingers crossed"?

   G: It _____ I wish you good _____.

   B: Thank you.

Listen & Talk 2 B

1. **A:** Two heads _____ better _____ one.

   B: _____ do you _____ _____ "Two heads are better than one"?

   A: I _____ working _____ is better _____ working _____.

2. **A:** _____ makes perfect.

   B: What do you _____ by "Practice makes perfect"?

   A: I _____ you learn something _____ _____ it _____ and over.

Conversation A

M: _____ _____ my dream, I went to many auditions, but I often _____. _____, I never gave _____. I _____ acting and dancing classes. _____, I _____ my goal. It's important that you _____ _____ up.

Conversation B

Hana: You _____ sad, Jiho. What's wrong?

Jiho: I don't think I can _____ my dream.

Amy: _____ _____ _____ _____ _____ _____ _____?

Jiho: I want to be an actor, but I always _____ _____. Maybe I have to _____ _____.

Amy: Do you know this actor?

Jiho: Sure. He's a _____ movie star.

Amy: He failed _____ _____ 100 auditions.

Jiho: Really? Maybe I should keep _____. I will _____ more for my next audition.

Hana: That's right! It's important that _____ _____ _____ _____.

해석

2. **B:** 나 내일 노래 경연 대회가 있어. 나는 정말 1등을 하고 싶어.
   G: 너에게 'keep my fingers crossed'할게.
   B: 'keep my fingers crossed'가 무슨 뜻이니?
   G: 그건 내가 너에게 행운을 빈다는 뜻이야.
   B: 고마워.

1. **A:** 두 개의 머리가 머리 하나보다 낫다.
   B: "두 개의 머리가 머리 하나보다 낫다."가 무슨 뜻이니?
   A: 함께 일하는 것이 혼자 일하는 것보다 낫다는 뜻이야.

2. **A:** 연습이 완벽함을 만든다.
   B: "연습이 완벽함을 만든다."가 무슨 뜻이니?
   A: 반복해서 무언가를 하면 배우게 된다는 뜻이야.

M: 내 꿈을 이루기 위해 나는 많은 오디션에 갔지만 자주 떨어졌다. 하지만 나는 절대 포기하지 않았다. 나는 연기와 춤 수업을 들었다. 마침내 나는 내 목표를 이뤘다. 절대 포기하지 않는 것이 중요하다.

하나: 너 슬퍼 보여, 지호야. 무슨 일이니?
지호: 내 생각에 나는 꿈을 이룰 수 없을 것 같아.
Amy: 그게 무슨 말이니?
지호: 나는 배우가 되고 싶지만 항상 오디션에서 떨어져. 어쩌면 나는 포기해야 할 거 같아.
Amy: 너 이 배우를 아니?
지호: 당연하지. 그는 유명한 영화배우잖아.
Amy: 그는 백 번 이상 오디션에서 떨어졌어.
지호: 정말? 그러면 나도 계속 노력해야겠구나. 나는 다음 오디션을 위해서 더 연습할 거야.
하나: 바로 그거야! 절대 포기하지 않는 것이 중요해.

Conversation 시험대비 기본평가

[01~02] 다음 대화의 빈칸에 알맞은 말은?

01

> G: Hey, Minho. Did you find the answer to the math problem?
> B: No. It's too hard for me. I'm not good at math.
> G: Let me see. _____
> B: Oh, I see. I'll use it.

① It's important to study math.

② It's important that you know many words.

③ It's important that you use this math rule to solve the problem.

④ It's important that you turn off the music when you study.

⑤ It's important that you decide what to do.

02

> G: Oh, this is hard to do.
> B: What's the matter?
> G: Can you teach me how to make cookies?
> B: Sure. It's a walk in the park.
> G: _____
> B: I mean it's easy to do.

① What do you mean by that? ② Where did you walk?

③ Why do you say so? ④ How is he doing?

⑤ What's the matter?

03 주어진 문장 다음에 이어질 대화의 순서로 알맞은 것을 고르시오.

> I have a singing contest tomorrow. I really want to win first place.

> (A) It means I wish you good luck.
> (B) What do you mean by "keep my fingers crossed"?
> (C) I'll keep my fingers crossed for you.
> (D) Thank you.

① (B) – (A) – (C) – (D) ② (B) – (C) – (A) – (D)

③ (C) – (A) – (B) – (D) ④ (C) – (B) – (A) – (D)

⑤ (C) – (D) – (B) – (A)

[01~03] 다음 대화를 읽고 물음에 답하시오.

G: Your poster looks great. (①)
B: Thanks, Kate. (②)
G: Not yet. I can't draw well. (③) How can I become good at drawing?
B: It takes (A)_____. (④) It's important that you draw as often as you can. (⑤)
G: You mean I should (B)_____ practicing?
B: That's right.

01 위 대화의 ①~⑤ 중 다음 주어진 말이 들어갈 알맞은 곳은?

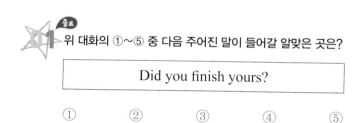

Did you finish yours?

①   ②   ③   ④   ⑤

02 빈칸 (A)와 (B)에 들어갈 말로 알맞은 것끼리 짝지어진 것을 고르시오.

	(A)	(B)
①	time	keep
②	time	enjoy
③	time	finish
④	money	keep
⑤	money	enjoy

03 위 대화의 내용과 일치하지 않는 것을 고르시오.

① The boy finished drawing his poster.
② The girl thinks the poster which the boy drew is great.
③ The boy knows how to be good at drawing.
④ The girl can draw as well as the boy.
⑤ The boy gives her some advice for drawing well.

[04~06] 다음 대화를 읽고 물음에 답하시오.

Hana: You look sad, Jiho. What's wrong? (①)
Jiho: I don't think I can ⓐachieve my dream.
Amy: What do you mean by that?
Jiho: I want to be an actor, but I ⓑnever fail auditions. (②)
Amy: Do you know this actor?
Jiho: Sure. He's a famous movie star. (③)
Amy: He failed more than 100 auditions. (④)
Jiho: Really? Maybe I should keep ⓒtrying. (⑤) I will practice ⓓmore for my next audition.
Hana: That's right! It's important that you ⓔnever give up.

04 위 대화의 ①~⑤ 중 다음 주어진 말이 들어갈 알맞은 곳은?

Maybe I have to give up.

①   ②   ③   ④   ⑤

05 위 대화의 ⓐ~ⓔ 중 흐름상 어색한 것을 고르시오.

① ⓐ   ② ⓑ   ③ ⓒ   ④ ⓓ   ⑤ ⓔ

06 위 대화의 내용과 일치하지 않는 것을 고르시오.

① Hana thinks it's important not to give up.
② Jiho wants to become an actor.
③ Amy told Jiho the story about the famous movie star.
④ Jiho failed auditions more than 100 times.
⑤ Jiho will keep trying for the next audition.

07 빈칸에 공통으로 들어갈 알맞은 말을 고르시오.

> A: (A)_____.
> B: What do you mean by "(B)_____"?
> A: I mean working together is better than working alone.

① keep my fingers crossed
② It's a walk in the park
③ Will is power
④ Practice makes perfect
⑤ Two heads are better than one

[08~09] 다음 짝지어진 대화가 <u>어색한</u> 것은?

08 ① A: I bought this bag at the mall. It's a steal.
   B: What do you mean by that?
   A: It's very cheap.
② A: Mina is really nice. She is all ears.
   B: What do you mean by that?
   A: She listens very carefully.
③ A: What is important to do to be an scientist?
   B: It's important to study math and science.
④ A: Practice makes perfect.
   B: What do you mean by "Practice makes perfect"?
   A: Yes, I do. I mean you learn something by doing it over and over.
⑤ A: I have an important exam tomorrow.
   B: I'll keep my fingers crossed for you!
   A: Thanks for saying that. I feel much better.

09 ① A: What is important to grow taller?
   B: It is important to drink much milk.
② A: Is it important that I should prepare a lot for the contest?
   B: Yes. I think practice makes perfect.
③ A: It's important to keep studying.
   B: I'll turn off the music.
④ A: What does "No sweat, no sweet" mean?
   B: It means "If you don't work hard, you can't achieve your goal."
⑤ A: What should we do to keep the air clean?
   B: First of all, it's important to use public transportation.

[10~11] 다음 대화를 읽고 물음에 답하시오.

> A: It's hard to be a good dancer. (A)_____
> B: (B) <u>절대 포기하지 않는 것이 중요해.</u> (is, never, important, it, give, you, that, up)
> A: Okay. I will not forget that.

10 빈칸 (A)에 알맞은 말을 고르시오.

① What are you going to do?
② What should I do?
③ What do you mean by that?
④ What are you talking about?
⑤ What do you want to be?

서답형
11 밑줄 친 (B)의 우리말에 맞게 괄호 안에 주어진 단어를 배열하여 영작하시오.

➡ _____

01 주어진 문장 이후에 이어질 대화의 순서를 바르게 배열하시오.

> Your poster looks great.

> (A) Not yet. I can't draw well. How can I become good at drawing?
> (B) That's right.
> (C) Thanks, Kate. Did you finish yours?
> (D) You mean I should keep practicing?
> (E) It takes time. It's important that you draw as often as you can.

➡ _____

[02~04] 다음 대화를 읽고 물음에 답하시오.

A: Please call me "Speedy Feet."
B: What do you mean (A)_____ "Speedy Feet"?
A: I mean I want to be a runner.
B: (B)달리기 선수가 되기 위해서 무엇을 하는 것이 중요하니? (to, become, runner, a, what, important, to, is, do)
A: (C)It's important what I practice to run every day.
B: I'm sure you'll make it.

02 빈칸 (A)에 알맞은 전치사를 쓰시오.

➡ _____

03 (B)의 밑줄 친 우리말에 맞게 괄호 안에 주어진 단어를 배열하여 영작하시오.

➡ _____

04 (C)에서 어법상 어색한 것을 고쳐서 완전한 문장을 쓰시오. (2개)

➡ _____

05 ⓐ~ⓔ 중 흐름상 어색한 것을 고치시오.

> G: Hey, Minho. ⓐDid you find the answer to the math problem?
> B: No. It's too hard for me. ⓑI'm good at math.
> G: ⓒLet me see. ⓓIt's important that you use this math rule to solve the problem.
> B: Oh, I see. ⓔI'll use it.

➡ _____

_____

06 다음 대화의 문맥상 또는 어법상 어색한 것을 고치시오. (2개)

> A: It's hard to make movies. What should I do?
> B: It's important that you think creative.
> A: Okay. I will forget that.

➡ (1) _____

_____

(2) _____

교과서

Grammar

1 'ask/want+A+to부정사' 구문

> **Other teams asked African American players to join them.**
> 다른 팀들은 아프리카계 미국인 선수들에게 자신들의 팀에 합류할 것을 요청했다.

- **'동사＋목적어＋to부정사' 구문**

  '주어＋동사＋목적어＋목적격보어'의 5형식 문장에서 want, ask, tell 등의 동사가 쓰이면 목적어와 목적격보어가 능동 관계일 때, 목적격보어로 to부정사가 온다.

  - Do you **want** me **to close** the shop? 내가 가게 문을 닫았으면 좋겠니?
  - He **asked** you **to wait** for him until 3:00. 그는 너에게 3시까지 기다려 달라고 부탁했어.

- **to부정사를 목적격보어로 취하는 동사**

  (1) 명령, 요청: tell, advise, warn, ask, request, allow 등
  - I **told** him **to do** it immediately. 나는 그에게 그것을 즉시 하라고 말했다.
  - Other players **advised** him **to stay** on the team. 다른 선수들은 그에게 팀에 남아 있으라고 충고했다.

  (2) 유도, 자극: lead, invite, encourage 등
  - He **encouraged** me **to write** poems. 그는 내게 시를 쓰도록 격려해 주었다.

  (3) 기대, 소망: like, expect, want, wish 등
  - Many people did not **expect** him **to do** well. 많은 사람들은 그가 잘하리라고 기대하지 않았다.

- **to부정사의 부정형은 'not[never]＋to 동사원형'이다.**

  - He **advised** me **not to go** there. 그는 나에게 거기에 가지 말라고 충고했다.
  - I **asked** him **not to tell** anybody. 나는 그에게 누구에게도 말하지 말라고 부탁했다.
  - The doctor **ordered** me **not to smoke**. 의사는 나에게 담배를 피우지 말라고 명령했다.

핵심 Check

1. 다음 우리말과 일치하도록 빈칸에 알맞은 말을 쓰시오.

   (1) 우리 부모님은 내가 그들과 함께 살기를 바라신다.
   ➡ My parents want me ＿＿＿＿＿ ＿＿＿＿＿ with them.

   (2) 나는 그에게 조심하라고 부탁했다.
   ➡ I asked him ＿＿＿＿＿ ＿＿＿＿＿ careful.

   (3) 어떻게 그런 생각을 하게 되었는가?
   ➡ What led you ＿＿＿＿＿ ＿＿＿＿＿ so?

② 목적격 관계대명사

• I will become a player **who** people like. 나는 사람들이 좋아하는 선수가 될 거야.

■ **목적격 관계대명사의 뜻**

관계대명사는 절과 절을 연결하는 접속사와 대명사의 기능 두 가지를 겸하는데, 관계대명사 앞의 명사(선행사)가 뒤 문장의 목적어 역할을 할 때 이 관계대명사를 '목적격 관계대명사'라고 한다.

This is the book **which** I have chosen. 이것이 내가 고른 책이다.

■ **목적격 관계대명사의 종류**

선행사가 사람일 때 'who(m),' 사물일 때 'which,' 사람과 사물 모두에 'that'을 쓸 수 있다.

선행사	사람	사물, 동물	사람, 사물, 동물
목적격 관계대명사	who(m)/that	which/that	that

That man over there is the dentist **whom** I told you about. 저기 있는 사람이 내가 너에게 얘기했던 그 치과 의사야.

■ **목적격 관계대명사의 생략**

목적격 관계대명사는 생략이 가능하다.

• I know the novelist (**who/whom/that**) he mentioned. 나는 그가 언급한 소설가를 알고 있다.

■ 목적격 관계대명사절에서는 앞에 있는 관계대명사가 동사의 목적어 역할을 하기 때문에 동사 뒤에 목적어가 없다는 것에 특히 주의해야 한다.

• I cannot find the book. I put it(=the book) on the table.
  = I cannot find the book (**which/that**) I put on the table. 나는 책상 위에 두었던 책을 찾을 수 없다.

■ 목적격 관계대명사가 전치사의 목적어인 경우 전치사는 관계대명사절의 끝에 오거나 관계대명사 앞에 올 수 있다. 전치사가 관계대명사절의 끝에 올 경우에는 관계대명사를 생략할 수 있지만 전치사가 관계대명사 앞에 올 경우에는 관계대명사를 생략하지 않으며 관계대명사 that을 쓸 수 없다.

• I had some animals (**which/that**) I took care **of**. (나는 내가 돌보던 동물들을 갖고 있었다.)
  = I had some animals **of which** I took care.
  = I had some animals of that I took care. (×)

핵심 Check

2. 다음 괄호 안에서 알맞은 말을 고르시오.

(1) He is the man (who / which) I met yesterday.

(2) The bag (whom / which) he is carrying is very old.

01 다음 문장에서 어법상 <u>어색한</u> 부분을 바르게 고치시오.

(1) My mother told me bring my umbrella.

_____ ➡ _____

(2) I asked Sam borrow the book from the library

_____ ➡ _____

(3) She is an actress which I wanted to meet.

_____ ➡ _____

(4) Did you find the book who you wanted?

_____ ➡ _____

[02~03] 다음 문장의 빈칸에 들어갈 알맞은 말은?

02

> Our English teacher advised us _____ harder.

① study   ② studies   ③ studied
④ studying   ⑤ to study

03

> The bag _____ he is carrying is very old.

① that   ② what   ③ who
④ whom   ⑤ whose

04 다음 우리말에 맞게 빈칸에 알맞은 말을 쓰시오.

(1) 너는 내가 그 이야기를 믿으라고 기대하는 거야?

➡ Do you expect me _____ _____ the story?

(2) 그는 그들로 하여금 궁핍한 사람들을 도우라고 장려했다.

➡ He encouraged them _____ _____ the poor and needy.

(3) 소년은 한번 본 그 소녀와 사랑에 빠졌다.

➡ The boy fell in love with a girl _____ he saw once.

(4) 내가 어제 산 치마를 너에게 보여줄게.

➡ I'll show you the skirt _____ I bought yesterday.

01 다음 빈칸에 알맞은 것은?

> My father told me _____ TV for an hour a day.

① watch   ② watches
③ watched   ④ watching
⑤ to watch

02 다음 〈보기〉의 밑줄 친 부분과 <u>다르게</u> 쓰인 것을 고르시오.

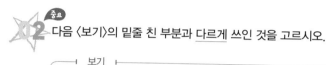
> ┌ 보기 ┐
> Everything <u>that</u> I said was true.

① The movie <u>which</u> I saw was interesting.
② The money was returned by the boy <u>that</u> found it.
③ Ted wants to marry the lady <u>whom</u> he loves.
④ This is the movie <u>that</u> I really wanted to watch.
⑤ I am looking for a man <u>who</u> I met at the park yesterday.

03 다음 빈칸에 들어갈 수 있는 말이 <u>다른</u> 하나는?

① The bag _____ I bought yesterday is blue.
② She is the scientist _____ I want to meet.
③ An orphan is a child _____ parents are dead.
④ This is the pen _____ was on the desk.
⑤ Kate is the writer _____ I like most.

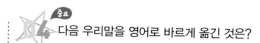
04 다음 우리말을 영어로 바르게 옮긴 것은?

> 그의 친구들은 그가 빚을 갚을 수 있도록 해줄 것이다.

① His friends will enable him pay his debts.
② His friends will enable him pays his debts.
③ His friends will enable him paying his debts.
④ His friends will enable him to pay his debts.
⑤ His friends will enable him to paying his debts.

05 다음 중 어법상 바르지 <u>않은</u> 것은?

> Mark ①<u>wanted</u> ②<u>me</u> ③<u>lend</u> ④<u>him</u> ⑤ <u>some money</u>.

①   ②   ③   ④   ⑤

서답형
06 다음 괄호 안에서 알맞은 말을 고르시오.

(1) The people (which / that) we met were very nice.
(2) The dress (who / which) she is wearing is pretty.
(3) This is the drama about (that / which) I spoke yesterday.
(4) His support helped Robinson (play / playing) harder.
(5) I (hoped / warned) the man to keep away from my dog.

07 다음 중 어법상 옳은 문장을 고르시오.

① But she had a dream who she couldn't give up.

② This is the house in that she lives.

③ We sometimes have to eat dishes whom we don't like.

④ Another important thing which we choose is time management.

⑤ There is something who you should remember.

08 다음 빈칸에 적절하지 않은 것은?

| Sena _____ me to start studying two weeks before the test. |

① watched   ② encouraged   ③ told
④ expected   ⑤ persuaded

09 다음 중 두 문장의 의미가 다른 것은?

① Mom expects that I will study hard.
→ Mom expects me to study hard.

② Sam advised her that she should not throw away the trash on the street.
→ Sam advised her not to throw away the trash on the street.

③ Ann told him that he must wear long clothes to protect himself from animals.
→ Ann told him to wear long clothes to protect himself from animals.

④ She allowed that I could eat ice cream for dessert.
→ I allowed her to eat ice cream for dessert.

⑤ Juliet told Romeo that he should come at once.
→ Juliet told Romeo to come at once.

10 다음 밑줄 친 that의 성격이 나머지 넷과 다른 것은?

① One idea is that a big rock from space hit the Earth.

② The phone that you picked up is mine.

③ An elephant is an animal that has a long nose.

④ Do you have some money that I can borrow?

⑤ The book that I read yesterday was very interesting.

11 괄호 안의 동사를 어법에 맞게 고쳐 쓰시오.

(1) They asked him (spend) the night in the house.

(2) Her doctors encouraged her (keep) learning Taekwondo.

(3) Why don't you help her (carry) the boxes?

(4) The teacher had the students (finish) their projects.

(5) We requested everyone in the office (assemble) in the lobby.

➡ (1) _____ (2) _____ (3) _____
(4) _____ (5) _____

12 다음 중 어법상 어색한 부분을 찾아 바르게 고친 것은?

| He warned Cindy keep away from his dog. |

① warned → has warned
② Cindy → Cindy's
③ keep → to keep
④ from → to
⑤ his → him

서답형

13 다음 문장에서 어법상 <u>어색한</u> 부분을 바르게 고쳐 다시 쓰시오.

(1) Sophie asked her dad help her to finish her homework.

➡ _____

(2) Mom wanted Lily coming home by 8.

➡ _____

(3) She invited me go to New York with her.

➡ _____

(4) The blue watch is the gift who I bought there for my brother.

➡ _____
_____

(5) The man which my mother is talking to is my art teacher.

➡ _____
_____

(6) The girl and her cat which I met this morning were playing in the park.

➡ _____
_____

14 괄호 안에 주어진 동사를 빈칸에 써 넣을 때 그 형태가 <u>다른</u> 하나는?

① The teacher wanted me _____ notes. (take)

② Jimin told me _____ a study group. (make)

③ Mom asked Rosa _____ some books to the library. (return)

④ Many people did not expect him _____ well. (do)

⑤ I feel something _____ up my back. (creep)

서답형

15 다음 문장에서 생략할 수 있는 것을 쓰시오.

(1) Mary is the girl who I met in Paris.

(2) My group thinks health is an important thing that we need for our dream.

(3) He is reading a book which is about the greenhouse gas.

➡ (1) _____ (2) _____ (3) _____

16 다음 중 어법상 <u>어색한</u> 것을 고르시오.

① The heavy rain caused the river overflow.

② Do not force them to agree to your opinion.

③ I warned him not to take any pictures here.

④ We want you to come and visit us.

⑤ After that season, other teams asked African American players to join them.

17 다음 두 문장을 한 문장으로 바르게 바꾸지 <u>않은</u> 것을 고르시오.

• Alice wishes to meet a boy.
• She went to the same school with him.

① Alice wishes to meet a boy she went to the same school with.

② Alice wishes to meet a boy who she went to the same school with.

③ Alice wishes to meet a boy that she went to the same school with.

④ Alice wishes to meet a boy with whom she went to the same school.

⑤ Alice wishes to meet a boy with that she went to the same school.

01 다음 문장에서 어법상 <u>어색한</u> 부분을 찾아 바르게 고쳐 다시 쓰시오.

(1) I want you are happy.

　➡ _____

(2) Jack asked his mother woke him up at 8 o'clock.

　➡ _____

(3) Tina told me finding a quiet place to study.

　➡ _____

(4) Jessy got her dad drop her off at the bus stop.

　➡ _____

(5) His teacher advised him not spend all his time on one subject.

　➡ _____

02 다음 두 문장을 관계대명사를 사용하여 한 문장으로 바꾸시오.

(1) • The man is my brother.
　• You met the man on Sunday.

　➡ _____

(2) • That is the computer.
　• I bought the computer last week.

　➡ _____

(3) • This is the cake.
　• It was made by Ann.

　➡ _____

(4) • I visited the church.
　• I took some pictures of the church.

　➡ _____

(5) • It is an experience.
　• I look forward the experience.

　➡ _____

(6) • Does Eddie have any friends?
　• He can depend on them.

　➡ _____

03 우리말에 맞게 괄호 안에 주어진 동사의 알맞은 형태를 빈칸에 쓰시오.

(1) 무엇을 가져오면 되나요?
　➡ What would you like me _____? (bring)

(2) 그녀는 그들을 대회에 참가하도록 만들었다.
　➡ She made them _____ part in the contest. (take)

(3) 무언가 탄내가 나는 것 같다.
　➡ I think I smell something _____. (burn)

04 다음 문장에서 어법상 어색한 부분을 찾아 바르게 고쳐 다시 쓰시오.

(1) This is the bridge who my father built.

➡ _____

(2) They are the people which I met in the plane.

➡ _____

(3) I like the new computer that I bought it last week.

➡ _____

(4) Can you tell me about the church of that you took the picture last weekend?

➡ _____

_____

_____

_____

05 다음 두 문장이 비슷한 의미를 갖도록 빈칸을 알맞은 말로 채우시오.

(1) Mom told me that I must come back home by tonight.

➡ Mom told me _____ back home by tonight.

(2) His boss told him that he should be more careful for the future.

➡ His boss ordered him _____ more careful for the future.

(3) The teacher told Maria that she should not give up her dream.

➡ The teacher encouraged Maria _____ _____ her dream.

06 두 문장을 관계대명사를 사용하여 한 문장으로 썼을 때, 빈칸에 해당하는 문장을 쓰시오.

(1) • _____

• My favorite author wrote it.

→ I bought a book that my favorite author wrote.

(2) • That is the girl.

• _____

→ That is the girl whom I invited to the party.

(3) • There are three things.

• _____

_____

→ There are three things that I need to do to achieve my dream.

(4) • _____

• The famous author wrote it.

→ Is the novel which the famous author wrote fun?

07 괄호 안에 주어진 어휘를 이용하여 우리말에 맞게 영작하시오.

(1) 그녀는 너에게 자기 방 청소를 부탁했다. (ask, clean)

➡ _____

(2) 엄마는 내가 강아지를 돌볼 거라고 예상하신다. (expect, take care of)

➡ _____

_____

(3) 우리가 만났던 사람들은 매우 친절했다. (the people, nice)

➡ _____

(4) 내가 어제 산 가방은 파란색이다. (bag, buy)

➡ _____

Jackie Robinson Breaks the Color Line

It was New York City on April 15, 1947. Jackie Robinson, an African
날짜 앞에는 전치사 on을 쓴다.   'Jackie Robinson'을 부연 설명하는 동격.

American, went on the field as second baseman for the Brooklyn
동격 앞에는 콤마(,)를 쓴다.   as: ~로(자격)

Dodgers. People couldn't believe their eyes. He was the first African
'~의 눈을 의심하다'라는 뜻. 놀람을 나타낼 때 쓰인다.

American player to play on a Major League team. That day, the color
to부정사의 형용사적 용법. on: 소속

line was broken.
수동태(be동사+과거분사). 과거시제이므로 be동사 was가 쓰였다.

Robinson faced many difficulties. Although Robinson was a talented
=Though

player and a gentle person, his teammates did not want to play with
wants는 to부정사를 목적어로 취하는 동사

him. Every hotel turned the team down because Robinson was on

the team. When he was at bat, people in the stands rudely shouted at

him. Robinson thought to himself, 'I need to keep calm and focus on
재귀대명사   'need to': '~해야 한다'. 뒤에 동사원형이 온다.

baseball. I will try and become a player who people like. Then, next
목적격 관계대명사로 who 뒤의 절이 'a player'를 꾸며 준다.

season, there will be more African American players in the league.'

Robinson put all his time and energy into baseball. With practice, he
with: ~함에 따라, ~와 더불어 with practice: 연습함에 따라서

became great at batting and base running.
at의 목적어로 동명사 batting과 'base running'이 쓰임.

American: 미국인, 미국의
baseman: (1, 2, 3) 루수
major: 주요한, 중대한
color line: 인종 차별
although: (비록) ~이긴 하지만
talented: (타고난) 재능이 있는
teammate: 팀 동료
rudely: 무례하게, 예의 없이, 버릇없이
turn down: ~을 거절하다, 거부하다
at bat: 타석에 서서
shout at: ~에게 소리치다
think to oneself: 조용히 생각하다,
마음속으로 생각하다
keep calm: 평정을 유지하다

🖇 확인문제

● 다음 문장이 본문의 내용과 일치하면 T, 일치하지 않으면 F를 쓰시오.

1 Jackie Robinson was the first African American player to play on a Major League
  team. ☐

2 On April 15, 1947, the color line was made. ☐

3 Robinson experienced many difficulties. ☐

4 Robinson's teammates wanted to play with him. ☐

5 When Robinson was at bat, people in the stands rudely shouted at him. ☐

6 Robinson put all his time and energy into breaking the color line. ☐

Robinson's effort moved his teammates. When people shouted at Robinson, one of his teammates walked up to Robinson and tapped him on the shoulder. "Do not listen to them. You're doing fine," he said. His support helped Robinson to play harder. Finally, Robinson earned the respect of other players and fans.

Thanks to Robinson, the Dodgers won the National League Championship in 1947. The league recognized Robinson's excellence and presented him with the Rookie of the Year Award in the same year. After that season, other teams asked African American players to join them.

Robinson's uniform number was 42. Baseball players in Major League teams no longer wear the number 42 to honor him. Every year, however, on April 15, every player wears the number that Robinson wore. The day is called "Jackie Robinson Day."

effort: 노력, 수고
support: 지지, 지원, 도움
recognize: 알아보다, 인정하다
excellence: 우수, 탁월, 뛰어남
earn the respect: 존경을 얻다
honor: 존경하다, 공경하다
no longer: 더 이상 ~ 아닌[하지 않는]

확인문제

● 다음 문장이 본문의 내용과 일치하면 T, 일치하지 않으면 F를 쓰시오.

1 Robinson's effort moved his teammates. ☐

2 Some of Robinson's teammates walked up to Robinson and tapped him on the shoulder. ☐

3 Thanks to Robinson, the Dodgers won the National League Championship in 1947. ☐

4 The league didn't recognize Robinson's excellence. ☐

5 Baseball players in Major League teams no longer wear the number 42 to honor Robinson. ☐

6 "Jackie Robinson Day" is April 5 of each year. ☐

● 우리말을 참고하여 빈칸에 알맞은 말을 쓰시오.

1 Jackie Robinson _____ _____ _____ _____

2 It was New York City _____ _____ _____, _____.

3 Jackie Robinson, an African American, went on the field _____ second baseman _____ the Brooklyn Dodgers.

4 People _____ _____ their eyes.

5 He was _____ _____ _____ _____ _____ to play on a Major League team.

6 That day, _____ _____ _____ _____ _____.

7 Robinson _____ _____ _____.

8 _____ Robinson was a talented player and a gentle person, his teammates did not want _____ _____ _____ _____.

9 Every hotel _____ _____ _____ _____ because Robinson was on the team.

10 When he _____ _____ _____, people in the stands rudely shouted at him.

11 Robinson _____ _____ _____, 'I need to keep calm and focus on baseball.

12 I will try and become a player _____ _____ _____.

13 Then, next season, _____ _____ _____ _____ African American players in the league.'

14 Robinson _____ all his time and energy _____ baseball.

---

1 Jackie Robinson 인종 차별을 깨다

2 1947년 4월 15일 뉴욕시에서였다.

3 아프리카계 미국인 Jackie Robinson은 브루클린 다저스의 2루수로 경기장에 나갔다.

4 사람들은 자신들의 눈을 의심했다.

5 그는 메이저리그 팀에서 경기한 최초의 아프리카계 미국인 선수였다.

6 그날 인종 차별이 깨졌다.

7 Robinson은 많은 어려움에 직면했다.

8 Robinson은 재능 있는 선수이고 온화한 사람이었지만 그의 팀원들은 그와 함께 경기하기를 원하지 않았다.

9 Robinson이 팀에 있었기 때문에 모든 호텔에서 그 팀을 거절했다.

10 그가 타석에 있을 때, 관중석에 있는 사람들이 그에게 무례하게 소리치기도 했다.

11 Robinson은 마음속으로 생각했다. '나는 평정심을 유지하고 야구에 집중해야 해.

12 나는 노력해서 사람들이 좋아하는 선수가 될 거야.

13 그러면 다음 시즌에는 아프리카계 미국인 선수가 리그에 더 많이 생길 거야.'

14 Robinson은 자신의 모든 시간과 에너지를 야구에 집중했다.

15 _____ _____, he became great at _____ and _____ _____.

16 Robinson's effort _____ his teammates.

17 When people shouted at Robinson, _____ _____ _____ _____ walked up to Robinson and _____ _____ _____ _____ shoulder.

18 "_____ _____ _____ _____ them.

19 You're doing _____," he said.

20 His support helped Robinson _____ _____ harder.

21 Finally, Robinson _____ _____ _____ of other players and fans.

22 _____ _____ Robinson, the Dodgers won the National League Championship in 1947.

23 The league _____ Robinson's excellence and _____ him _____ the Rookie of the Year Award in the same year.

24 After that season, other teams _____ African American players _____ _____ them.

25 Robinson's _____ _____ was 42.

26 Baseball players in Major League teams _____ _____ wear the number 42 _____ _____ _____.

27 Every year, _____, on April 15, every player wears the number that Robinson _____.

28 The day _____ _____ "Jackie Robinson Day."

15 연습을 함으로써 그는 타격과 주루를 잘하게 되었다.

16 Robinson의 노력은 그의 팀원들을 감동시켰다.

17 사람들이 Robinson에게 소리쳤을 때, 그의 팀 동료 중 한 명이 Robinson에게 다가가 어깨를 두드렸다.

18 "그들 말을 듣지 마.

19 너는 잘하고 있어."라고 그가 말했다.

20 그의 지지는 Robinson이 더 열심히 경기하는 데 도움이 됐다.

21 마침내, Robinson은 다른 선수들과 팬들의 존경을 받았다.

22 Robinson 덕분에 다저스는 1947년에 내셔널리그 챔피언십에서 우승하게 되었다.

23 리그에서는 Robinson의 탁월함을 인정했고, 같은 해에 그에게 신인상을 수여했다.

24 그 시즌 이후, 다른 팀들은 아프리카계 미국인 선수들에게 자신들의 팀에 합류할 것을 요청했다.

25 Robinson의 등 번호는 42번이었다.

26 메이저리그 팀의 야구 선수들은 그에 대한 존경을 보여 주기 위해 더 이상 42번을 달지 않는다.

27 하지만 매년 4월 15일, 모든 선수들은 Robinson이 달았던 번호를 단다.

28 이 날을 '재키 로빈슨 데이'라고 부른다.

● 우리말을 참고하여 본문을 영작하시오.

1 Jackie Robinson 인종 차별을 깨다

➡ _____

2 1947년 4월 15일 뉴욕시에서였다.

➡ _____

3 아프리카계 미국인 Jackie Robinson은 브루클린 다저스의 2루수로 경기장에 나갔다.

➡ _____

4 사람들은 자신들의 눈을 의심했다.

➡ _____

5 그는 메이저리그 팀에서 경기한 최초의 아프리카계 미국인 선수였다.

➡ _____

6 그날 인종 차별이 깨졌다.

➡ _____

7 Robinson은 많은 어려움에 직면했다.

➡ _____

8 Robinson은 재능 있는 선수이고 온화한 사람이었지만 그의 팀원들은 그와 함께 경기하기를 원하지 않았다.

➡ _____

9 Robinson이 팀에 있었기 때문에 모든 호텔에서 그 팀을 거절했다.

➡ _____

10 그가 타석에 있을 때, 관중석에 있는 사람들이 그에게 무례하게 소리치기도 했다.

➡ _____

11 Robinson은 마음속으로 생각했다. '나는 평정심을 유지하고 야구에 집중해야 해.

➡ _____

12 나는 노력해서 사람들이 좋아하는 선수가 될 거야.

➡ _____

13 그러면 다음 시즌에는 아프리카계 미국인 선수가 리그에 더 많이 생길 거야.'

➡ _____

14 Robinson은 자신의 모든 시간과 에너지를 야구에 집중했다.

➡ _____

15 연습을 함으로써 그는 타격과 주루를 잘하게 되었다.

➡ _____

16 Robinson의 노력은 그의 팀원들을 감동시켰다.

➡ _____

17 사람들이 Robinson에게 소리쳤을 때, 그의 팀 동료 중 한 명이 Robinson에게 다가가 어깨를 두드렸다.

➡ _____

18 "그들 말을 듣지 마.

➡ _____

19 너는 잘하고 있어."라고 그가 말했다.

➡ _____

20 그의 지지는 Robinson이 더 열심히 경기하는 데 도움이 됐다.

➡ _____

21 마침내, Robinson은 다른 선수들과 팬들의 존경을 받았다.

➡ _____

22 Robinson 덕분에 다저스는 1947년에 내셔널리그 챔피언십에서 우승하게 되었다.

➡ _____

23 리그에서는 Robinson의 탁월함을 인정했고, 같은 해에 그에게 신인상을 수여했다.

➡ _____

24 그 시즌 이후, 다른 팀들은 아프리카계 미국인 선수들에게 자신들의 팀에 합류할 것을 요청했다.

➡ _____

25 Robinson의 등 번호는 42번이었다.

➡ _____

26 메이저리그 팀의 야구 선수들은 그에 대한 존경을 보여 주기 위해 더 이상 42번을 달지 않는다.

➡ _____

27 하지만 매년 4월 15일, 모든 선수들은 Robinson이 달았던 번호를 단다.

➡ _____

28 이 날을 '재키 로빈슨 데이'라고 부른다.

➡ _____

[01~03] 다음 글을 읽고 물음에 답하시오.

It was New York City __(A)__ April 15, 1947. Jackie Robinson, an African American, went on the field ⓐas second baseman for the Brooklyn Dodgers. People couldn't believe their eyes. He was the first African American player to play __(B)__ a Major League team. That day, the color line was broken.

서답형

01 위 글의 빈칸 (A)와 (B)에 공통으로 들어갈 알맞은 전치사를 쓰시오.

➡ _____

02 위 글의 밑줄 친 ⓐas와 같은 의미로 쓰인 것을 고르시오.

① Leave it as it is.
② Yesterday he attended the meeting as a reporter.
③ Her anger grew as she talked.
④ As I was tired, I soon fell asleep.
⑤ He trembled as he spoke.

중요

03 위 글을 읽고 Jackie Robinson에 대해 알 수 없는 것을 고르시오.

① 혈통   ② 국적
③ 수비 위치   ④ 가족 관계
⑤ 소속팀

[04~06] 다음 글을 읽고 물음에 답하시오.

Robinson faced many difficulties. Although Robinson was a talented player and a gentle person, his teammates did not want to play with him. Every hotel turned the team down (A)[because / because of] Robinson was on the team. ⓐ그가 타석에 있을 때, people in the stands rudely shouted at him.

Robinson thought to (B)[him / himself], 'I need to keep calm and focus on baseball. I will try and become a player who people like. Then, next season, there will be more African American players in the league.' Robinson put all his time and energy into baseball. With practice, he became (C)[great / greatly] at batting and base running.

서답형

04 위 글의 괄호 (A)~(C)에서 어법상 알맞은 낱말을 골라 쓰시오.

➡ (A)_____ (B)_____ (C)_____

서답형

05 위 글의 밑줄 친 ⓐ의 우리말을 5단어로 쓰시오.

➡ _____

중요

06 위 글을 읽고 대답할 수 없는 질문은?

① Did Robinson have difficulties during his career as a major leaguer?
② Why did every hotel turn the team down?
③ When Robinson was at bat, did people in the stands welcome him?
④ Thanks to Robinson's effort, how many African American players could play on the Major League teams?
⑤ How did Robinson become a good batter and base runner?

[07~10] 다음 글을 읽고 물음에 답하시오.

Robinson's uniform number was 42. Baseball players in Major League teams no longer wear the number 42 ⓐto honor him. Every year, (A) , on April 15, every player wears the number that Robinson wore. ⓑThe day is called "Jackie Robinson Day."

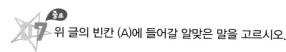 위 글의 빈칸 (A)에 들어갈 알맞은 말을 고르시오.

① therefore   ② however
③ for example   ④ in fact
⑤ in addition

08 아래 〈보기〉에서 위 글의 밑줄 친 ⓐto honor와 문법적 쓰임이 같은 것의 개수를 고르시오.

┌─── 보기 ───┐
① He wept to see the sight.
② My hope is to work as a doctor in Africa.
③ I want something to write with.
④ I have nothing to do this afternoon.
⑤ I was very happy to hear the news.
└────────┘

① 1개   ② 2개   ③ 3개   ④ 4개   ⑤ 5개

서답형
09 Why do baseball players in Major League teams no longer wear the number 42? Fill in the blanks with a suitable word.

➡ They do so in order to _____ Robinson.

서답형
10 위 글의 밑줄 친 ⓑ를 능동태로 고치시오.

➡ _____

[11~13] 다음 글을 읽고 물음에 답하시오.

Robinson thought to himself, 'I need to keep calm and focus on baseball. I will try and become a player ___ⓐ___ people like. Then, next season, there will be more African American players in the league.' Robinson put all his time and energy into baseball. With practice, he became great at batting and base running.

11 위 글의 빈칸 ⓐ에 들어갈 알맞은 말을 모두 고르시오.

① what   ② who
③ whom   ④ which
⑤ that

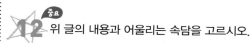 위 글의 내용과 어울리는 속담을 고르시오.

① Better late than never.
② A stitch in time saves nine.
③ Do to others as you would be done by.
④ Practice makes perfect.
⑤ Look before you leap.

13 위 글의 내용과 일치하지 않는 것은?

① Robinson은 평정심을 유지하고 야구에 집중해야 한다고 마음속으로 생각했다.
② Robinson은 노력해서 사람들이 좋아하는 선수가 되려고 결심했다.
③ Robinson 덕분에 다음 시즌에 아프리카계 미국인 선수가 리그에 더 많이 생겼다.
④ Robinson은 자신의 모든 시간과 에너지를 야구에 집중했다.
⑤ 연습을 함으로써 Robinson은 타격과 주루를 잘하게 되었다.

[14~17] 다음 글을 읽고 물음에 답하시오.

How I Will Achieve My Dream

I want to be a designer. There are ⓐthree things (A)[that / what] I need to do ⓑto achieve my dream. I need to be healthy, be creative, and never give up. Being healthy will help me (B)[keep / keeping] going for my dream. Being creative will help me do something different. Plus, I will always tell myself never ___(A)___ because it will make me (C)[try / to try] harder.

서답형
14 위 글의 빈칸 (A)에 들어갈 알맞은 말을 쓰시오.

➡ _____

서답형
15 위 글의 괄호 (A)~(C)에서 어법상 알맞은 낱말을 골라 쓰시오.

➡ (A)_____ (B)_____ (C)_____

16 위 글의 밑줄 친 ⓐ에 해당하지 않는 것은? (2개)

① to be healthy
② to work well with others
③ to be creative
④ never to give up
⑤ to help others

중요
17 위 글의 밑줄 친 ⓑ를 바꿔 쓴 것으로 옳지 않은 것을 고르시오.

① so as to achieve my dream
② in order that I can achieve my dream
③ achieving my dream
④ so that I can achieve my dream
⑤ in order to achieve my dream

[18~20] 다음 글을 읽고 물음에 답하시오.

Robinson's effort ⓐmoved ①his teammates. When people shouted at Robinson, one of ②his teammates walked up to Robinson and tapped ③him on the shoulder. "Do not listen to them. ④You're doing fine," he said. ⑤His support helped Robinson to play harder. ⓑFinally, Robinson earned the respect of other players and fans.

18 위 글의 밑줄 친 ⓐmoved와 같은 의미로 쓰인 것을 고르시오.

① He moved towards the window.
② I moved the meeting to Wednesday.
③ Their deep friendship moved us a great deal.
④ They moved into a new house.
⑤ We moved our chairs a little nearer.

중요
19 밑줄 친 ①~⑤ 중에서 가리키는 대상이 나머지 넷과 다른 것은?

①   ②   ③   ④   ⑤

20 위 글의 밑줄 친 ⓑFinally와 바꿔 쓸 수 없는 말을 고르시오.

① Lastly   ② In the long run
③ Eventually   ④ In the end
⑤ At last

[21~22] 다음 글을 읽고 물음에 답하시오.

A: It's important that I manage my time well, practice hard, and have a strong ⓐwill to achieve my dream. How about you?
B: ⓑI think being healthy, working well with others, and being creative is important.

21 위 글의 밑줄 친 ⓐwill과 같은 의미로 쓰인 것을 고르시오.

① How long will you stay in Paris?

② Her decision shows great strength of will.

③ Will you send this letter for me, please?

④ It will be fine tomorrow.

⑤ I ought to draw up my will before I die.

서답형
22 위 글의 밑줄 친 ⓑ에서 어법상 틀린 부분을 찾아 고치시오.

➡ _____

[23~24] 다음 글을 읽고 물음에 답하시오.

Robinson's effort moved his teammates. (①) When people shouted at Robinson, one of his teammates walked up to Robinson and tapped him on the shoulder. (②) "Do not listen to them. (③) You're doing fine," he said. (④) Finally, Robinson earned the respect of other players and fans. (⑤)

Thanks to Robinson, the Dodgers won the National League Championship in 1947. The league recognized Robinson's (A) and presented him with the Rookie of the Year Award in the same year. After that season, other teams asked African American players to join them.

서답형
23 위 글의 빈칸 (A)에 excellent를 알맞은 형태로 쓰시오.

➡ _____

중요
24 위 글의 흐름으로 보아, 주어진 문장이 들어가기에 가장 적절한 곳은?

His support helped Robinson to play harder.

①　　②　　③　　④　　⑤

[25~27] 다음 글을 읽고 물음에 답하시오.

How I Will Achieve My Dream
I want to be a chef. There are ⓐthree things that I need to do to achieve my dream. I need to practice hard, work well with others, and manage my time well. (A)_____ hard will help me cook well and easily. (B)_____ well with others will make ⓑit easier to work at a restaurant. Plus, I will always tell myself (C)_____ my time well because it will help me make food in time to serve.

서답형
25 위 글의 빈칸 (A)~(C)에 들어갈 말을 각각 알맞은 형태로 쓰시오.

➡ (A) _____
　　(B) _____
　　(C) _____

서답형
26 위 글의 밑줄 친 ⓐthree things가 가리키는 것을 본문에서 찾아 쓰시오.

➡ _____
_____

27 위 글의 밑줄 친 ⓑit과 문법적 쓰임이 같은 것을 모두 고르시오.

① It is very hard to give up smoking.

② It is easy to get a bad habit.

③ It is quite difficult to master a foreign language.

④ I found it useless to teach him English.

⑤ I make it a rule to take a walk early in the morning.

[01~03] 다음 글을 읽고 물음에 답하시오.

It was New York City on ⓐApril 15, 1947. Jackie Robinson, an African American, went on the field as second baseman for the Brooklyn Dodgers. People couldn't believe their eyes. He was the first African American player to play on a Major League team. That day, the (A)c_____ l_____ was broken.

 중요

01 주어진 영영풀이를 참고하여 빈칸 (A)에 주어진 철자로 시작하는 단어를 쓰시오.

> barrier preventing blacks from participating in various activities with whites

➡ _____

02 위 글의 밑줄 친 ⓐ를 영어로 읽는 법을 쓰시오.

➡ _____

03 Why couldn't people believe their eyes when Jackie Robinson came out into the field? Fill in the blanks with suitable words.

➡ Because there was no _____ to play on a Major League team before him.

[04~07] 다음 글을 읽고 물음에 답하시오.

Thanks to Robinson, the Dodgers won the National League Championship in 1947. The league recognized Robinson's excellence and ⓐpresented him with the Rookie of the Year Award in the same year. After that season, other teams asked African American players __(A)__ ⓑthem.

04 위 글의 빈칸 (A)에 join을 알맞은 형태로 쓰시오.

➡ _____

05 위 글의 밑줄 친 ⓐ를 다음과 같이 바꿔 쓸 때 빈칸에 들어갈 알맞은 말을 쓰시오.

➡ presented the Rookie of the Year Award _____ him

06 위 글의 밑줄 친 ⓑ가 가리키는 것을 본문에서 찾아 쓰시오.

➡ _____

중요

07 When did Robinson win the Rookie of the Year Award? Answer in English in a full sentence. (5 words)

➡ _____

[08~10] 다음 글을 읽고 물음에 답하시오.

Robinson faced many difficulties. Although Robinson was a talented player and a gentle person, his teammates did not want to play with him. ⓐ모든 호텔에서 그 팀을 거절했다 because Robinson was on the team. When he was at bat, people in the stands rudely shouted at him.

08 위 글에서 'gifted'와 바꿔 쓸 수 있는 단어를 찾아 쓰시오.

➡ _____

9 위 글의 밑줄 친 ⓐ의 우리말에 맞게 주어진 어휘를 이용하여 6단어로 영작하시오.

> Every, turned

➡ _____

_____

10 본문의 내용과 일치하도록 다음 빈칸 (A)와 (B)에 알맞은 단어를 쓰시오.

> In spite of his talent and (A)_____ personality, Robinson experienced many (B)_____. For example, his teammates did not want to play with him.

[11~14] 다음 글을 읽고 물음에 답하시오.

ⓐRobinson's effort moved his teammates. When people shouted at Robinson, one of his teammates walked up to Robinson and tapped him on the shoulder. "Do not listen to ⓑthem. You're doing fine," he said. ⓒHis support helped Robinson to play harder. Finally, ⓓRobinson은 다른 선수들과 팬들의 존경을 받았다.

11 위 글의 밑줄 친 ⓐ를 수동태로 고치시오.

➡ _____

_____

12 위 글의 밑줄 친 ⓑthem이 가리키는 것을 본문에서 찾아 쓰시오.

➡ _____

13 다음 빈칸 (A)와 (B)에 알맞은 단어를 넣어 ⓒHis support에 대한 설명을 완성하시오.

> One of Robinson's (A)_____ walked up to Robinson, tapped him on the shoulder, and told him not to listen to the people who (B)_____ _____ him, adding "You're doing fine."

14 위 글의 밑줄 친 ⓓ의 우리말에 맞게 주어진 어휘를 이용하여 9단어로 영작하시오.

> earn, respect, of

➡ _____

[15~17] 다음 글을 읽고 물음에 답하시오.

Robinson ⓐ마음속으로 생각했다, 'I need to keep calm and focus on baseball. ⓑI will try and become a player who people like. Then, next season, there will be more African American players in the league.' Robinson put all his time and energy into baseball. With practice, he became great at (A)_____ and (B)_____.

15 위 글의 빈칸 (A)와 (B)에 bat와 base run을 각각 알맞은 형태로 쓰시오.

➡ (A) _____ (B) _____

16 위 글의 밑줄 친 ⓐ의 우리말을 세 단어로 쓰시오.

➡ _____

17 위 글의 밑줄 친 ⓑ에서 생략할 수 있는 단어를 생략하고 문장을 다시 쓰시오.

➡ _____

교과서

구석구석

해석

Language in Use

I visited three countries last year. France was the first country which I visited.
　　　　　　　　　　　　　　　　　　　　 the+서수　　　목적격 관계대명사(= that)

Mary is the girl who I met in Paris. The blue watch is the gift which I bought
　　　　　목적격 관계대명사(= whom/that)　　　　　　　　　　 목적격 관계대명사(= that)

there for my brother.
= in Paris　buy A B(4형식) = buy B for A(3형식): A에게 B를 사주다

구문해설　· gift: 선물

작년에 나는 3개국을 방문했다. 프랑스가 내가 방문한 첫 번째 국가였다. Mary는 내가 파리에서 만났던 소녀이다. 그 파란 시계는 그곳에서 내 동생을 위해 산 선물이다.

Enjoy Writing B

How I Will Achieve My Dream

I want to be a designer. There are three things that I need to do to achieve my
　　 명사적 용법의 to부정사　　　　　　　　　　　　　목적격 관계대명사　　　부사적 용법의 to부정사

dream. I need to be healthy, be creative, and never give up. Being healthy will
　　　　　　　　　　　　　　　　　　　　　　　　　　　　　동명사 주어

help me keep going for my dream. Being creative will help me do something
　　　 = to keep　　　　　　　　　　　　　　　help+목적어+to부정사(원형부정사)

different. Plus, I will always tell myself never to give up because it will make
　　　　　　　　　주어와 목적어가 같으면 재귀대명사를 씀　　tell+목적어+to부정사

me try harder.
make+목적어+원형부정사

구문해설　· achieve: 성취하다　· creative: 창의적인　· give up: ~을 포기하다　· keep going: (힘들거나 고통스러워도) 계속 살아가다[견디다]

어떻게 나의 꿈을 성취할 것인가

나는 디자이너가 되기를 원한다. 나의 꿈을 성취하기 위해 내가 할 필요가 있는 세 가지가 있다. 나는 건강해야 하고, 창의적이어야 하고, 그리고 결코 포기하지 말아야 한다. 건강한 것은 나의 꿈을 계속 유지하도록 도와줄 것이다. 창의적인 것은 내가 무언가 다른 것을 하도록 도와줄 것이다. 더하여, 내 스스로에게 결코 포기하지 말라고 항상 말할 것인데, 이는 내가 더 열심히 노력하도록 해 줄 것이기 때문이다.

Wrap Up 2

B: It's difficult to learn English.
　　 가주어　　　　　 진주어

G: Rome was not built in a day.
　　　　 be not p.p.(부정문 수동태)　하루 사이에, 하루 아침에

B: What do you mean by that?
그게 무슨 뜻이니? (= What is that exactly? = What exactly do you mean? = Could you explain about that in detail?)

G: I mean it takes time to achieve something.
　　　 take+시간: (얼마의 시간이) 걸리다　to부정사의 부사적 용법(목적): ~하기 위해서 (진주어로 쓰인 명사적 용법으로 볼 수도 있음)

B: I see.
= I understand.

B: 영어를 배우는 것은 어려워.
G: 로마는 하루아침에 이루어지지 않았어.
B: 그게 무슨 뜻이니?
G: 무언가를 이루는 데 시간이 걸린다는 뜻이야.
B: 알겠어.

01 다음 빈칸에 들어갈 말이 순서대로 바르게 짝지어진 것은?

> • They gave _____ the game without scoring even one point.
> • I met a lot of nice people, thanks _____ you.

① in – to
② in – for
③ up – to
④ up – for
⑤ up – at

02 다음 중 밑줄 친 부분의 뜻풀이가 바르지 않은 것은?

① Sorry, we can no longer help you. (더 이상 ~ 아닌)
② I never expected your support. (지지)
③ No pain, no gain. (고통)
④ They will present him with an award for good citizenship. (선물)
⑤ She has a gentle heart. (점잖은)

03 다음 밑줄 친 부분과 의미가 가장 가까운 것을 주어진 철자로 시작하여 쓰시오.

> In the end, we all decided to organize a concert for Easter.

➡ F_____

04 다음 빈칸에 알맞은 말을 고르시오.

> One of the ways to _____ the respect is by showing responsibility for the community.

① believe
② present
③ keep
④ earn
⑤ win

[05~06] 다음 대화를 읽고 물음에 답하시오.

B: I have a singing contest tomorrow. I really want to win first place.
G: I'll keep my fingers crossed for you.
B: What do you mean by "keep my fingers crossed"?
G: It means (A)_____.
B: Thank you.

05 빈칸 (A)에 알맞은 말을 고르시오.

① it's easy to do
② working together is better than working alone
③ you learn something by doing it over and over
④ it takes time to achieve something
⑤ I wish you good luck

06 위 대화를 읽고 대답할 수 없는 질문은?

① Does the girl know the meaning of "keep my fingers crossed"?
② What does the boy want at a singing contest?
③ What kind of contest is the boy going to have?
④ Where is a singing contest held?
⑤ When is there a singing contest?

[07~08] 다음 대화를 읽고 물음에 답하시오.

A: (A)_____.
B: What do you mean ⓐ_____ "(B)_____"?
A: I mean you learn something ⓑ_____ doing it over and over.

07 빈칸 (A)와 (B)에 공통으로 들어갈 말을 고르시오.

① Practice makes perfect
② Rome was not built in a day
③ Will is power
④ Two heads are better than one
⑤ It's a walk in the park

08 빈칸 ⓐ와 ⓑ에 공통으로 들어갈 전치사를 쓰시오.

➡ _____

[09~10] 다음 대화를 읽고 물음에 답하시오.

G: Your poster looks great. (①)
B: Thanks, Kate. (②) Did you finish yours?
G: Not yet. I can't draw well. (③)
B: It takes time. (④) It's important that
  (A)_____. (⑤)
G: You mean I should keep practicing?
B: That's right.

09 위 대화의 ①~⑤ 중 다음 주어진 말이 들어갈 알맞은 곳은?

> How can I become good at drawing?

①   ②   ③   ④   ⑤

10 빈칸 (A)에 알맞은 말을 고르시오.

① you take an art class
② you draw as often as you can
③ you see a lot of pictures
④ you go to an art gallery
⑤ you buy expensive pictures

11 다음 상황에 어울리는 말이 아닌 것을 고르시오.

> You and your friend are watching a soccer game in a stadium. Your friend shouts loudly, "Way to go!" but you do not know what he means. So, you want to ask him what it means.

① What is "Way to go" exactly?
② Will you "Way to go"?
③ What exactly do you mean by "Way to go"?
④ What do you mean by "Way to go"?
⑤ Could you explain about "Way to go" in detail?

12 다음 빈칸에 들어갈 말이 순서대로 바르게 짝지어진 것은?

> B: It's difficult to learn English.
> G: Rome was not built in a day.
> B: What do you mean by that?
> G: I mean it _____ time to _____ something.
> B: I see.

① takes	mean
② takes	achieve
③ does	mean
④ does	achieve
⑤ does	expect

Grammar

13 다음 우리말을 주어진 어휘를 이용하여 영작하시오.

(1) 부모님이 내게 사 주신 컴퓨터가 고장 났다.
(buy, for, break)

➡ _____

_____

(2) 내가 사진을 찍어 준 남자와 그의 개가 1등을 차지했다. (the man, that, take a picture, win the first prize)

➡ _____

_____

(3) 네가 일요일에 만난 그 남자는 내 남동생이다. (meet, brother)

➡ _____

(4) 그의 가족은 그가 수영 대회에 참가하기를 원했다. (take part in, the swimming competition)

➡ _____

_____

(5) 그녀는 나에게 파리에 함께 가자고 권유했다. (invite, go, her)

➡ _____

(6) 나는 그에게 시끄럽게 하지 말라고 말했다. (tell, make a noise)

➡ _____

14 다음 중 두 문장을 한 문장으로 만들었을 때 그 의미가 **다른** 하나는?

① It turned out to be a tiger shark. + It attacked her that morning.
  → It turned out to be a tiger shark which attacked her that morning.

② Those are the flowers. + Rebecca grows them in her garden.
  → Those are the flowers Rebecca grows in her garden.

③ Alice will send a letter to Alex. + Alice met him at the party.
  → Alice will send a letter to Alex whom she met at the party.

④ I will become a player. + People like the player.
  → I will become a player who people like.

⑤ The bag was sent to Wendy. + I bought the bag yesterday.
  → Wendy sent the bag that I bought yesterday.

15 다음 중 어법상 올바른 것은?

① I didn't expect him talk to you.
② They asked John did something for them.
③ Mom wanted Sam finishing his homework.
④ It will enable Jane to complete her project.
⑤ His doctor ordered Simon to takes some rest.

16 〈보기〉의 밑줄 친 that과 용법이 **다른** 하나는?

┌─ 보기 ─┐
France was the first country that I visited last year.
└──────┘

① The man who I admire the most is King Sejong.
② This is the dog which he often found in his garden.
③ Tom bought a backpack which has two side pockets.
④ You are the only person that I can trust.
⑤ This is the bike that Emily lost yesterday.

17 다음 ⓐ~ⓗ 중 옳은 것을 모두 고르면?

> ⓐ I told you to not make any noise.
> ⓑ My parents want me live with them.
> ⓒ I'll let you to go home early.
> ⓓ His wife asked him to wash the dishes.
> ⓔ His support helped Robinson to play harder.
> ⓕ He is the man which gave me a drink.
> ⓖ I didn't enjoy the movie which I saw it yesterday.
> ⓗ I will become a player that people like.

① ⓐ, ⓒ
② ⓑ, ⓒ, ⓓ
③ ⓑ, ⓓ, ⓗ
④ ⓓ, ⓔ, ⓖ
⑤ ⓓ, ⓔ, ⓗ

18 괄호 안에 주어진 어휘를 이용하여 우리말에 맞게 영작하시오.

(1) 그는 나에게 자기를 병원에 데려다 달라고 부탁했다. (ask, take, the hospital)

➡ _____

(2) 너는 그녀가 나가는 소리를 들었니? (hear, go out)

➡ _____

(3) 나는 로마에서 만난 그 여인을 잊을 수 없다. (forget, met, woman, Rome)

➡ _____

_____

Reading

[19~20] 다음 글을 읽고 물음에 답하시오.

It was New York City on April 15, 1947. Jackie Robinson, an African American, went on the field as second baseman for the Brooklyn Dodgers. People couldn't believe their eyes. He was the first African American player ⓐto play on a Major League team. That day, the color line was broken.

19 위 글의 밑줄 친 ⓐto play와 to부정사의 용법이 다른 것을 모두 고르시오.

① He must be brave to do such a thing.
② At first, he had no friends to practice baseball together.
③ There are many African American players to play on a Major League team.
④ His dream was to be a major leaguer.
⑤ He put all his energy into baseball to become a player who people liked.

20 본문의 내용과 일치하도록 다음 빈칸 (A)와 (B)에 알맞은 단어를 쓰시오.

> On April 15, 1947, when (A)_____ _____ went on the field as second baseman for the Brooklyn Dodgers, the (B)_____ _____ was broken.

[21~23] 다음 글을 읽고 물음에 답하시오.

Robinson faced many difficulties. ⓐ Robinson was a talented player and a gentle person, his teammates did not want to play with him. Every hotel turned the team down because Robinson was on the team. When he was at bat, people in the stands rudely shouted at him.

(①) Robinson thought to himself, 'I need to keep calm and focus on baseball. (②) Then, next season, there will be more African American players in the league.' (③) Robinson put all his time and energy into baseball. (④) With practice, he became great at batting and base running. (⑤)

21 위 글의 빈칸 ⓐ에 들어갈 알맞은 말을 고르시오.

① As
② Although
③ If
④ Because
⑤ Since

22 위 글의 흐름으로 보아, 주어진 문장이 들어가기에 가장 적절한 곳은?

> I will try and become a player who people like.

①   ②   ③   ④   ⑤

23 위 글의 마지막 부분에서 알 수 있는 'Robinson'의 성격으로 가장 알맞은 것을 고르시오.

① curious   ② outgoing
③ sociable   ④ diligent
⑤ creative

[24~26] 다음 글을 읽고 물음에 답하시오.

Robinson's effort moved his teammates. When people shouted at Robinson, one of his teammates walked up to Robinson and tapped him ⓐ the shoulder. "Do not listen to them. You're doing fine," he said. His support helped Robinson to play harder. Finally, Robinson earned the respect of other players and fans.

Thanks to Robinson, the Dodgers won the National League Championship in 1947. The league recognized Robinson's excellence and presented him ⓑ the Rookie of the Year Award in the same year. After that season, ⓒ다른 팀들은 아프리카계 미국인 선수들에게 자신들의 팀에 합류할 것을 요청했다.

24 위 글의 빈칸 ⓐ와 ⓑ에 들어갈 전치사가 바르게 짝지어진 것은?

① on – with   ② by – to
③ in – for   ④ by – with
⑤ on – to

25 위 글의 밑줄 친 ⓒ의 우리말에 맞게 한 단어를 보충하여, 주어진 어휘를 알맞게 배열하시오.

> them / players / teams / asked / American / join / other / African

➡ _____

_____

26 위 글의 주제로 알맞은 것을 고르시오.

① Robinson's effort made him famous.
② Robinson earned people's recognition through his effort.
③ A teammate encouraged Robinson not to be disappointed.
④ The Dodgers won the National League Championship in 1947.
⑤ Robinson won the Rookie of the Year Award in 1947.

[27~28] 다음 글을 읽고 물음에 답하시오.

Robinson's uniform number was 42. Baseball players in Major League teams no longer wear the number 42 to honor him. Every year, however, on April 15, every player ⓐ_____ the number that Robinson ⓑ_____. The day is called "Jackie Robinson Day."

27 위 글의 빈칸 ⓐ와 ⓑ에 wear를 알맞은 형태로 쓰시오.

➡ ⓐ _____ ⓑ _____

28 다음 문장에서 위 글의 내용과 다른 부분을 찾아서 고치시오.

> Baseball players in Major League teams want to wear the number 42 to honor him.

➡ _____

01 다음 짝지어진 두 단어의 관계가 <u>다른</u> 하나를 고르시오.

① different – difference
② important – importance
③ silent – silence
④ allow – allowance
⑤ excellent – excellence

02 다음 중 밑줄 친 부분의 뜻풀이가 바르지 <u>않은</u> 것은?

① Writing a book requires a lot of time and <u>effort</u>. (노력)
② Everyone <u>recognized</u> his skill. (인정했다)
③ How many things do you <u>recycle</u> at your school? (재활용하다)
④ This is one of the <u>major</u> sources of energy. (주요한)
⑤ I know that they <u>face</u> lots of problems. (얼굴)

03 다음 빈칸에 알맞은 단어를 고르시오.

> I thought _____, "I'm in trouble."

① to me
② for me
③ to myself
④ for myself
⑤ in me

04 두 문장에 공통으로 들어갈 수 있는 단어를 고르시오.

> • She _____ first place in the swimming competition.
> • She _____ the Best Actress award.

① won
② made
③ went
④ took
⑤ realized

05 다음 대화의 빈칸에 들어갈 말을 〈보기〉에서 골라 순서대로 바르게 배열한 것은?

> G: Oh, this is hard to do.
> B: _____
> G: _____
> B: _____
> G: _____
> B: I mean it's easy to do.

┤ 보기 ├

(A) Can you teach me how to make cookies?
(B) Sure. It's a walk in the park.
(C) What's the matter?
(D) What do you mean by that?

① (B) – (A) – (C) – (D)
② (B) – (C) – (A) – (D)
③ (C) – (A) – (B) – (D)
④ (C) – (B) – (A) – (D)
⑤ (C) – (D) – (B) – (A)

[06~07] 다음 글을 읽고 물음에 답하시오.

W: Do you want to ⓐachieve your dream? Remember! Great people ⓑalways stop learning. The best way ⓒto learn is by reading. Even ⓓwhen you are busy, you have to find time to read. However, 네가 읽을 알맞은 책을 고르는 것도 중요하다. (choose, to, it's, that, books, read, important, you, the, right) Here is ⓔwhat to choose the right books.

06 위 글에서 문맥상 또는 어법상 어색한 것을 모두 고르시오.

① ⓐ　　② ⓑ　　③ ⓒ　　④ ⓓ　　⑤ ⓔ

07 다음 밑줄 친 우리말에 맞게 주어진 단어를 바르게 배열하시오.

➡ _____

08 다음 대화의 빈칸에 들어갈 수 없는 것은?

> B: I have a singing contest tomorrow. I really want ⓐ_____ first place.
> G: I'll ⓑ_____ my fingers ⓒ_____ for you.
> B: What do you ⓓ_____ by "ⓑ_____ my fingers ⓒ_____"?
> G: ⓔ_____ I wish you good luck.
> B: Thank you.

① lucky　　　　② It means
③ to win　　　　④ mean
⑤ keep

[09~11] 다음 글을 읽고 물음에 답하시오.

> M: To achieve my dream, I went to many auditions, but I often failed. (A)_____, I never gave up. I took acting and dancing classes. (B)_____, I (C)_____ my goal. (D)절대 포기하지 않는 것이 중요합니다.

09 빈칸 (A)와 (B)에 들어갈 말로 알맞은 것끼리 짝지어진 것을 고르시오.

	(A)	(B)
①	However	Though
②	Therefore	Especially
③	However	Finally
④	Therefore	Especially
⑤	In addition	Finally

10 빈칸 (C)에 알맞은 말을 위의 대화에 나온 단어를 이용해서 채우시오.

➡ _____

11 밑줄 친 (D)의 우리말을 영작하시오.

➡ _____

12 다음 대화의 순서를 바르게 배열하시오.

> (A) It's important that you never give up.
> (B) Okay. I will not forget that.
> (C) It's hard to be a good dancer. What should I do?

➡ _____

13 다음 중 어법상 올바른 것은?

① Her parents were worried and asked her stop surfing.
② He also ordered us to tell the truth and never to lie.
③ Mr. Johnson told us shook hands after the game.
④ His parents encouraged him has an interest in art.
⑤ I didn't expect you understanding me at all.

14 다음 중 어법상 <u>어색한</u> 문장은?

① I love the watch which my uncle bought for me.

② Paul is the boy who I often play soccer with.

③ Is this the book you were talking about it at that time?

④ I went to the office in which Anne was working.

⑤ Do you know the man your mother is talking to?

15 다음 중 밑줄 친 that과 바꿔 쓸 수 있는 것은?

> The chair that I sat on was not comfortable.

① whom   ② whose   ③ who

④ which   ⑤ what

[16~18] 다음 글을 읽고 물음에 답하시오.

It was New York City on April 15, 1947. Jackie Robinson, an African American, went on the field as second baseman for the Brooklyn Dodgers. People couldn't believe their eyes. He was the first @아프리카계 미국인 player to play on a Major League team. ⓑ That day, the color line __(A)__ .

16 위 글의 빈칸 (A)에 들어갈 알맞은 말을 고르시오.

① was drawn   ② happened

③ was broken   ④ was made

⑤ appeared

17 위 글의 밑줄 친 @의 우리말을 두 단어로 쓰시오.

➡ _____

18 위 글의 밑줄 친 ⓑThat day가 가리키는 것을 본문에서 찾아 쓰시오.

➡ _____

[19~21] 다음 글을 읽고 물음에 답하시오.

Robinson @faced many difficulties. Although Robinson was a talented player and a gentle person, his teammates did not want ⓑto play with him. Every hotel ⓒturned the team down because Robinson was on the team. When he was at bat, people in the stands rudely shouted at him.

19 위 글의 밑줄 친 @faced와 바꿔 쓸 수 있는 말을 고르시오.

① expressed   ② encountered

③ accepted   ④ looked into

⑤ solved

20 위 글의 밑줄 친 ⓑto play와 to부정사의 용법이 <u>다른</u> 것을 고르시오.

① I think it wrong to tell a lie.

② I decided to go to Madrid.

③ He wanted to buy a new smartphone.

④ This water is not good to drink.

⑤ It is necessary to finish the work now.

21 위 글의 밑줄 친 ⓒturned the team down을 다음과 같이 바꿔 쓸 때 빈칸에 들어갈 알맞은 말을 쓰시오.

➡ _____ the team

[22~24] 다음 글을 읽고 물음에 답하시오.

Robinson's effort @moved his teammates. When people shouted at Robinson, one of his teammates walked up to Robinson and tapped him on the shoulder. "Do not listen to them.

You're doing fine," he said. His support helped Robinson to play harder. Finally, Robinson earned the respect of other players and fans.

Thanks to Robinson, the Dodgers won the National League Championship in 1947. The league recognized Robinson's excellence and presented him with the Rookie of the Year Award in the same year. After that season, other teams asked African American players to join them.

출제율 100%

22 위 글의 제목으로 가장 알맞은 것을 고르시오.

① How to Earn the Respect of Others
② Robinson's Effort Bore Fruit
③ How Did the Dodgers Win the National League Championship?
④ Who Won the Rookie of the Year Award in 1947?
⑤ Many Teams Wanted African American Players.

출제율 90%

23 위 글의 밑줄 친 ⓐmoved와 바꿔 쓸 수 있는 단어를 쓰시오.

➡ _____

출제율 95%

24 위 글의 내용과 일치하지 않는 것은?

① When people shouted at Robinson, one of his teammates encouraged him.
② The teammate's support helped Robinson to play harder.
③ At last, other players and fans came to respect Robinson.
④ Thanks to the Dodgers, Robinson won the National League Championship in 1947.
⑤ After that season, other teams gave African American players a chance to join them.

[25~26] 다음 글을 읽고 물음에 답하시오.

Robinson's uniform number was 42. ⓐBaseball players in Major League teams no longer wear the number 42 to honor him. Every year, however, on April 15, every player wears the number ⓑthat Robinson wore. The day is called "Jackie Robinson Day."

출제율 90%

25 위 글의 밑줄 친 ⓐ를 바르게 바꿔 쓴 문장을 모두 고르시오.

① Baseball players in Major League teams no more wear the number 42 to honor him.
② Baseball players in Major League teams don't wear the number 42 no longer to honor him.
③ Baseball players in Major League teams don't wear the number 42 any more to honor him.
④ Baseball players in Major League teams don't wear the number 42 no more to honor him.
⑤ Baseball players in Major League teams don't wear the number 42 any longer to honor him.

출제율 90%

26 위 글의 밑줄 친 ⓑthat과 문법적 쓰임이 같은 것을 모두 고르시오.

① Those are the books that you lent me.
② I am so tired that I cannot go on.
③ This is the house that we live in.
④ It is the movie that I want to see.
⑤ The trouble is that we have no money.

01 밑줄 친 우리말을 주어진 단어를 이용하여 영작하시오.

> A: Two heads are better than one.
> B: What do you mean by "Two heads are better than one"?
> A: <u>함께 일하는 것이 혼자 일하는 것보다 낫다는 뜻이야.</u> (alone, together, working)

➡ _____

_____

[02~03] 다음 대화를 읽고 물음에 답하시오.

> G: Hey, Minho. ⓐDid you find the answer to the math problem?
> B: No. ⓑIt's too easy for me. ⓒI'm not good at math.
> G: ⓓLet me see. (A)<u>네가 그 문제를 풀기 위해선 이 수학 공식을 이용하는 것이 중요해.</u> (it's, that, rule, solve)
> B: Oh, I see. ⓔI'll use it.

02 ⓐ~ⓔ 중 흐름상 어색한 부분을 찾아 고치시오.

➡ _____

중요
03 밑줄 친 우리말 (A)를 주어진 단어를 이용하여 영작하시오.

➡ _____

_____

중요
04 밑줄 친 우리말을 주어진 단어를 이용하여 영작하시오.

> A: Practice makes perfect.
> B: What do you mean by "Practice makes perfect"?
> A: <u>반복해서 무언가를 하면 배우게 된다는 뜻이야.</u> (over, by, I, something, learn) (11 words)

➡ _____

05 다음 두 문장을 관계대명사를 사용하여 한 문장으로 바꾸시오.

(1) • The Korean dishes tasted yummy.
　　• We had them last night.

➡ _____

_____

(2) • I have a dog.
　　• I take a walk with it every night.

➡ _____

_____

중요
06 다음 빈칸을 알맞은 말로 채워 비슷한 뜻을 갖는 문장으로 바꾸어 쓰시오.

(1) July told her daughter that she should not go out alone at night.
　➡ July ordered her daughter _____ _____.

(2) We hope that Amy will win first prize at the singing contest.
　➡ We expect Amy _____ _____.

[07~09] 다음 글을 읽고 물음에 답하시오.

Robinson faced ⓐmany difficulties. Although Robinson was a talented player and a gentle person, his teammates did not want to play with him. Every hotel turned the team (A)[down / up] because Robinson was on the team. When he was at bat, people in the stands (B)[rude / rudely] shouted at him.

Robinson thought to himself, 'I need to keep (C)[calm / calmly] and focus on baseball. I will try and become a player who people like. ⓑThen, next season, there will be more African American players in the league.' Robinson put all his time and energy into baseball. With practice, he became great at batting and base running.

07 위 글의 밑줄 친 ⓐmany difficulties의 예를 본문에서 찾아 우리말로 쓰시오.

➡ (1) _____

(2) _____

(3) _____

_____

08 위 글의 괄호 (A)~(C)에서 문맥이나 어법상 알맞은 낱말을 골라 쓰시오.

➡ (A)_____ (B)_____ (C)_____

09 위 글의 밑줄 친 ⓑThen이 가리키는 내용을 본문에서 찾아 다음 빈칸에 알맞게 쓰시오.

➡ If _____

[10~12] 다음 글을 읽고 물음에 답하시오.

Robinson's effort moved his teammates. When people shouted at Robinson, one of his teammates walked up to Robinson and tapped him on the shoulder. "Do not listen to them. You're doing fine," he said. ⓐHis support helped Robinson playing harder. Finally, Robinson earned the respect of other players and fans.

ⓑThanks to Robinson, the Dodgers won the National League Championship in 1947. The league recognized Robinson's excellence and presented him with the Rookie of the Year Award in the same year. After that season, other teams asked African American players to join them.

10 위 글의 밑줄 친 ⓐ에서 어법상 틀린 부분을 찾아 고치시오.

➡ _____

11 위 글을 읽고 1947년에 Robinson과 관련하여 일어난 일 두 가지를 우리말로 쓰시오.

➡ (1) _____

_____

(2) _____

_____

12 위 글의 밑줄 친 ⓑ를 다음과 같이 바꿔 쓸 때 빈칸에 들어갈 알맞은 말을 쓰시오

➡ Robinson's effort enabled the Dodgers _____ _____ the National League Championship in 1947.

창의사고력 서술형 문제

01 다음 대화의 밑줄 친 우리말을 영작하시오. (주어진 어휘를 이용할 것)

A: Are you studying now?
B: Yes, I am.
A: But you're listening to music now.
B: Yes. 음악이 공부를 더 잘할 수 있게 도와준다고 생각해요. (study, help, better)_____
A: I don't think so. 네가 공부할 때는 집중하는 것이 중요하다. (focus, when, it)
_____
B: Okay. 음악 소리를 줄일게요. (I'll, the music) _____

02 〈보기〉를 참고하여 다른 사람에게 기대하는 것을 expect를 이용하여 어법에 맞게 3 문장 이상 쓰시오.

┌─ 보기 ─────────────────────────────┐
I expect my friend Sora to become a scientist.
└───────────────────────────────────┘

(1) _____
(2) _____
(3) _____

03 다음 내용을 바탕으로 꿈을 이루기 위한 나의 다짐을 표현하는 글을 쓰시오.

Q1 What is your dream? My dream is to become a chef.
Q2 How can you achieve your dream?
☑ practicing hard, ☑ working well with others, ☑ managing my time well
Q3 How can things from Q2 help you?
☑ practicing hard
It will help me cook well and easily.
☑ working well with others
It will make it easier to work at a restaurant.
☑ managing my time well
It will help me make food in time to serve.

How I Will Achieve My Dream
   I want to be a chef. There are three things that I need to do to achieve my dream. I need (A)_____, work well with others, and manage my time well. Practicing hard will help me (B)_____. Working well with others will make it easier (C)_____. Plus, I will always tell myself to manage my time well because it will help me (D)_____.

단원별 모의고사

01 다음 빈칸에 들어갈 말로 적절한 것을 고르시오.

> Why do you always shout _____ me?

① at　② by　③ of　④ from　⑤ to

02 빈칸 (A)와 (B)에 알맞은 것끼리 짝지어진 것을 고르시오.

> • As a doctor, she (A)_____ the respect of her patients.
> • If you have a dream, never (B)_____ up and pursue your passion.

	(A)	(B)
①	earned	give
②	accepted	give
③	earned	grow
④	accepted	grow
⑤	earned	count

03 우리말 해석을 보고 주어진 단어를 이용하여 빈칸을 채우시오.

(1) I'd like to have a strong will to overcome _____ like her. (나는 그녀처럼 어려움을 극복하는 강한 의지를 갖고 싶다.) (difficult)

(2) He got a prize for _____ in B-boy dancing. (그는 B-boy 댄스 부분에서 우수상을 탔다.) (excellent)

04 주어진 영영풀이의 어휘를 빈칸에 써 넣으시오.

> help and kindness that you give to someone who is having a difficult time

> I need his help and _____.

[05~06] 다음 대화를 읽고 물음에 답하시오.

> A: (A)Will is power.
> B: What do you mean by "Will is power"?
> A: (B)강한 의지로 꿈을 이룰 수 있다는 뜻이야.
> (mean, achieve, with)

05 위 대화의 밑줄 친 (A)'Will'과 같은 의미로 사용되지 <u>않은</u> 것을 고르시오.

① The decision was made of her free <u>will</u>.
② He <u>will</u> finish the report immediately.
③ The stronger <u>will</u> you have, the more you will learn.
④ Humans have the freedom of the <u>will</u>.
⑤ Where there is a <u>will</u>, there is a way.

06 밑줄 친 (B)의 우리말을 주어진 단어를 이용하여 영작하시오.

➡ _____

_____

07 주어진 대화 이후에 이어질 대화의 순서를 바르게 배열하시오.

> A: Please call me "The Wizard of Goyang."
> B: What do you mean by "The Wizard of Goyang"?

> (A) What is important to do to become an inventor?
> (B) I'm sure you'll make it.
> (C) I mean I want to be an inventor.
> (D) It's important that I think creatively.

➡ _____

08 ①~⑤ 중 다음 주어진 말이 들어갈 알맞은 곳은?

> Do you want to achieve your dream? Remember! (①) Great people never stop learning. (②) The best way to learn is by reading. (③) Even when you are busy, you have to find time to read. (④) Here is how to choose the right books. (⑤)

> However, it's important that you choose the right books to read.

①   ②   ③   ④   ⑤

[09~12] 다음 대화를 읽고 물음에 답하시오.

> **Hana:** You look (A)_____, Jiho. What's wrong?
> **Jiho:** I don't think I can achieve my dream.
> **Amy:** (B)_____ that?
> **Jiho:** I want to be an actor, but I always fail auditions. Maybe I have to give up.
> **Amy:** Do you know this actor?
> **Jiho:** Sure. He's a famous movie star.
> **Amy:** (C)He failed much than 100 auditions.
> **Jiho:** Really? Maybe I should keep trying. I will practice more for my next audition.
> **Hana:** That's right! It's important that you never (D)_____.

09 빈칸 (A)에 알맞은 말을 고르시오.

① sleepy   ② happy   ③ sad
④ lonely   ⑤ lucky

10 빈칸 (B)에 알맞은 말을 고르시오.

① When are you going to tell me about
② Why are you telling him
③ What do you mean by
④ How do you know
⑤ Where did you hear about

11 밑줄 친 (C)에서 어법상 또는 문맥상 어색한 것을 찾아 바르게 고쳐서 완벽한 문장으로 쓰시오.

➡ _____

12 빈칸 (C)에 들어갈 말을 위의 대화에서 찾아 쓰시오.

➡ _____

13 다음 두 문장을 관계대명사를 사용하여 한 문장으로 바꾸시오.

(1) • She is the girl.
     • I love her.
     ➡ _____

(2) • Have you ever fallen in love with a lady?
     • You haven't even talked to her.
     ➡ _____
     _____
     _____
     _____

14 주어진 동사를 어법에 맞게 빈칸에 쓰시오.

(1) Mom asked David _____ the dishes. (do)
(2) Her dad allowed her _____ to the concert. (go)

(3) It caused them _____ on their freedom. (insist)

(4) I warned him _____ late. (be)

15 다음 중 어법상 어색한 문장은?

① Please allow me to stay here one more day.

② Becky asked you to clean your room.

③ He encouraged her to reveal her true feelings.

④ Everything that I said was true.

⑤ I love the jacket whom Hana is wearing.

16 다음 중 어법상 적절한 것을 고르시오.

① I will always tell myself manage my time well because it will help me to make food in time to serve.

② This is because people wanted her to become a role model for young people.

③ I like the cake who my mother made for my birthday.

④ Ryan sells oranges who he grew himself.

⑤ I will invite the friends who I met them at the party last weekend.

17 다음 문장에서 어법상 어색한 것을 바르게 고치시오.

(1) The doctor advised her drank more water.

➡ _____

(2) The teacher encouraged her trying again.

➡ _____

(3) He was not sure whether he wished her stay or go.

➡ _____

(4) What is the name of the program who he is watching?

➡ _____

[18~20] 다음 글을 읽고 물음에 답하시오.

Robinson faced many difficulties. ⓐ Although Robinson was a talented player and a gentle person, his teammates did not want to play with him. Every hotel turned the team down because Robinson was on the team. When he was at bat, people in the stands rudely shouted ①at him.

Robinson thought to himself, 'I need to keep calm and focus ②on baseball. I will try and become a player who people like. Then, next season, there will be more African American players in the league.' Robinson put all his time and energy ③into baseball. ④With practice, he became great ⑤for ⓑbatting and base running.

18 위 글의 밑줄 친 ⓐ를 다음과 같이 바꿔 쓸 때 빈칸에 들어갈 알맞은 말을 쓰시오.

➡ Robinson was a talented player and a gentle person, _____ his teammates did not want to play with him.

19 위 글의 밑줄 친 전치사 ①~⑤ 중에서 쓰임이 옳지 않은 것을 찾아 고치시오.

➡ _____

20 아래 〈보기〉에서 위 글의 밑줄 친 ⓑbatting과 문법적 쓰임이 같은 것의 개수를 고르시오.

┌─── 보기 ├───
① Kids are <u>playing</u> on the sand.
② I'm proud of <u>being</u> Korean.
③ Sally's hobby is <u>talking</u> about entertainers.
④ <u>Being</u> on time is very important in the business world.
⑤ Do you know the woman <u>standing</u> at the gate?
└─────────────

① 1개 ② 2개 ③ 3개 ④ 4개 ⑤ 5개

23 위 글을 읽고 대답할 수 없는 질문은?

① Who told Robinson not to listen to people who shouted at him?
② Could Robinson earn the respect of other players and fans?
③ When did the Dodgers win the National League Championship?
④ What award did Robinson win in 1947?
⑤ How many African American players joined other teams after that season?

[21~23] 다음 글을 읽고 물음에 답하시오.

Robinson's effort moved his teammates. When people shouted at Robinson, one of his teammates walked up to Robinson and tapped him on the shoulder. "Do not listen to them. You're doing fine," he said. His support helped Robinson to play harder. Finally, Robinson earned the respect of other players and fans.

Thanks to Robinson, the Dodgers won the National League Championship in 1947. The league recognized Robinson's excellence and presented him with the Rookie of the Year Award in the same year. After that season, other teams asked African American players to ⓐ<u>join</u> them.

21 위 글의 밑줄 친 ⓐjoin과 바꿔 쓸 수 있는 어구들을 쓰시오.

➡ _____

22 위 글의 내용과 어울리는 속담을 고르시오.

① Sincerity moves heaven.
② Haste makes waste.
③ Don't cry over spilt milk.
④ Everybody's business is nobody's business.
⑤ Too many cooks spoil the broth.

[24~25] 다음 글을 읽고 물음에 답하시오.

Robinson's uniform number was 42. Baseball players in Major League teams no longer wear the number 42 to honor him. Every year, however, on April 15, every player wears ⓐ<u>the number</u> (A) Robinson wore. The day is called "Jackie Robinson Day."

24 위 글의 빈칸 (A)에 들어갈 알맞은 말을 모두 고르시오.

① who ② what
③ that ④ whom
⑤ which

25 위 글의 밑줄 친 ⓐthe number가 가리키는 것을 본문에서 찾아 쓰시오.

➡ _____

Lesson 8

Science Is Making Big Changes

 의사소통 기능

- 놀람 표현하기
  I'm surprised that you can recommend books.

- 요청하기
  Can you recommend one, please?

 언어 형식

- 현재완료
  Have you ever **thought** about these changes?

- 조동사 may
  Let's see what our lives **may** be like in the near future.

Words & Expressions

Key Words

- □ **add** [æd] 동 더하다
- □ **advance** [ædvǽns] 명 발전
- □ **AI** 인공지능(= **artificial intelligence**)
- □ **app** [æp] 명 스마트폰 앱, 어플리케이션(**application**)
- □ **automatically** [ɔ̀ːtəmǽtikəli] 부 자동적으로
- □ **bottle** [bátl] 명 병
- □ **charge** [tʃɑːrdʒ] 동 (지불, 대금 등을) 청구하다
- □ **condition** [kəndíʃən] 명 상태, 조건
- □ **counter** [káuntər] 명 계산대
- □ **cover** [kʌ́vər] 동 덮다
- □ **decorate** [dékərèit] 동 장식하다, 꾸미다
- □ **deliver** [dilívər] 동 배달하다
- □ **difference** [dífərns] 명 차이, 차이점
- □ **drone** [droun] 명 (원격 조종의) 드론
- □ **drop** [drɑp] 동 떨어뜨리다
- □ **ever** [évər] 부 어느 때고, 언제든, 한번이라도
- □ **experience** [ikspíəriəns] 명 경험
- □ **fancy** [fǽnsi] 형 화려한, 공들인, 고급의
- □ **fit** [fit] 동 (치수·모양 등이) 꼭 맞다
- □ **gravity** [grǽvəti] 명 중력
- □ **guess** [ges] 동 추측하다
- □ **heavily** [hévili] 부 심하게, 아주 많이
- □ **huge** [hjuːdʒ] 형 거대한
- □ **later** [léitər] 부 나중에, 후에
- □ **law** [lɔ:] 명 법칙, 법
- □ **librarian** [laibréəriən] 명 사서
- □ **list** [list] 명 목록, 리스트
- □ **lower** [lóuər] 동 낮추다

- □ **material** [mətíəriəl] 명 재료
- □ **medicine** [médisn] 명 약
- □ **method** [méθəd] 명 방법, 방식
- □ **offer** [ɔ́ːfər] 동 ~을 제공하다
- □ **patient** [péiʃənt] 명 환자
- □ **pay** [pei] 동 (돈을) 지불하다
- □ **price** [prais] 명 가격
- □ **print** [print] 동 ~을 인쇄하다
- □ **purchase** [pə́ːrtʃəs] 명 구입(품)
- □ **real** [ríːəl] 형 진짜의
- □ **recommend** [rèkəménd] 동 ~을 추천하다
- □ **rescue** [réskjuː] 동 구조하다
- □ **return** [ritə́ːrn] 동 돌아가다
- □ **save** [seiv] 동 구하다
- □ **since** [sins] 접 ~ 이후로
- □ **skill** [skil] 명 기술
- □ **society** [səsáiəti] 명 사회
- □ **station** [stéiʃən] 명 역, 정류장
- □ **suit** [suːt] 동 (입맛, 취향 등에) 맞다
- □ **taste** [teist] 동 맛보다
- □ **technology** [teknálədʒi] 명 과학 기술, 생산 기술
- □ **temperature** [témpərətʃər] 명 온도
- □ **tube** [tjuːb] 명 튜브
- □ **UFO** 미확인 비행 물체(= **Unidentified Flying Object**)
- □ **virtual** [və́ːrtʃuəl] 형 가상의
- □ **with** [wið] 전 ~을 써서, ~을 이용하여
- □ **work** [wəːrk] 동 작동하다

Key Expressions

- □ **add up** 합산하다
- □ **be good at** ~을 잘하다
- □ **be interested in** ~에 관심이 있다
- □ **be ready for** ~할 준비가 되다
- □ **be worried about** ~에 대해 걱정하다
- □ **by** 동명사 ~함으로써
- □ **don't have to** 동사원형 ~할 필요가 없다
- □ **forget to** 동사원형 ~할 것을 잊다
- □ **get lost** 길을 잃다
- □ **in space** 공중에
- □ **in the future** 미래에
- □ **in trouble** 곤경에 빠져서, 난처하여

- □ **look at** ~을 보다
- □ **look for** ~을 찾다
- □ **may + 동사원형** ~일지도 모른다(추측)
- □ **move around** 돌아다니다
- □ **put on** 입다, 쓰다, 신다
- □ **take care of** ~을 돌보다
- □ **take place** 일어나다, 개최되다
- □ **talk to** ~ ~에게 말을 걸다
- □ **turn off** (전기·가스·수도 등을) 끄다
- □ **turn on** (전기·가스·수도 등을) 켜다
- □ **wait in line** 줄을 서서 기다리다
- □ **would like to** 동사원형 ~하고 싶다

Word Power

※ 명사에 접미사 -al을 붙여 형용사가 되는 어휘들

□ **culture**(문화) – **cultural**(문화의, 문화적인)

□ **music**(음악) – **musical**(음악의, 음악적인)

□ **tradition**(전통) – **traditional**(전통의, 전통적인)

□ **industry**(산업) – **industrial**(산업의)

□ **person**(사람, 개인) – **personal**(개인의, 개인적인)

□ **nation**(국가) – **national**(국가의)

※ 비슷한 의미를 가진 어휘들

□ **deliver**(배달하다) – **carry**(나르다, 운반하다)

□ **heavily**(심하게, 아주 많이) – **excessively**(지나치게, 심히)

□ **huge**(거대한) – **large**(큰)

□ **material**(재료) – **matter**(물질, 물체)

□ **offer**(~을 제공하다) – **provide**(공급하다)

□ **put on**(입다, 쓰다, 신다) – **wear**(입다)

□ **guess**(추측하다) – **estimate**(추정하다)

□ **law**(법칙, 법) – **principle**(원칙, 법칙)

□ **method**(방법, 방식) – **manner**(방법, 방식)

□ **take place**(일어나다) – **happen**(발생하다)

※ 반대 의미를 가진 어휘들

□ **difference**(차이, 차이점) ↔ **similarity**(유사점)

□ **ever**(어느 때고, 언제든, 한번이라도) ↔ **never**(지금까지[어느 때건] 한 번도 ~ 않다)

□ **lower**(낮추다) ↔ **heighten**(강화하다, 높이다)

English Dictionary

□ **advance** 발전
→ progress or an instance of progress in science, technology, human knowledge, etc.
과학, 기술, 인간의 지식의 진보나 그러한 순간

□ **app** 애플리케이션
→ a piece of computer software that is designed to do a particular job
특별한 작업을 하기 위해 만들어진 컴퓨터 소프트웨어

□ **automatically** 자동적으로
→ with operating by itself
저절로 작동되는

□ **charge** (지불, 대금 등을) 청구하다
→ to ask someone to pay an amount of money for something that you are selling to them or doing for them
어떤 것을 팔거나, 어떤 일을 한 것에 대한 돈을 지불하라고 누군가에게 요청하다

□ **decorate** 장식하다, 꾸미다
→ to add ornaments, etc. to something to make it more attractive 어떤 것을 더 매력적으로 만들기 위해서 장식을 더하다

□ **deliver** 배달하다
→ to take something to somewhere to give it to someone 누군가에게 주기 위해 어딘가로 어떤 것을 가지고 가다

□ **drone** (원격 조종의) 드론
→ an unmanned aircraft or ship guided by remote control or onboard computers
원격조종이나 내장 컴퓨터로 조종되는 무인의 항공기나 배

□ **law** 법칙, 법
→ a statement of fact concerning what always happens in certain circumstances; a scientific principle
특정한 조건에서 항상 발생하는 것에 관련된 사실의 설명; 과학적 원리

□ **material** 재료
→ a substance that is used for a particular purpose
특별한 목적을 위해 사용되는 물질

□ **medicine** 약
→ a substance that you take to cure an illness
병을 치료하기 위해 먹는 물질

□ **method** 방법, 방식
→ a way of doing something, especially a planned way
어떤 것을 하기 위한 방법, 특히 계획된 방법

□ **patient** 환자
→ someone who is receiving medical treatment
의학적 치료를 받고 있는 사람

□ **recommend** ~을 추천하다
→ to speak in favor of something
어떤 것을 지지하여 말하다

□ **rescue** 구조하다
→ to save someone or something from danger or harm
위험이나 손상으로부터 누군가나 어떤 것을 구하다

□ **station** 역, 정류장
→ a place where a bus or train stops to allow passengers to get on and off
버스나 기차가 승객을 태우거나 내리도록 멈추는 장소

□ **virtual** 가상의
→ created by computers, or appearing on computers or the Internet
컴퓨터에 의해 만들어진 또는 컴퓨터나 인터넷에 나타나는

서답형

01 다음 〈보기〉와 같은 관계가 되도록 빈칸에 알맞은 말을 쓰시오.

┌─ 보기 ─┐
huge – large

(1) wear – _____ (2 단어)
(2) happen – _____ (2 단어)

[02~03] 다음 빈칸에 들어갈 말로 적절한 것은?

02
He always tried to protect people _____ trouble.

① at   ② for   ③ on   ④ in   ⑤ to

03
It rained _____ last night, so it is a little cold today.

① nearly   ② heavily
③ poorly   ④ short
⑤ difficult

중요
04 다음 중 밑줄 친 부분의 뜻풀이가 바르지 <u>않은</u> 것은?

① The <u>advances</u> in medicine are surprising. (발전)
② This is how the product <u>works</u>. (일하다)
③ I'm sorry, but can you tell me what the <u>difference</u> is? (차이점)
④ You can ask the woman at the <u>counter</u>. (계산대)
⑤ The door locks <u>automatically</u> when it is shut. (자동적으로)

[05~06] 다음 빈칸에 공통으로 들어갈 말로 알맞은 것은?

05
• I don't think I'll ever be ready _____ the exam tomorrow!
• I looked _____ my bag for three hours and finally found it.

① for   ② at   ③ to   ④ on   ⑤ like

중요
06
• I need someone to _____ care of my daughter after school.
• A lot of cultural festivals _____ place during autumn.

① take   ② give   ③ get
④ find   ⑤ have

중요
07 〈보기〉의 밑줄 친 'may'와 같은 의미로 쓰인 것을 고르시오.

┌─ 보기 ─┐
He's absent today. He <u>may</u> be sick.

① If you're finished, <u>may</u> I use the phone?
② <u>May</u> I come in two hours late tomorrow morning?
③ I <u>may</u> be late, so don't wait for me.
④ You <u>may</u> use this room.
⑤ <u>May</u> I use this computer for a while?

01 다음 밑줄 친 부분과 의미가 가장 가까운 것을 쓰시오. (3단어)

> We need not change the meeting place.

➡ _____

02 다음 짝지어진 단어의 관계가 같도록 빈칸에 알맞은 말을 주어진 철자를 시작하여 쓰시오.

> ever : never – difference : s_____

03 주어진 우리말에 맞게 빈칸을 채우시오. (철자가 주어진 경우 그 철자로 시작할 것)

(1) 그들은 박물관에 들어가는 데 너에게 20달러를 청구한다.

➡ They c_____ you $20 to get in the museum.

(2) 돌은 흔히 건축 재료로 사용된다.

➡ Stone is often used as a building m_____.

(3) 나의 친구가 이 레스토랑을 추천했다.

➡ My friend r_____ this restaurant.

(4) 이 가방이 내 취향에 가장 잘 맞는다.

➡ This bag s_____ my taste best.

(5) 이것을 할 수 있는 다른 방법이 있나요?

➡ Is there any other m_____ to do this?

04 빈칸에 들어갈 수 있는 단어를 〈보기〉에서 골라 쓰시오.

> ┌─ 보기 ┐
> as at by for of in on to

(1) In the summer, we turn _____ the fan to keep cool.

(2) Who takes care _____ the children while you're away?

(3) They can learn responsibility _____ doing their homework.

(4) I waited _____ line to buy a ticket.

05 우리말과 일치하도록 괄호 안에 주어진 단어를 알맞게 배열하시오.

(1) 지구는 태양 주위를 돈다.

(moves, the Sun, the Earth, around)

➡ _____

(2) 꽃집으로 가는 도중 길을 잃어버렸어.

(shop, lost, to, on, the, I, my, got, way, flower)

➡ _____

(3) 사람들은 대기 오염에 대해 걱정하지 않는다.

(are, pollution, people, about, worried, not, air)

➡ _____

(4) 안전 헬멧과 구명조끼를 입는 것을 명심해라.

(safety, life, sure, jackets, be, to, on, and, put, helmets)

➡ _____

Conversation

① 놀람 표현하기

I'm surprised that you can recommend books. 네가 책을 추천해 줄 수 있다니 놀라워.

- 예상하지 못한 일에 대한 놀라움을 나타낼 때 'I'm surprised that ~.'라고 말할 수 있다.
  접속사 that 다음에는 절(주어+동사)이 와야 하며, 명사구가 오는 경우에는 be surprised at을 쓴다.
  surprised 대신에 amazed나 shocked를 사용해도 된다.

- 비슷한 표현으로 'What a surprise!', 'How surprising!'이나 'I can't believe it.' 등이 있다.

놀람 표현하기

- I'm surprised that 주어 동사 ~. (~하는 것이 놀라워.)
- How surprising! (놀랍구나!)
- That's amazing! (놀랍구나!)
- What a surprise! (놀랍구나!)
- That's[It's] surprising! (놀랍구나!)
- I (just) can't believe this. (이걸 믿을 수 없어!)

핵심 Check

1. 다음 우리말과 일치하도록 빈칸에 알맞은 말을 쓰시오.

   A: _____ it has such a creative shape. (나는 그것이 그렇게 창의적인 형태를 가지고 있는 것에 놀랐어.)

   B: So am I. (나도 그래.)

2. 대화의 순서를 바르게 배열하시오.

   (A) Sure. I heard it from her.

   (B) No, I didn't. Is that true?

   (C) Wow! I'm surprised that Kate speaks four languages.

   (D) Did you know that Kate speaks four languages?

   ➡ _____

3. 괄호 안의 단어를 순서대로 배열하여 대화를 완성하시오.

   A: I think I need to study more. (나는 더 공부를 할 필요가 있는 것 같아.)

   B: _____ (so, I'm, that, surprised, think, you)

   (나는 네가 그렇게 생각하는 것이 놀라워.)

② 요청하기

Can you recommend one, please? (하나 추천해 줄 수 있니?)

■ 상대방에게 어떤 행동을 요청할 때는 'Can you 동사 ~?'로 말할 수 있다. 대답을 할 때는 긍정이면 'Sure.', 'Of course.' 등으로, 부정이면 'Sorry, I can't.' 등으로 말할 수 있다.

요청하기

- Can[Could/Will/Would] you 동사 ~? (~해 줄 수 있니?)
- Can[Could] I ask you to 동사 ~? (~을 부탁해도 될까?)
- Do[Would] you mind 동명사 ~? (~해 줄 수 있니?)

- (Please,) 동사 ~. (~해 줘.)

■ 'Do you mind 동명사 ~?'의 질문에 대답할 때 주의해야 할 점은 요청을 수락할 때 부정으로 대답해야 한다는 점이다. 즉, 'No, I don't (mind).', 'No problem.', 'Of course not.' 등으로 대답하는 것이 요청을 수락한 것이고, 요청을 거절할 때는 'Yes, I do.', 'I'm sorry I do.'라고 답한다.

요청에 답하기

수락
- Yes!
- Okay!
- Sure!
- All right!
- Of course.
- No problem.
- (That) Sounds good.

거절
- Of course not.
- Sorry, but ~.
- Thank you, but ~.
- (I'm) Sorry but I can't.
- I'm afraid I can't ~.

핵심 Check

4. 다음 우리말과 일치하도록 빈칸에 알맞은 말을 쓰시오.

A: Can _____ with my English homework? (내 영어 숙제 좀 도와 줄 수 있니?)

B: Of course. (물론이지.)

A: Can you _____? (지금 내게 가르쳐 줄 수 있니?)

B: _____ I have to go to the piano practice. (미안하지만, 못 할 것 같아. 피아노 연습에 가야 해.)

5. 괄호 안의 단어를 순서대로 배열하여 대화를 완성하시오.

A: _____? (the, ask, could, door, to, I, you, open)

(문 여는 것을 부탁해도 될까?)

B: Sure! (물론이지!)

Listen & Speak 1 A-1

G: ❶Oh, I forgot to turn off the heater before I left home.

B: Really? Then do you ❷need to return home?

G: No. I can ❸turn it off ❹with my smartphone.

B: Wow, ❺I'm surprised that you can turn off the heater with your smartphone.

G: 아, 나는 집에서 나오기 전에 히터 끄는 것을 잊어버렸어.
B: 정말? 그러면 넌 집으로 돌아가야 하니?
G: 아니. 나는 내 스마트폰으로 히터를 끌 수 있어.
B: 우와, 나는 네가 스마트폰으로 히터를 끌 수 있다는 게 놀라워.

❶ forget+to동사원형: ~할 것을 잊다 turn off: (전기·가스·수도 등을) 끄다 / 여기서 before 뒤에 주어(I)+동사(left)가 나온 것으로 보아, before는 접속사로 사용되었다.
❷ need to 동사원형: ~할 필요가 있다 return: 돌아가다 need to 대신 should나 have to를 쓸 수도 있다.
❸ turn off는 이어동사로 '동사+부사(on, off, up, over 등)'로 이루어져 있다. '동사+부사+목적어'의 어순이나 '동사+목적어+부사'의 어순 둘 다 가능하다. 하지만 목적어 자리에 인칭대명사(it, them)가 올 때는 반드시 '동사+목적어+부사'의 어순으로 쓴다.
❹ with: ~을 써서[이용하여]
❺ I'm surprised that 주어 동사 ~: ~하는 것이 놀라워

Check(√) True or False

(1) The girl can turn the heater off with her smartphone.　　　　T ☐ F ☐

(2) The boy is not surprised that the girl can turn off the heater with her smartphone.　　T ☐ F ☐

Listen & Speak 2 A-1

W: ❶May I help you?

B: Hi, I'm ❷looking for a smart watch. ❸Can you show me one?

W: Sure. ❹Look at this one. It can play music for you.

B: ❺Sounds cool.

W: ❻Also, you can search for anything just by talking to it.

B: That's great. I will ❼take it.

W: 도와드릴까요?
B: 안녕하세요, 저는 스마트 워치를 찾고 있어요. 하나 보여 주실래요?
W: 물론이죠. 이것을 보세요. 그것은 당신을 위해 음악을 연주할 수 있어요.
B: 멋지네요.
W: 또한 그것에게 말만 하면 어떤 것이든 검색할 수 있어요.
B: 멋지네요. 그것을 살게요.

❶ 어떤 일을 하기 전에 상대방에게 허락을 요청할 때는 'May I ~?', 'Can I ~?' 등을 사용할 수 있다.
❷ look for: ~을 찾다
❸ Can you 동사 ~?: ~해 줄 수 있니? show는 4형식 동사로 간접목적어(me)와 직접목적어(one)를 취한다.
❹ look at: ~을 보다
❺ sound+형용사: ~하게 들리다 cool: 멋진
❻ search for: ~을 찾다 just: 단지 by 동명사: ~함으로써
❼ take: 선택하다, 사다

Check(√) True or False

(3) The boy wants to buy a smart watch.　　　　T ☐ F ☐

(4) The smart watch can't play music.　　　　T ☐ F ☐

Listen & Speak 1 A-2

W: ❶Welcome to VR World. ❷Would you like to visit Niagara Falls?

B: Sure.

W: Okay, ❸put this on.

B: All right. Wow, it ❹looks so real.

W: It is ❺huge, isn't it?

B: Yes, and ❻I'm surprised that I feel water on my face.

❶ Welcome to: ~에 오신 것을 환영합니다
❷ would like to 동사원형: ~하고 싶다 visit: 방문하다
❸ put on: 입다, 쓰다, 신다
❹ look+형용사: ~하게 보이다 real: 진짜의
❺ huge: 거대한
❻ I'm surprised that 주어 동사 ~: ~하는 것이 놀라워

 Listen & Speak 2 A-2

M: Welcome. This is our new smart light. You ❶ don't have to use your hands ❷to turn it on and off.

W: Really? Then ❸can you tell me how to do it?

M: Just say, "Light on!" or "Light out!"

W: Light on or light out? That's very simple.

❶ don't have to 동사원형: ~할 필요가 없다
❷ to부정사의 부사적 용법(목적)으로 '~하기 위해서'로 해석한다. off 앞에 turn it이 생략되어 있다. turn on: (전기·가스·수도 등을) 켜다 turn off: (전기·가스·수도 등을) 끄다
❸ Can you 동사 ~?: ~해 줄 수 있니? tell+간접목적어(me)+직접목적어 (how to do it): 나에게 그것을 하는 방법을 말해주다

 Conversation A

M: ❶These days, many things can work like humans. Some cars can travel without a human driver. We can ❷make smartphones do simple work only ❸by talking to them. ❹I'm surprised that we're already living in the future.

❶ these days: 요즘, 오늘날 like는 전치사로 '~처럼'의 의미이다.
❷ make(사역동사)+목적어+목적격보어(동사원형): …에게 ~하게 하다
❸ by 동명사: ~함으로써 talk to ~: ~에게 말을 걸다 them은 smartphones를 받는 대명사이다
❹ I'm surprised that 주어 동사 ~: ~하는 것이 놀라워 in the future: 미래에

 Conversation B

Amy: Wow, ❶there are so many books in this library.

Hana: You're right. Where can we find books about ❷gravity?

Terry: Hi, I'm Terry, the AI ❸librarian. Can I help you?

Amy: Hi. ❹We're looking for books about gravity. ❺Can you recommend one, please?

Terry: We have fifty seven books about gravity in this library. I think *The Law of Gravity* will be the best one for you.

Hana: I'm surprised that you can recommend books.

Amy: Right. That's ❻amazing. Where is the book, Terry?

Terry: It's ❼on the third floor. Come with me.

❶ there are 복수명사: ~가 있다
❷ gravity: 중력
❸ librarian: 사서
❹ look for: ~을 찾다
❺ Can you 동사 ~?: ~해 줄 수 있니? recommend: ~을 추천하다 one = a book
❻ amazing: 놀라운
❼ on the 서수 floor: ~층에

 Communication Task Step 3

A: ❶Can you tell us about your item, please?

B: Sure. These are future shoes. People will run 100 meters in 5 seconds with these shoes.

C: Wow, ❷I'm surprised that humans will run that fast.

❶ 'Can you tell us about ~?'는 어떤 것에 대한 설명을 요청할 때 사용하는 표현이다. 요청이나 부탁의 표현을 할 때는 조동사 can 대신에 could, will, would를 사용하여 말할 수 있다.
❷ that: 그렇게

● 다음 우리말과 일치하도록 빈칸에 알맞은 말을 쓰시오.

Listen & Speak 1 A

1. **G:** Oh, I forgot _____ _____ _____ the heater before I left home.

   B: Really? Then do you need _____ _____ home?

   G: No. I can _____ it _____ with my smartphone.

   B: Wow, I'm _____ _____ you can turn _____ the heater with your smartphone.

2. **W:** Welcome to VR World. Would you like _____ visit Niagara Falls?

   B: Sure.

   W: Okay, _____ this on.

   B: All right. Wow, it looks so real.

   W: It is huge, isn't it?

   B: Yes, and _____ _____ that I feel water on my face.

Listen & Speak 1 B

1. **A:** Is _____ anything in these pictures that _____ you?

   B: Yes. I'm _____ that this drone can _____ a dog.

2. **A:** Is _____ _____ in these pictures _____ _____ you?

   B: Yes. _____ _____ _____ this car can drive _____ automatically.

Listen & Talk 2 A

1. **W:** May I _____ you?

   B: Hi, I'm _____ _____ a smart watch. Can you show me one?

   W: Sure. Look at this one. It can play music _____ you.

   B: Sounds cool.

   W: Also, you can _____ _____ anything just _____ talking to it.

   B: That's great. I will take it.

2. M: Welcome. This is our new smart light. You _____ _____ to use your hands to turn it on and off.

W: Really? Then can you _____ me _____ to do it?

M: Just say, "Light on!" or "Light out!"

W: Light _____ or light out? That's very simple.

Listen & Talk 2 B

1. A: I want to _____ go. Can you _____ go with me, please?
   B: Sure.

2. A: My room is _____. Can you _____ it, please?
   B: Sure.

3. A: The dog wants to go _____. Can you _____ the dog, please?
   B: Sure.

Conversation A

M: These days, many things can _____ _____ humans. Some cars can _____ without a human driver. We can make smartphones do _____ work only _____ _____ _____ them. _____ _____ _____ we're already _____ in the future.

Conversation B

Amy: Wow, there _____ so many _____ in this library.

Hana: You're right. _____ _____ we find books about _____?

Terry: Hi, I'm Terry, the AI _____. Can I help you?

Amy: Hi. We're _____ _____ books about _____. Can you _____ one, please?

Terry: We have fifty seven books about gravity in this library. I think *The Law of Gravity* will be the best one for you.

Hana: I'm surprised _____ _____ _____ _____ _____ _____ _____.

Amy: Right. That's _____. Where is the book, Terry?

Terry: It's _____ the third floor. Come with me.

[01~02] 다음 대화의 빈칸에 알맞은 말은?

01

> G: Oh, I forgot to turn off the heater before I left home.
>
> B: Really? Then do you need to return home?
>
> G: No. I can turn it off with my smartphone.
>
> B: Wow, I'm _____ that you can turn off the heater with your smartphone.

① interesting   ② boring   ③ exciting
④ surprised   ⑤ satisfied

02

> W: May I help you?
>
> B: Hi, I'm looking for a smart watch. _____
>
> W: Sure. Look at this one. It can play music for you.
>
> B: Sounds cool.
>
> W: Also, you can search for anything just by talking to it.
>
> B: That's great. I will take it.

① Can you tell me how to do it?   ② Can you show me one?
③ Can you show me how it works?   ④ Can I recommend one?
⑤ Can I clean it?

03 주어진 문장 다음에 이어질 대화의 순서로 알맞은 것을 고르시오.

> Are you ready for your trip to London?

> (A) Can you show me one?
>
> (B) Yes, but I'm worried about getting lost. I'm not good at finding places.
>
> (C) Don't worry. There are many good smartphone apps you can use.
>
> (D) Sure. Use this one. It shows you a map of the city and pictures of streets.

① (B) – (A) – (C) – (D)   ② (B) – (C) – (A) – (D)
③ (C) – (A) – (B) – (D)   ④ (C) – (B) – (A) – (D)
⑤ (C) – (D) – (B) – (A)

[01~03] 다음 대화를 읽고 물음에 답하시오.

W: Welcome to VR World. Would you like to visit Niagara Falls?

B: Sure.

W: Okay, (A)_____.

B: All right. Wow, it looks so real.

W: It is huge, isn't it?

B: Yes, and (B)_____

01 빈칸 (A)에 들어갈 말로 알맞은 것을 고르시오.

① work this out
② put this away
③ put this on
④ give this up
⑤ turn it down

02 빈칸 (B)에 들어갈 말로 알맞은 것을 고르시오.

① I'm surprised that you did that.
② I'm surprised to learn that I can visit Niagara Falls.
③ I'm surprised that you can help me.
④ I'm surprised that I won the game.
⑤ I'm surprised that I feel water on my face.

03 위 대화의 내용과 일치하지 않는 것을 고르시오. (2개)

① 남자아이는 VR을 이용해 나이아가라 폭포를 보고 있다.
② VR을 통해 본 나이아가라 폭포는 진짜처럼 보인다.
③ 남자아이는 나이아가라 폭포에 직접 갔다.
④ VR을 통해 본 나이아가라 폭포는 그리 크지 않다.
⑤ VR을 통해 나이아가라 폭포를 볼 때 남자아이는 물을 느꼈다.

04 다음 중 짝지어진 대화가 어색한 것은?

① A: Can you help me to do this?
   B: I'm sorry. I can't.

② A: Did you know that Nick speaks four languages?
   B: No, I didn't. I'm surprised that he speaks four languages.

③ A: Can you come to my house this weekend?
   B: Of course.

④ A: Can you go to the store for me?
   B: Sure. I'm busy now.

⑤ A: Did you see Tom at the school festival?
   B: Yeah, I was surprised that he was like a real singer.

05 빈칸 (A)와 (B)에 공통으로 들어갈 말로 알맞은 것을 고르시오.

A: Is there anything in these pictures (A)_____ surprises you?

B: Yes. I'm surprised (B)_____ this car can drive itself automatically.

① which
② what
③ that
④ how
⑤ why

06 대화의 빈칸에 들어갈 말을 〈보기〉에서 골라 순서대로 바르게 배열한 것은?

> W: May I help you?
> B: _____
> W: _____
> B: _____
> W: _____
> B: That's great. I will take it.

> ┤ 보기 ├
> (A) Also, you can search for anything just by talking to it.
> (B) Sounds cool.
> (C) Hi, I'm looking for a smart watch. Can you show me one?
> (D) Sure. Look at this one. It can play music for you.

① (B) – (A) – (C) – (D)
② (B) – (C) – (A) – (D)
③ (C) – (A) – (B) – (D)
④ (C) – (B) – (A) – (D)
⑤ (C) – (D) – (B) – (A)

[07~08] 다음 대화를 읽고 물음에 답하시오.

> M: Welcome. (①) This is our new smart light. (②) You don't have to use your hands to turn it on and off. (③)
> W: Really? (④)
> M: Just say, "Light on!" or "Light out!" (⑤)
> W: Light on or light out? That's very simple.

07 위 대화의 ①~⑤ 중 다음 주어진 말이 들어갈 알맞은 곳은?

> Then can you tell me how to do it?

①   ②   ③   ④   ⑤

08 위 대화의 내용과 일치하지 <u>않는</u> 것을 고르시오.

① The man knows how to turn on and off the new smart light.
② The woman should use her hands to turn on and off the new smart light.
③ The woman at first didn't know the way to turn on and off the new smart light.
④ The woman thinks that the way to turn on and off the new smart light is simple.
⑤ By saying "Light on", the woman can turn the new smart light on.

[09~10] 다음 대화를 읽고 물음에 답하시오.

> G: Oh, I forgot to turn off the heater before I left home. (①)
> B: Really? (②) Then do you need to return home? (③)
> G: No. (④)
> B: Wow, I'm surprised that you can turn off the heater with your smartphone. (⑤)

09 위 대화의 ①~⑤ 중 다음 주어진 말이 들어갈 알맞은 곳은?

> I can turn it off with my smartphone.

①   ②   ③   ④   ⑤

10 위 대화의 내용과 일치하는 것을 고르시오.

① The girl is in her house now.
② The girl is going to return home to turn off the heater.
③ The boy already knows that the heater can be turned off by the smartphone.
④ The boy forgot to turn the heater off.
⑤ The boy is surprised to learn that the girl can turn off the heater with her smartphone.

01 다음 대화의 (A)~(C)에서 적절한 것을 고르시오.

> G: Oh, I forgot to turn (A)[on / off] the heater before I left home.
> B: Really? Then do you need to return home?
> G: (B)[Yes / No]. I can turn it off with my smartphone.
> B: Wow, I'm (C)[surprised / frustrated] that you can turn off the heater with your smartphone.

➡ (A) _____ (B) _____ (C) _____

02 다음 우리말에 맞게 주어진 단어를 바르게 배열하시오.

> A: Is there anything in these pictures that surprises you?
> B: Yes. 나는 이 드론이 물건을 배달할 수 있다는 게 놀라워. (this, things, I'm, can, that, deliver, surprised, drone)

➡ _____

03 ⓐ~ⓔ 중 흐름상 어색한 것을 고치시오.

> M: Welcome. ⓐThis is our new smart light. ⓑYou have to use your hands to turn it on and off.
> W: Really? ⓒThen can you tell me how to do it?
> M: ⓓJust say, "Light on!" or "Light out!"
> W: ⓔLight on or light out? That's very simple.

➡ _____

[04~05] 다음 대화를 읽고 물음에 답하시오.

> Amy: Wow, there are so many books in this library.
> Hana: You're right. Where can we find books about gravity?
> Terry: Hi, I'm Terry, the AI librarian. Can I help you?
> Amy: Hi. We're looking for books about gravity. (A)Can you recommend one, please?
> Terry: We have fifty seven books about gravity in this library. I think *The Law of Gravity* will be the best one for you.
> Hana: (B)나는 네가 책을 추천해 줄 수 있다니 놀라워. (you, I'm, recommend, that, books, surprised, can)
> Amy: Right. That's amazing. Where is the book, Terry?
> Terry: It's on the third floor. Come with me.

04 밑줄 친 (A)와 같은 의미를 가진 문장으로 쓰고자 한다. 주어진 단어를 이용해 문장을 만드시오.

➡ (1) _____ (can, ask)
  (2) _____ (mind)
  (3) _____ (will)

05 (B)의 밑줄 친 우리말에 맞게 괄호 안에 주어진 단어를 배열하여 영작하시오.

➡ _____

Grammar

① 현재완료

Have you ever **thought** about these changes?
여러분은 이러한 변화들에 대해 생각해 본 적이 있는가?

- 현재완료는 'have[has]+과거분사'의 형태로 과거의 어느 한 시점에 일어난 일이 현재까지 영향을 미칠 때 사용한다.

- 의문문은 'Have[Has]+주어+과거분사 ~?'이며, 부정문은 'have[has]+not[never]+과거분사'로 나타낸다.

  • I **haven't forgotten** his warning yet. 나는 그의 경고를 아직 잊지 않았다.

  • How many times **have** you **done** this kind of work? 이런 일을 몇 번이나 해보셨어요?

- 현재완료는 의미에 따라 완료(막[벌써] ~했다), 경험(~한 적이 있다), 계속(~해 왔다), 결과(~해 버렸다) 등으로 구분할 수 있다.

  완료 용법은 과거에 시작한 일이 이미 끝난 것을 나타내며, 보통 'just(막, 방금), already(이미, 벌써), yet(아직, 벌써)' 등과 같은 부사와 쓰이고, 경험 용법은 과거에서부터 지금까지의 경험을 나타내며, 'ever(이제껏), never(한 번도 ~ 아닌), before(전에), once(한 번), twice(두 번), three times(세 번)' 등과 같은 부사(구)와 함께 쓰이며, 계속 용법은 과거에 일어난 일이 현재까지 계속되고 있는 것을 나타내며, 보통 'for(~ 동안)+기간 명사'나 'since(~부터, ~ 이래로)+시간 명사'와 함께 쓰인다. 결과 용법은 과거의 일이 원인이 되어, 그 결과가 현재에 영향을 미칠 때 쓴다.

  • I **have never been** here before. <경험> 저는 전에 이곳에 와 본 적이 없습니다.

  • He **has studied** Japanese for three years. <계속> 그는 3년 동안 일본어를 공부하고 있다.

  • The man **has lost** his cowboy hat. <결과> 그 남자는 그의 카우보이 모자를 잃어버렸다. (그 결과 (그의 카우보이 모자가) 지금 없다.)

- 현재완료는 과거에 시작된 동작과 그 동작의 현재 상태를 동시에 표현하므로 명백한 과거를 나타내는 yesterday, ~ ago, last week 등의 부사(구)나 의문사 when과는 함께 쓰이지 않는다.

  • I **was** ill yesterday. (○) 나는 어제 아팠다.
    I have been ill yesterday. (×)

  *have[has] been to vs. have[has] gone to
  have[has] been to는 '~에 가 본 적이 있다'는 경험을 나타내고, have[has] gone to는 '~에 가고 없다'는 결과를 나타낸다. 그러므로 have[has] gone to는 3인칭만 주어로 쓸 수 있다.

핵심 Check

1. 주어진 동사를 빈칸에 어법에 맞게 쓰시오.
   (1) She _____ already _____ all her money. (spend)
   (2) I _____ not _____ from my brother for about two months. (hear)
   (3) _____ you ever _____ about becoming a teacher? (think)

② 조동사 may

Let's see what our lives **may** be like in the near future.
가까운 미래에 우리의 삶이 어떻게 될지 살펴보자.

- 'may'는 조동사로 뒤에 'be'동사나 일반동사와 함께 쓰이며, 이때 'be'동사와 일반동사는 동사원형으로 쓴다.
  - You **may** do as you like. 너 하고 싶은 대로 해도 괜찮다.
- 조동사 '**may**'의 의미
  (1) '추측'을 나타내어 '~일지도 모른다, 아마 ~일 것이다'의 뜻을 나타낸다.
  - A friend today **may** turn against you tomorrow. 오늘의 친구가 내일의 적이 될지도 모른다.
  (2) '허가'를 나타내어 '~해도 좋다'의 뜻을 나타낸다.
  - If you're finished, **may** I use the phone? 전화 끝나셨으면 제가 좀 써도 될까요?
- 부정문은 'may' 다음에 'not'을 쓰고 의문문은 may를 문두에 둔다.
  - You **may not** believe it, but that's true. 믿지 않을지 모르지만 그것은 사실이다.
  - **May** I ask where you bought it? 그걸 어디서 샀는지 물어봐도 될까요?

핵심 Check

2. 다음 괄호 안에서 알맞은 말을 고르시오.

(1) He worked a lot today. He (may / can) be tired now.

(2) May I (use / using) your phone?

(3) The math problem may (be / is) easy for him.

01 다음 대화의 빈칸에 알맞은 말을 쓰시오.

> M: _____ I speak to Mr. Kim, please?
> W: Wait a moment, please.

02 다음 두 문장을 한 문장으로 바르게 연결한 것은?

> • Robert went to America.
> • And he is there now.

① Robert went to America.
② Robert went to America already.
③ Robert hasn't been to America yet.
④ Robert hasn't come back to America.
⑤ Robert has gone to America.

03 다음 빈칸에 알맞은 것을 고르시오.

> It is possible that they are in the garden.
> = They _____ in the garden.

① may be   ② must be   ③ have been
④ are   ⑤ were

04 다음 대화의 빈칸에 들어갈 말로 알맞은 것은?

> M: Did you finish doing the dishes?
> W: I'm sorry, but I have not finished doing the dishes _____.

① for   ② since   ③ just
④ yet   ⑤ already

05 다음 빈칸에 가장 알맞은 것은?

> He didn't take a rest for long. He _____ tired.

① has   ② has been   ③ may be
④ may is   ⑤ should be

01 다음 중 어법상 바르지 <u>않은</u> 것은?

① Melanie has gone to her home country already.
② Most people have never heard of these laws.
③ She has studied Spanish for three years.
④ When have you parked your car at the garage?
⑤ Ann has caught a big fish at the lake.

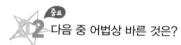 다음 중 어법상 바른 것은?

① He mays know my e-mail address.
② It may not raining in Seoul.
③ Paul may do not be in the classroom.
④ Jane may not is at home now.
⑤ I may not be able to work again.

03 다음 빈칸에 알맞은 말이 바르게 짝지어진 것은?

> • _____ you finished your homework already?
> • What do you think may _____ in the future?

① Is – happen
② Is – happens
③ Have – happen
④ Have – happens
⑤ Has – happening

 다음 괄호 안에서 알맞은 말을 고르시오.

(1) Jack (have / has) just drawn her portrait.
(2) I (don't have / haven't) improved much in speaking English.
(3) Matthew is not here. He has (been / gone) to a far country over the sea.
(4) A lot of things (have happened / happened) in 2010.
(5) Something good may (happens / happen) to you.
(6) Tony (not may / may not) be interested in music.

05 다음 질문에 대한 응답으로 알맞은 것은?

> • Has Charlotte lived a difficult life since childhood?

① Yes, she is.
② Yes, she has.
③ Yes, she does.
④ No, she doesn't.
⑤ No, she may be.

06 다음 우리말을 영어로 옮길 때, 빈칸에 알맞은 말을 고르시오.

> Smith 씨와 통화할 수 있을까요?
> _____ I speak to Mr. Smith?

① May
② Am
③ Must
④ Will
⑤ Do

서답형

07 다음 문장에서 어법상 어색한 부분을 바르게 고치시오.

(1) People have already start to pay with virtual cards.

_____ ➡ _____

(2) What have you done last week, Allen?

_____ ➡ _____

(3) How long do you have been employed here?

_____ ➡ _____

(4) I haven't heard from him for last year.

_____ ➡ _____

(5) I have been out of work since five months.

_____ ➡ _____

중요

08 다음 중 밑줄 친 부분의 의미가 다른 하나는?

① How <u>may</u> I help you?
② You <u>may</u> not use my pen.
③ You <u>may</u> play computer games after you finish your homework.
④ <u>May</u> I call you later tonight?
⑤ Jason worked all day. He <u>may</u> be tired now.

09 다음 빈칸에 알맞은 말이 순서대로 짝지어진 것은?

• She has lived in a 3D printed house _____ 5 years.
• She has lived in a 3D printed house _____ 2025.

① after – for
② for – after
③ since – for
④ for – since
⑤ as – for

[10~11] 다음 우리말에 맞게 영작한 것을 고르시오.

10

내 여동생은 중국에 가 본 적이 있다.

① My sister went to China.
② My sister was in China.
③ My sister has been to China.
④ My sister has gone to China.
⑤ My sister has went to China.

11

드론들이 학교에서 학생들과 선생님들을 도와줄지도 모른다.

① Drones must help students and teachers at schools.
② Drones may help students and teachers at schools.
③ Drones can help students and teachers at schools.
④ Drones will help students and teachers at schools.
⑤ Drones should help students and teachers at schools.

중요

12 다음 중 어법상 어색한 문장은?

① Julie has known Mr. Brown since ten years.
② Don't you mean that Peter has met a famous person before?
③ He has never played tennis.
④ Something bad may happen to you when you are alone.
⑤ When it rains heavily, people may cover the whole city with the huge umbrella.

13 다음 〈보기〉의 밑줄 친 부분과 용법이 같은 것은?

> ┤ 보기 ├
> He <u>has managed</u> the small but nice hotel for about 10 years.

① She <u>has lost</u> her smartphone on the bus.
② Mike <u>has been</u> in the hospital since last month.
③ Julie <u>has been</u> to Amsterdam ten times.
④ Andy <u>has</u> just <u>finished</u> decorating his bedroom.
⑤ Linda has <u>gone back</u> to her home country.

14 다음 문장에서 어법상 어색한 부분을 바르게 고치시오.

(1) She mays be angry with me.

_____ ➡ _____

(2) Look at the sky. It may rains soon.

_____ ➡ _____

(3) She does not may use my computer.

_____ ➡ _____

(4) She may is upset with you.

_____ ➡ _____

15 다음 글의 밑줄 친 ⓐ, ⓑ를 알맞은 형태로 바꿔 쓰시오.

> • Christine and Thomas ⓐ<u>has visited</u> the Technology Fair yesterday. But we have never ⓑ<u>gone</u> there.

➡ ⓐ _____ ⓑ _____

16 주어진 어휘를 이용하여 다음 두 문장을 비슷한 뜻을 가진 한 문장으로 바꿔 쓰시오.

(1) Bill first knew Alice in 2017. He still knows her. (since)

➡ _____

(2) Olivia started to live in Seoul three years ago. And she still lives there. (for)

➡ _____

17 다음 밑줄 친 부분과 바꾸어 쓸 수 있는 것을 고르시오.

> <u>May</u> I help you?

① Do   ② Must   ③ Will
④ Can   ⑤ Should

18 다음 문장을 지시한 대로 바꾸어 쓰시오.

(1) Cleaning drones may help students at school. (부정문으로)

➡ _____

(2) I may see your passport. (의문문으로)

➡ _____

19 다음 밑줄 친 부분의 쓰임이 나머지 넷과 다른 것은?

① We <u>have known</u> each other since 2004.
② He <u>has taught</u> math for 20 years.
③ Sasha <u>has been</u> in Seoul for long.
④ I <u>have been</u> to Japan before.
⑤ Jack <u>has grown</u> tomatoes since then.

01 다음 우리말에 맞게 주어진 어휘를 이용하여 영작하시오.

(1) 그는 15살 이래로 부산에 살고 있다.
(live, Busan, old)

➡ _____

(2) 너는 기린을 본 적이 있니? (see, giraffes)

➡ _____

(3) 나는 아직 숙제를 끝내지 못했다. (finish, my)

➡ _____

(4) 나는 내 일기장을 잃어버렸다. (그래서 지금 일기장이 없다.) (lose)

➡ _____

(5) Paul은 교실에 없을지도 모른다. (be, classroom)

➡ _____

(6) 제가 에어컨을 켜도 될까요? (turn, the air conditioner)

➡ _____

02 주어진 두 문장을 한 문장으로 바꿔 쓰시오.

(1) • It began to rain last Thursday.
• It still rains.

➡ _____

(2) • Did William go to buy sandwiches?
• So, he isn't here now.

➡ _____

03 그림을 보고, 주어진 어휘를 이용하여 자신의 경험에 대해 쓰시오. (현재완료 시제로 주어와 동사를 갖춘 완전한 문장으로 쓸 것.)

(1) (use, naver, drone)

➡ _____

(2) (to, the tomato festival)

➡ _____

04 다음 밑줄 친 단어의 의미를 쓰시오.

(1) Students <u>may</u> learn many different subjects that are not taught now such as 3D printing, drone design, etc.

➡ _____

(2) You <u>may</u> go for a swim this afternoon.

➡ _____

05 다음 두 문장이 비슷한 뜻을 갖도록 빈칸에 알맞은 말을 쓰시오.

(1) It is probable that she will come to the party.

➡ She _____ to the party.

(2) You can't park your car here.

➡ You _____ your car here.

(3) Maybe they will sell delicious food.

➡ They _____ delicious food.

06 다음 문장을 어법에 맞게 고쳐 쓰시오.

(1) When have you started working at the company?

➡ _____

(2) She has worked as a drone designer for 2035.

➡ _____

(3) Have you ever gone to Vietnam before?

➡ _____

(4) So there maybe traffic lights for drones in the sky.

➡ _____

(5) Schools may are open only three days a week, so students don't may go to school every day.

➡ _____

_____

07 다음 문장을 부정문과 의문문으로 각각 바꿔 쓰시오.

> You have ever thought of how schools may change over the next 20 years.

부정문: _____

_____

의문문: _____

_____

08 다음 우리말을 괄호 안에 주어진 어휘를 이용하여 영작하시오.

(1) 나는 6년 동안 영어를 공부해 왔다. (study, years, 7 단어)

➡ _____

(2) 나는 그 편지를 아직 보내지 않았다. (send, the letter, 7 단어)

➡ _____

(3) 너는 바다에서 수영해 본 적이 있니? (ever, the sea, 7 단어)

➡ _____

(4) 어떤 변화들은 이미 일어나기 시작했고 반면 다른 것들은 가까운 미래에 일어날지도 모른다. (some, take place, while, 16 단어)

➡ _____

_____

09 두 문장의 의미가 같도록 빈칸에 알맞은 말을 쓰시오.

(1) I visited the restaurant again. It was my fourth visit.

= I _____ the restaurant _____.

(2) It is likely to rain today.

= We _____ rain today.

Changing Society

Advances in science and technology have caused many changes in
<u>have+과거분사</u>: 현재완료 계속 용법
our lives so far. In the future, science and technology will make more
지금까지
changes. Let's see what our lives may be like in the near future.
간접의문문: 의문사+주어(our lives)와 조동사(may). may: ~일지도 모른다(추측)

Sangho in the Shopping Center

Shopping is <u>much</u> easier. There are no lines and no counters.
비교급 강조('훨씬')
Sangho enters a shop with his smartphone <u>which</u> has a special
주격 관계대명사
shopping app. In the shop, he takes the items he wants. The items <u>are</u>
'the items'와 'he' 사이에 목적격 관계대명사 'which[that]'가 생략.
<u>automatically added</u> to a virtual card on his smartphone. If Sangho puts
수동태(be동사+과거분사)
an item back, <u>it is</u> automatically removed from his list of purchases.
if가 쓰인 문장의 주절에는 일반적으로 조동사가 쓰이지만, 어떤 조건이 주어졌을 때 예외 없이 발생하는 상황을 묘사할 때는 조동사 생략 가능. it = an item
When he finishes <u>shopping</u>, Sangho does not need to wait in line <u>to</u>
finish는 목적어로 동명사를 취한다.
<u>pay</u>. His virtual card adds up all the prices and will charge him <u>later</u>.
부사적 용법(목적)   latter(X)
Isn't that fancy?

society: (공동체를 이루는 일반적인) 사회
advance: 발전, 진보, 발달
technology: 과학 기술, 생산 기술
counter: 계산대, 판매대
app: 스마트폰 앱, 어플리케이션
(=application)
automatically: 자동(적)으로
virtual: (컴퓨터를 이용한) 가상의
list: 목록, 리스트
purchase: 구입; 구입하다
charge: 청구하다
fancy: 멋진
wait in line: 줄을 서서 기다리다
add up: 더하다

📎 확인문제

- 다음 문장이 본문의 내용과 일치하면 T, 일치하지 않으면 F를 쓰시오.

1 Advances in science and technology have caused many changes in our lives until now. ☐

2 Shopping has become more complex. ☐

3 Sangho enters a shop with his smartphone which has a special shopping app. ☐

4 When he finishes shopping, Sangho needs to wait in line to pay. ☐

Sumin's 3D Printed House and Clothes

Sumin lives in a 3D printed house. Building a 3D printed house is

집이 3D 프린트로 만들어진 것임(수동의 의미)　동명사 주어
faster and cheaper than building a house with traditional methods.

비교급+than　　　동명사
Sumin's house looks fantastic because of its unique design. A 3D

감각동사+형용사　　because of+명사구
printer can produce house shapes that people cannot make with

목적격 관계대명사(= which), 생략 가능
traditional building methods and materials. Sumin also likes to make

her clothes at home by using a 3D printer. She can choose colors and

by+동명사
materials and can design clothes that fit her body and suit her tastes.

주격 관계대명사로 생략 불가능
Sumin is now a fashion designer!

Dongmin in the Hospital

Dongmin is visiting his grandfather in the hospital. An AI nurse

현재진행형
enters the room. It moves around the room and checks the patients'

conditions. When the AI nurse finds that Dongmin's grandfather

명사절을 이끄는 접속사
has a high temperature, it gives him some medicine to lower his

4형식 문장　　　부사적 용법(목적)
temperature.

Have you ever thought about these changes? Some changes have

현재완료(경험), 의문문은 Have+주어+과거분사 ~?
already started to take place while others may start in the near future.

현재완료(완료)　　　　　　~할지도 모른다(추측)
Can you imagine other changes? Take some time to think about them.

= other changes

method: 방법
material: 재료
fit: (모양 · 크기가 어떤 사람 · 사물에) 맞다
suit: (~에게) 맞다, 어울리다
AI: 인공 지능(= artificial intelligence)
patient: 환자; 인내심이 있는
medicine: 약
ever: 어느 때고, 언제든, 한번이라도
move around: 돌아다니다
take place: 일어나다(= happen), 개최되다

확인문제

● 다음 문장이 본문의 내용과 일치하면 T, 일치하지 않으면 F를 쓰시오.

1 Sumin's house looks strange because of its unique design. ☐

2 Sumin designs clothes for others by using a 3D printer. ☐

3 An AI nurse moves around the room and checks the patients' conditions. ☐

4 When the AI nurse finds that Dongmin's grandfather has a low temperature, it gives some medicine to raise his temperature. ☐

5 Some changes have already started to happen while others may start in the near future. ☐

● 우리말을 참고하여 빈칸에 알맞은 말을 쓰시오.

1 _____ Society

2 _____ in science and technology _____ _____ many changes in our lives _____ _____.

3 In the future, science and technology will _____ _____ _____.

4 Let's see what our lives _____ _____ _____ in the near future.

5 Sangho in the _____ _____

6 Shopping is _____ _____.

7 There are _____ _____ and _____ _____.

8 Sangho enters a shop with his smartphone which has a _____ _____ _____.

9 In the shop, he _____ _____ _____ he wants.

10 The items _____ _____ _____ _____ _____ a virtual card on his smartphone.

11 If Sangho _____ an item _____, it _____ _____ _____ _____ his list of purchases.

12 When he finishes _____, Sangho does not need to wait _____ _____ to pay.

13 His virtual card _____ _____ all the prices and will _____ him later.

14 Isn't that _____?

---

1 변화하는 사회

2 과학과 기술의 발전은 지금까지 우리의 삶에 많은 변화를 초래해 왔다.

3 미래에 과학 기술은 더 많은 변화를 만들 것이다.

4 가까운 미래에 우리의 삶이 어떻게 될지 살펴보자.

5 쇼핑 센터에 있는 상호

6 쇼핑이 훨씬 쉽다.

7 줄도 없고 계산대도 없다.

8 상호는 특별한 쇼핑 앱이 있는 스마트폰을 가지고 가게로 들어간다.

9 가게에서 그는 그가 원하는 물건들을 집는다.

10 그 물건들은 자동으로 그의 스마트폰에 있는 가상 카드에 더해진다.

11 만약 상호가 물건을 되돌려 놓으면 그것은 자동으로 그의 구매 목록에서 제거된다.

12 쇼핑을 끝냈을 때 상호는 돈을 지불하기 위해 줄을 설 필요가 없다.

13 그의 가상 카드가 모든 가격을 더해서 나중에 그에게 청구할 것이다.

14 정말 멋지지 않은가?

15 Sumin's _____ _____ House and Clothes

16 Sumin lives in a _____ _____ house.

17 _____ a 3D printed house is _____ _____ _____ than building a house _____ _____ _____.

18 Sumin's house _____ _____ because of its unique design.

19 A 3D printer can produce _____ _____ that people cannot make with _____ _____ _____ _____ _____.

20 Sumin also likes to make her clothes at home _____ _____ a 3D printer.

21 She can choose colors and materials and can design clothes _____ _____ her body and _____ her tastes.

22 Sumin is now a _____ _____ !

23 Dongmin _____ _____ _____

24 Dongmin _____ _____ his grandfather in the hospital.

25 _____ _____ nurse enters the room.

26 It moves around the room and _____ the patients' _____ .

27 When the AI nurse finds that Dongmin's grandfather has a _____ _____ , it gives him some medicine _____ _____ his temperature.

28 _____ _____ _____ _____ about these changes?

29 Some changes have already started to _____ _____ while others may start _____ _____ _____ _____ .

30 Can you _____ other changes?

31 _____ _____ _____ to think about them.

15 수민이의 3D 프린터로 만든 집과 옷

16 수민이는 3D 프린터로 만든 집에 산다.

17 3D 프린터로 집을 짓는 것은 전통적인 방법으로 집을 짓는 것보다 더 빠르고 저렴하다.

18 수민이의 집은 독특한 디자인 때문에 멋져 보인다.

19 3D 프린터는 사람들이 전통 건축 방법과 재료들로 만들 수 없는 집 모양을 만들어 낼 수 있다.

20 수민이는 또한 집에서 3D 프린터를 사용해 옷을 만드는 것을 좋아한다.

21 그녀는 색깔과 재료를 고를 수 있고 자신의 몸과 취향에 맞는 옷을 디자인할 수 있다.

22 수민이는 이제 패션 디자이너다!

23 병원에 있는 동민

24 동민이는 병원에 계시는 그의 할아버지를 방문하고 있다.

25 AI 간호사가 병실로 들어온다.

26 그것은 병실을 돌아다니고, 환자들의 상태를 확인한다.

27 AI 간호사가 동민이 할아버지가 열이 높다는 것을 알았을 때 그것은 그의 체온을 낮추기 위해 그에게 약을 준다.

28 여러분은 이러한 변화에 대해 생각해 본 적 있는가?

29 어떤 변화는 이미 일어나기 시작했고 반면 다른 것들은 가까운 미래에 일어날지도 모른다.

30 여러분은 다른 변화들을 상상할 수 있는가?

31 그것들에 대해 잠깐 생각해 보자.

● 우리말을 참고하여 본문을 영작하시오.

1 변화하는 사회
➡ _____

2 과학과 기술의 발전은 지금까지 우리의 삶에 많은 변화를 초래해 왔다.
➡ _____

3 미래에 과학 기술은 더 많은 변화를 만들 것이다.
➡ _____

4 가까운 미래에 우리의 삶이 어떻게 될지 살펴보자.
➡ _____

5 쇼핑 센터에 있는 상호
➡ _____

6 쇼핑이 훨씬 쉽다.
➡ _____

7 줄도 없고 계산대도 없다.
➡ _____

8 상호는 특별한 쇼핑 앱이 있는 스마트폰을 가지고 가게로 들어간다.
➡ _____

9 가게에서 그는 그가 원하는 물건들을 집는다.
➡ _____

10 그 물건들은 자동으로 그의 스마트폰에 있는 가상 카드에 더해진다.
➡ _____

11 만약 상호가 물건을 되돌려 놓으면 그것은 자동으로 그의 구매 목록에서 제거된다.
➡ _____

12 쇼핑을 끝냈을 때 상호는 돈을 지불하기 위해 줄을 설 필요가 없다.
➡ _____

13 그의 가상 카드가 모든 가격을 더해서 나중에 그에게 청구할 것이다.
➡ _____

14 정말 멋지지 않은가?
➡ _____

15 수민이의 3D 프린터로 만든 집과 옷
➡ _____

16 수민이는 3D 프린터로 만든 집에 산다.
➡ _____

17 3D 프린터로 집을 짓는 것은 전통적인 방법으로 집을 짓는 것보다 더 빠르고 저렴하다.
➡ _____

18 수민이의 집은 독특한 디자인 때문에 멋져 보인다.

➡ _____

19 3D 프린터는 사람들이 전통 건축 방법과 재료들로 만들 수 없는 집 모양을 만들어 낼 수 있다.

➡ _____

20 수민이는 또한 집에서 3D 프린터를 사용해 옷을 만드는 것을 좋아한다.

➡ _____

21 그녀는 색깔과 재료를 고를 수 있고 자신의 몸과 취향에 맞는 옷을 디자인할 수 있다.

➡ _____

22 수민이는 이제 패션 디자이너이다!

➡ _____

23 병원에 있는 동민

➡ _____

24 동민이는 병원에 계시는 그의 할아버지를 방문하고 있다.

➡ _____

25 AI 간호사가 병실로 들어온다.

➡ _____

26 그것은 병실을 돌아다니고, 환자들의 상태를 확인한다.

➡ _____

27 AI 간호사가 동민이 할아버지가 열이 높다는 것을 알았을 때 그것은 그의 체온을 낮추기 위해 그에게 약을 준다.

➡ _____

28 여러분은 이러한 변화에 대해 생각해 본 적 있는가?

➡ _____

29 어떤 변화는 이미 일어나기 시작했고 반면 다른 것들은 가까운 미래에 일어날지도 모른다.

➡ _____

30 여러분은 다른 변화들을 상상할 수 있는가?

➡ _____

31 그것들에 대해 잠깐 생각해 보자.

➡ _____

[01~03] 다음 글을 읽고 물음에 답하시오.

Advances in science and technology @have caused many changes in our lives so far. In the future, science and technology will make more changes. Let's see what our lives may be like in the near future.

01 위 글의 밑줄 친 @have caused와 현재완료의 용법이 다른 것을 모두 고르시오.

① She has been in Seoul since 2000.
② We have visited Paris before.
③ Have you solved it yet?
④ We have known her for a long time.
⑤ He has lost his pen.

02 위 글의 제목으로 알맞은 것을 고르시오.

① Too Much Information in Changing Society
② Changes Due to Advances in Science and Technology
③ Various Kinds of Advances
④ What Changes Do You Like Most?
⑤ Rapid Advances in Science and Technology

03 위 글의 뒤에 올 내용으로 가장 알맞은 것을 고르시오.

① 과학과 기술의 발전이 지금까지 우리의 삶에 가져온 변화
② 현재의 과학과 기술이 발전하는 모습
③ 전 세계의 과학과 기술의 발전 가능성
④ 가까운 미래의 우리 삶의 모습
⑤ 과학 기술 발전의 장단점

[04~06] 다음 글을 읽고 물음에 답하시오.

Sumin's 3D Printed House and Clothes

Sumin lives in a 3D printed house. @Building a 3D printed house is faster and cheaper than building a house with traditional methods. ⓑ수민이의 집은 독특한 디자인 때문에 멋져 보인다. A 3D printer can produce house shapes (A) people cannot make with traditional building methods and materials. Sumin also likes to make her clothes at home by using a 3D printer. She can choose colors and materials and can design clothes (B) fit her body and suit her tastes. Sumin is now a fashion designer!

04 위 글의 빈칸 (A)와 (B)에 공통으로 들어갈 알맞은 말을 모두 고르시오.

① that   ② who
③ what   ④ which
⑤ whom

05 위 글의 밑줄 친 @Building과 문법적 쓰임이 다른 것을 모두 고르시오.

① The sleeping girl is so pretty.
② I heard him singing on the stage.
③ He enjoyed studying with his friends.
④ Look at the boy sitting under the tree.
⑤ Thank you for showing me the way to the subway station.

서답형
06 위 글의 밑줄 친 ⓑ의 우리말에 맞게 주어진 어휘를 이용하여 9단어로 영작하시오.

fantastic, because, unique

➡ _____

[07~09] 다음 글을 읽고 물음에 답하시오.

Dongmin in the Hospital

Dongmin is visiting his grandfather in the hospital. An AI nurse enters the room. It moves around the room and checks the patients' conditions. When the AI nurse finds that Dongmin's grandfather has a high temperature, ⓐit gives him some medicine ⓑto lower his temperature.

Have you ever thought about these changes? __(A)__ changes have already started to take place while __(B)__ may start in the near future. Can you imagine other changes? Take some time to think about them.

07 위 글의 빈칸 (A)와 (B)에 들어갈 말로 바르게 짝지어진 것은?

① Some – other
② Another – other
③ Some – others
④ Another – others
⑤ One – the other

서답형

08 위 글의 밑줄 친 ⓐit이 가리키는 것을 본문에서 찾아 쓰시오.

➡ _____

서답형

09 위 글의 밑줄 친 ⓑ를 다음과 같이 바꿔 쓸 때 빈칸에 들어 갈 알맞은 말을 쓰시오.

➡ _____ it _____ his temperature

[10~12] 다음 글을 읽고 물음에 답하시오.

Sangho in the Shopping Center

Shopping is ⓐmuch easier. There are no lines and no counters. Sangho enters a shop with his smartphone which has a special shopping app. In the shop, he takes the items he wants. The items are automatically added __(A)__ a virtual card on his smartphone. If Sangho puts an item back, it is automatically removed __(B)__ his list of purchases. When he finishes shopping, Sangho does not need to wait in line to pay. His virtual card adds up all the prices and will charge him later. Isn't that fancy?

10 위 글의 빈칸 (A)와 (B)에 들어갈 전치사가 바르게 짝지어진 것은?

① to – from
② at – for
③ at – from
④ on – by
⑤ to – for

11 위 글의 밑줄 친 ⓐmuch와 바꿔 쓸 수 없는 말을 고르시오.

① even　　② far　　③ still
④ very　　⑤ a lot

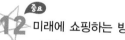

12 미래에 쇼핑하는 방법으로 위 글의 내용과 일치하지 않는 것은?

① 특별한 쇼핑 앱이 있는 스마트폰을 가지고 가게로 들어간다.
② 원하는 물건들을 집으면, 그 물건들은 자동으로 스마트폰에 있는 가상 카드에 더해진다.
③ 물건을 되돌려 놓으면, 나중에 그 금액을 반환받으면 된다.
④ 돈을 지불하기 위해 줄을 설 필요가 없다.
⑤ 가상 카드가 모든 가격을 더해서 나중에 청구할 것이다.

[13~15] 다음 글을 읽고 물음에 답하시오.

Sumin's 3D Printed House and Clothes

Sumin lives in a 3D printed house. Building a 3D printed house is faster and cheaper than building a house with traditional methods. Sumin's house looks fantastic because of its unique design. A 3D printer can produce house shapes ⓐthat people cannot make with traditional building methods and materials. Sumin also likes to make her clothes at home by using a 3D printer. She can choose colors and materials and can design clothes ⓑthat fit her body and suit her tastes. Sumin is now a fashion designer!

서답형

13 다음 보기에서 위 글의 밑줄 친 ⓐthat, ⓑthat과 문법적 쓰임이 같은 것을 각각 고르시오.

① This is the pen that you gave me yesterday.
② The dog that is running there is mine.
③ I want to read the book that he was reading.
④ He is the man that wants to see you.
⑤ Where's the letter that came yesterday?

➡ ⓐthat과 같은 것: _____
　 ⓑthat과 같은 것: _____

서답형

14 Which is faster and cheaper, building a 3D printed house or building a house with traditional methods? Answer in English in a full sentence. (9 words)

➡ _____

중요

15 위 글을 읽고 대답할 수 없는 질문은?

① What kind of house does Sumin live in?
② How long does it take to build a 3D printed house?
③ Why does Sumin's house look fantastic?
④ How does Sumin make her clothes at home?
⑤ Who chooses colors and materials of Sumin's clothes?

[16~19] 다음 글을 읽고 물음에 답하시오.

Sangho in the Shopping Center

Shopping is much easier. There are no lines and no counters. (①) Sangho enters a shop with his smartphone which has a special shopping (A)[app / list]. (②) In the shop, he takes the items he wants. (③) If Sangho puts an item back, it is automatically removed from his list of purchases. (④) When he finishes shopping, Sangho (B)[needs / does not need] to wait in line to pay. (⑤) His virtual card adds up all the prices and will ⓐcharge him (C)[later / latter]. Isn't that fancy?

중요

16 위 글의 흐름으로 보아, 주어진 문장이 들어가기에 가장 적절한 곳은?

The items are automatically added to a virtual card on his smartphone.

①　　②　　③　　④　　⑤

서답형

17 위 글의 괄호 (A)~(C)에서 문맥상 알맞은 낱말을 골라 쓰시오.

➡ (A)_____ (B)_____ (C)_____

18 위 글의 밑줄 친 ⓐcharge와 같은 의미로 쓰인 것을 고르시오.

① We will charge at the enemy.
② We won't charge you for delivery.
③ He took charge of the farm after his father's death.
④ You can use it free of charge.
⑤ I need to charge a storage battery.

위 글의 주제로 알맞은 것을 고르시오.

① The use of the smartphone will increase.
② Many fancy shopping apps are now available.
③ Using a virtual card will increase.
④ It's difficult to live without a smartphone.
⑤ Shopping will be a lot easier in the future.

[20~21] 다음 글을 읽고 물음에 답하시오.

Schools in 20 Years

ⓐHave you ever thought of how schools may change over the next 20 years? Students may learn drone design. Cleaning drones may help students at school. ⓑ모든 학교에 AI 선생님들 교무실이 있을지도 모릅니다. Students may go to school only two or three times a week.

20 아래 〈보기〉에서 위 글의 밑줄 친 ⓐ와 현재완료의 용법이 같은 것의 개수를 고르시오.

— 보기 —

① He has just broken the window.
② She has never eaten spaghetti.
③ He has studied English for three hours.
④ I have lost my key.
⑤ How many times have you seen it?

① 1개 ② 2개 ③ 3개 ④ 4개 ⑤ 5개

서답형
21 위 글의 밑줄 친 ⓑ의 우리말에 맞게 주어진 어휘를 이용하여 10단어로 영작하시오.

| there, AI teachers' room |

➡ _____

[22~24] 다음 글을 읽고 물음에 답하시오.

Dongmin in the Hospital

Dongmin is visiting his grandfather in the hospital. An AI nurse enters the room. It moves around the room and checks the patients' conditions. When the AI nurse finds that Dongmin's grandfather has a high temperature, ⓐit gives him some medicine to lower his temperature.

Have you ever thought about these changes? Some changes have already started to take place ⓑwhile others may start in the near future. Can you imagine other changes? Take some time to think about them.

서답형
22 위 글의 밑줄 친 ⓐ를 3형식 문장으로 고치시오.

➡ _____

23 위 글의 밑줄 친 ⓑwhile과 같은 의미로 쓰인 것을 고르시오.

① Strike while the iron is hot.
② Did anyone call while I was away?
③ While you are eating, you shouldn't speak.
④ Her parents died while she was still at school.
⑤ I've read fifty pages, while he's read only twenty.

서답형
24 본문의 내용과 일치하도록 다음 빈칸 (A)와 (B)에 알맞은 단어를 쓰시오.

The AI nurse gives Dongmin's grandfather some medicine to (A)_____ his temperature when it finds that he has a (B)_____ temperature.

[01~03] 다음 글을 읽고 물음에 답하시오.

Advances in science and technology ⓐ_____ many changes in our lives so far. In the future, science and technology will make more changes. ⓑLet's see what our lives may be like in the near future.

01 위 글의 빈칸 ⓐ에 cause를 알맞은 형태로 쓰시오.

➡ _____

02 본문의 내용과 일치하도록 다음 빈칸 (A)와 (B)에 알맞은 단어를 쓰시오.

> Because of (A)_____ in science and technology, there have been many (B)_____ in our lives so far.

03 위 글의 밑줄 친 ⓑ를 다음과 같이 바꿔 쓸 때 빈칸에 들어갈 알맞은 말을 쓰시오.

(1) How about _____ what our lives may be like in the near future?

(2) _____ _____ _____ see what our lives may be like in the near future?

[04~06] 다음 글을 읽고 물음에 답하시오.

Sangho in the Shopping Center

Shopping is much easier. There are no lines and no counters. Sangho enters a shop with his smartphone which has a special shopping app. ⓐIn the shop, he takes the items he wants. The items are automatically added to a virtual card on his smartphone. If Sangho puts an item back, it is automatically removed from his list of purchases. When he finishes shopping, ⓑ돈을 지불하기 위해 줄을 설 필요가 없다. His virtual card adds up all the prices and will charge him later. Isn't that fancy?

04 위 글을 읽고 상호가 쇼핑 센터에서 장을 보는 방법을 우리말로 쓰시오.

➡ (1) _____

(2) _____

(3) _____

_____

(4) _____

_____

05 위 글의 밑줄 친 문장 ⓐ에 생략된 단어를 넣어 문장을 다시 쓰시오.

➡ _____

06 위 글의 밑줄 친 ⓑ의 우리말에 맞게 주어진 어휘를 이용하여 10단어로 영작하시오.

> need, line, to

➡ _____

[07~09] 다음 글을 읽고 물음에 답하시오.

Sumin's 3D Printed House and Clothes

Sumin lives in a 3D printed house. Building a 3D printed house is faster and cheaper than building a house with traditional methods. Sumin's house looks fantastic because of its unique design. A 3D printer can produce house shapes that people cannot make with traditional building methods and materials. Sumin also likes to make her clothes at home by using a 3D printer. ⓐShe can choose colors and materials and can design clothes that fits her body and suits her tastes. Sumin is now a fashion designer!

07 본문의 내용과 일치하도록 다음 빈칸에 알맞은 단어를 쓰시오.

The _____ _____ of Sumin's house makes it look fantastic.

08 위 글의 밑줄 친 ⓐ에서 어법상 틀린 부분을 찾아 고치시오. (두 군데)

➡ _____ , _____

09 위 글을 읽고 수민이가 집에서 자신의 옷을 만드는 방법을 우리말로 쓰시오.

➡ (1) _____
　　(2) _____
　　(3) _____

[10~12] 다음 글을 읽고 물음에 답하시오.

Sangho in the Shopping Center

Shopping is much easier. There are no lines and no counters. Sangho enters a shop with his smartphone which has a special shopping ⓐapp. In the shop, he takes the items he wants. The items are automatically added to a virtual card on his smartphone. If Sangho puts an item back, ⓑit is automatically removed from his list of purchases. ⓒWhen he finishes to shop, Sangho does not need to wait in line to pay. His virtual card adds up all the prices and will charge him later. Isn't that fancy?

10 위 글의 밑줄 친 ⓐapp을 줄이지 않은 본래 형태로 쓰시오.

➡ _____

11 다음 빈칸에 알맞은 단어를 넣어 위 글의 밑줄 친 ⓑit이 가리키는 것을 완성하시오.

the _____ that Sangho puts back

12 위 글의 밑줄 친 ⓒ에서 어법상 틀린 부분을 찾아 고치시오.

➡ _____

[13~15] 다음 글을 읽고 물음에 답하시오.

Schools in 20 Years

Have you ever thought of ⓐ다음 20년에 걸쳐 학교의 모습이 어떻게 변할지? Students __(A)__ learn 3D printing. AI teachers __(B)__ help students at school. There __(C)__ be a drone station in every school. ⓑStudents may not carry paper textbooks anymore.

13 위 글의 빈칸 (A)~(C)에 공통으로 들어갈 알맞은 조동사를 쓰시오.

➡ _____

14 위 글의 밑줄 친 ⓐ의 우리말에 맞게 한 단어를 보충하여, 주어진 어휘를 알맞게 배열하시오.

may / 20 years / schools / over / the / how / change

➡ _____

15 위 글의 밑줄 친 ⓑ를 다음과 같이 바꿔 쓸 때 빈칸에 들어갈 알맞은 말을 쓰시오.

➡ Students may _____ _____ carry paper textbooks.

Enjoy Writing B

Schools in 20 Years

Have you ever thought of how schools may change over the next 20 years?
간접의문문: 의문사+주어+동사

Students may learn drone design. Cleaning drones may help students at
추측을 나타내는 조동사

school. There may be an AI teachers' room in every school. Students may go
~이 있을지도 모른다

to school only two or three times a week.
배수: ~번   일주일에(=per week)

구문해설 • over: [기간] … 동안, …에 걸쳐 • teachers' room: 교무실 • two or three times: 두세 번

20년 후 학교의 모습

다음 20년에 걸쳐 학교의 모습이 어떻게 변할지 생각해 본 적이 있나요? 학생들은 드론 디자인을 배울지도 모릅니다. 청소 드론이 학교에서 학생들을 도울지도 모릅니다. 모든 학교에 AI 선생님들 교무실이 있을지도 모릅니다. 학생들은 일주일에 오직 두세 번만 학교에 갈지도 모릅니다.

Project

Have you ever imagined life in the future? People may use personal drones in
          현재완료(경험)   추측

their daily lives. So there may be traffic lights for drones in the sky. A lot of AI
        life의 복수형   추측   = Many

helpers may be created soon and they may help humans in lots of ways.
        추측   수동태   추측   = many

구문해설 • personal: 개인의 • daily life: 일상 생활

미래의 삶을 상상해 본 적이 있나요? 사람들은 매일의 삶에서 개인 드론을 사용할지도 모릅니다. 그래서 하늘에는 드론들을 위한 교통 신호등이 있을지도 모릅니다. 많은 AI 도우미들이 곧 만들어져서 많은 방식으로 인간을 도울지도 모릅니다.

Wrap Up 1

G: Are you ready for your trip to London?
   be ready for: ~의 준비가 되다

B: Yes, but I'm worried about getting lost. I'm not good at finding places.
        be worried about: ~에 대해 걱정하다 get lost: 길을 잃다 be good at: ~을 잘하다

G: Don't worry. There are many good smartphone apps you can use.
            There are+복수명사: ~가 있다   apps와 you can use 사이에 목적격
                                            관계대명사(which, that)가 생략되어 있다.

B: Can you show me one?
   Can you 동사 ~?: ~해 줄 수 있니?[요청하기] one = a smartphone app

G: Sure. Use this one. It shows you a map of the city and pictures of streets.
          shows(4형식 동사)+간접목적어(you, ~에게)+직접목적어(a map of the city and picture of streets, ~을.를)

B: Oh, thanks.

G: 너의 런던 여행은 준비됐니?
B: 응. 하지만 나는 길을 잃는 것에 대해 걱정하고 있어. 나는 장소 찾는 것을 잘 못해.
G: 걱정 마. 네가 사용할 수 있는 좋은 스마트폰 앱이 많이 있어.
B: 나에게 하나 보여줄 수 있니?
G: 물론이지. 이것을 사용해 봐. 그것은 도시의 지도와 길의 사진을 보여줘.
B: 오, 고마워.

01 다음 짝지어진 단어의 관계가 나머지와 <u>다른</u> 하나는?

① difference – similarity
② ever – never
③ law – principle
④ lower – heighten
⑤ true – false

02 다음 중 〈보기〉에 있는 단어를 사용하여 자연스러운 문장을 만들 수 <u>없는</u> 것은? (형태 변화 가능하며 필요하다면 대문자를 쓸 것)

┌─ 보기 ─┐
add get move wait
└────────┘

① You don't _____ to bring your lunch.
② They are _____ in line to order food.
③ _____ up the following numbers.
④ If you _____ lost, call my mobile phone at 010-744-2996.
⑤ We _____ around classrooms for every subject.

[03~04] 다음 빈칸에 알맞은 말을 고르시오.

03

Seawater _____ about 70 percent of the Earth's surface.

① spreads ② covers ③ grows
④ charges ⑤ fits

04

He enjoyed the work which _____ his personality perfectly.

① saved ② worked ③ paid
④ lowered ⑤ suited

05 다음 대화에서 흐름상 <u>어색한</u> 것을 고르시오.

G: ⓐAre you ready for your trip to London?
B: Yes, but I'm worried about getting lost. ⓑI'm good at finding places.
G: ⓒDon't worry. There are many good smartphone apps you can use.
B: ⓓCan you show me one?
G: Sure. Use this one. ⓔIt shows you a map of the city and pictures of streets.
B: Oh, thanks.

① ⓐ ② ⓑ ③ ⓒ ④ ⓓ ⑤ ⓔ

[06~07] 대화의 순서를 바르게 배열하시오.

06

(A) Sure. These are future shoes. People will run 100 meters in 5 seconds with these shoes.
(B) Wow, I'm surprised that humans will run that fast.
(C) Can you tell us about your item, please?

➡ _____

07

(A) Oh, I forgot to turn off the heater before I left home.

(B) No. I can turn it off with my smartphone.

(C) Wow, I'm surprised that you can turn off the heater with your smartphone.

(D) Really? Then do you need to return home?

➡ _____

08 다음 대화에서 어법상 알맞은 것을 고르시오.

W: Welcome to VR World. Would you like ⓐvisiting Niagara Falls?

B: Sure.

W: Okay, ⓑput on this.

B: All right. Wow, it looks so ⓒreally.

W: It is huge, ⓓdoesn't it?

B: Yes, and ⓔI'm surprised that I feel water on my face.

① ⓐ   ② ⓑ   ③ ⓒ   ④ ⓓ   ⑤ ⓔ

[09~12] 다음 대화를 읽고 물음에 답하시오.

G: Uncle Jack! Your new drone looks cool.

M: Thanks. I designed it to (A)_____ people's lives.

G: (B)_____ people's lives?

M: Yes. It watches the ocean. 만약 곤경에 빠진 사람이 있다면 그것은 날아가서 튜브를 떨어뜨린단다. (drops, is, it, if, and, a person, a tube, over, in, there, flies, trouble)

G: I'm surprised that drones can rescue people. (C)Can you show me how it works?

M: Sure. Watch this.

09 빈칸 (A)와 (B)에 공통으로 들어갈 말로 적절한 것을 고르시오. (대·소문자 무시)

① spend   ② charge   ③ take
④ save   ⑤ deliver

10 다음 영영풀이에 해당하는 단어를 대화에서 찾아 쓰시오.

to save someone or something from danger or harm

➡ _____

11 밑줄 친 우리말과 같은 뜻이 되도록 괄호 안의 어구를 바르게 배열하시오.

➡ _____
_____

12 밑줄 친 (C)와 같은 의미가 되도록 주어진 단어를 이용해 문장을 완성하시오.

➡ _____
(ask, can)

[13~14] 다음 대화를 읽고 물음에 답하시오.

G: Are you ready (A)____ your trip to London?

B: Yes, but I'm worried (B)____ getting lost. I'm not good (C)____ finding places.

G: Don't worry. There are many good smartphone apps you can use.

B: Can you show me one?

G: Sure. Use this one. It shows you a map of the city and pictures of streets.

B: Oh, thanks.

13 빈칸 (A)~(C)에 알맞은 말을 〈보기〉에서 골라 쓰시오.

> ┌─ 보기 ─┐
> about at for from in along

➡ (A)_____ (B)_____ (C)_____

14 위 대화를 읽고 답할 수 없는 질문을 고르시오.

① What is the boy worried about?
② Where is the boy going to travel?
③ What isn't the boy good at?
④ What does the app that the girl recommends to the boy show?
⑤ How many apps can the boy use?

Grammar

15 다음 빈칸에 들어갈 표현이 순서대로 바르게 짝지어진 것을 고르시오.

> He _____ the bridge since he _____ 42 years old.

① has built — was
② has built — has been
③ is building — was being
④ built — was
⑤ built — has been

---

16 다음 ⓐ~ⓗ 중 옳은 것을 모두 고르면?

> ⓐ He mays be late for school.
> ⓑ There may are other people that I don't know.
> ⓒ I've never gone to Paris before.
> ⓓ They may invite me to the party.
> ⓔ I have eaten traditional Korean food before.
> ⓕ Jim has worked at the company for 2015.
> ⓖ She may not use my computer.
> ⓗ He has met his old roommate for dinner last week.

① ⓐ, ⓒ
② ⓑ, ⓒ, ⓓ
③ ⓑ, ⓓ, ⓗ
④ ⓓ, ⓔ, ⓗ
⑤ ⓓ, ⓔ, ⓖ

17 밑줄 친 부분의 쓰임이 나머지 넷과 다른 것은?

① They <u>may</u> know my name.
② The news <u>may</u> be true.
③ I think schools <u>may</u> change a lot over the next 20 years.
④ Buses and trains <u>may</u> run at 500km per hour.
⑤ <u>May</u> we have a short break now?

18 다음 문장에서 어법상 어색한 것을 바르게 고쳐 쓰시오.

(1) I have bought it only a couple of hours ago.
➡ _____

(2) She has studied science and technology since 10 years.
➡ _____

(3) Have you ever gone to Paris?
➡ _____

(4) There may is an AI teachers' room in every school.
➡ _____

19 다음 우리말을 주어진 어휘를 이용하여 영작하시오.

(1) 그는 복권을 사 본 적이 없다. (never, a lottery ticket)

➡ _____

(2) 나는 공항에서 여권을 잃어버렸다. (지금 여권이 없다.) (lose, my passport, at)

➡ _____

(3) 우리는 1999년부터 서로 알고 지냈다. (know, each, 7 단어)

➡ _____

(4) 그는 과학 프로젝트를 막 마쳤다. (finish, his science project, just)

➡ _____

(5) 그들은 내일 돌아올지도 모른다. (come back)

➡ _____

(6) 제가 당신의 스마트폰을 써도 될까요? (use)

➡ _____

Reading

[20~21] 다음 글을 읽고 물음에 답하시오.

ⓐ과학과 기술의 발전은 지금까지 우리의 삶에 많은 변화를 초래해 왔다. In the future, science and technology will make more changes. Let's see what our lives ⓑmay be like in the near future.

20 위 글의 밑줄 친 ⓐ의 우리말에 맞게 한 단어를 보충하여, 주어진 어휘를 알맞게 배열하시오.

advances / in our lives / so far / many changes / in science and technology / caused

➡ _____

_____

21 위 글의 밑줄 친 ⓑmay와 같은 의미로 쓰인 것을 모두 고르시오.

① May I come in?
② He works so that he may succeed.
③ It may rain at any moment.
④ May she rest in peace.
⑤ It may be true.

[22~24] 다음 글을 읽고 물음에 답하시오.

Sangho in the Shopping Center
Shopping is much easier. There are no lines and no counters. Sangho enters a shop with his smartphone which has a special shopping app. In the shop, he takes the items he wants. The items are automatically (A)[adding / added] to a virtual card on his smartphone. ⓐIf Sangho puts an item back, it automatically removes from his list of purchases. When he finishes shopping, Sangho does not need to wait in line to pay. His (B)[actual / virtual] card adds up all the prices and will (C)[change / charge] him later. Isn't that fancy?

22 위 글의 괄호 (A)~(C)에서 문맥이나 어법상 알맞은 낱말을 골라 쓰시오.

➡ (A)_____ (B)_____ (C)_____

23 위 글의 밑줄 친 ⓐ에서 어법상 틀린 부분을 찾아 고치시오.

➡ _____

24 다음 문장에서 위 글의 내용과 다른 부분을 찾아서 고치시오.

> • When Sangho finishes shopping, he needs to pay at the counter.

➡ _____

_____

[25~27] 다음 글을 읽고 물음에 답하시오.

Sumin's 3D Printed House and Clothes

Sumin lives in a 3D printed house. ⓐBuilding a 3D printed house is faster and cheaper than building a house with traditional methods. Sumin's house looks fantastic because of its unique design. ⓑA 3D printer can produce house shapes that people cannot make them with traditional building methods and materials. Sumin also likes to make her clothes at home by using a 3D printer. She can choose colors and materials and can design clothes that fit her body and suit her tastes. Sumin is now a fashion designer!

25 위 글의 밑줄 친 문장 ⓐ를 바르게 바꿔 쓴 문장을 <u>모두</u> 고르시오.

① To build a 3D printed house is faster and cheaper than to build a house with traditional methods.

② Building a house with traditional methods is faster and cheaper than building a 3D printed house.

③ Building a 3D printed house is not as fast and cheap as building a house with traditional methods.

④ Building a house with traditional methods is not as fast and cheap as building a 3D printed house.

⑤ Building a 3D printed house is as fast and cheap as building a house with traditional methods.

26 위 글의 밑줄 친 ⓑ에서 어법상 <u>틀린</u> 부분을 찾아 고치시오.

➡ _____

27 위 글의 내용과 일치하지 <u>않는</u> 것은?

① 수민이는 3D 프린터로 만든 집에 산다.

② 수민이의 집은 독특한 디자인 때문에 멋져 보인다.

③ 3D 프린터는 사람들이 전통적인 건축 방법과 재료들로 만들 수 있는 집 모양을 만들어 낼 수 없다.

④ 수민이는 또한 집에서 3D 프린터를 사용해 옷을 만드는 것을 좋아한다.

⑤ 수민이는 자신의 몸과 취향에 맞는 옷을 디자인할 수 있다.

[28~29] 다음 글을 읽고 물음에 답하시오.

Dongmin in the Hospital

Dongmin is visiting his grandfather in the hospital. An AI nurse enters the room. It moves around the room and checks the patients' conditions. When the AI nurse finds that Dongmin's grandfather has a high temperature, it gives ⓐhim some medicine to __(A)__ his temperature.

Have you ever thought about these changes? Some changes have already started to take place while others may start in the near future. Can you imagine other changes? Take some time to think about ⓑthem.

28 위 글의 빈칸 (A)에 low를 알맞은 형태로 쓰시오.

➡ _____

29 위 글의 밑줄 친 ⓐhim과 ⓑthem이 가리키는 것을 본문에서 찾아 쓰시오.

➡ ⓐ _____ ⓑ _____

01 출제율 90%

다음 짝지어진 단어의 관계가 같도록 빈칸에 알맞은 말을 주어진 철자로 시작하여 쓰시오.

(1) | farm : farmer – library : l_____ |

(2) | material : matter – provide : o_____ |

02 출제율 95%

다음 빈칸에 들어갈 말로 적절한 것은?

I haven't played rugby _____ I left university.

① when   ② before   ③ as
④ since   ⑤ although

03 출제율 100%

다음 우리말에 맞게 빈칸에 알맞은 말을 쓰시오.

(1) 나는 드론에 관심이 있다.
   ➡ I'm _____ _____ _____.

(2) 십대들은 새로운 과학 기술을 이용하는 데 어려움이 없다.
   ➡ Teens have no difficulty using new _____.

(3) 나의 선생님은 많은 다른 교육 자료를 사용한다.
   ➡ My teacher uses a lot of different teaching _____.

(4) 그녀는 화려한 스포츠카를 갖고 있다.
   ➡ She has a f_____ sports car.

04 출제율 90%

우리말과 일치하도록 주어진 단어를 바르게 배열하시오.

(1) 기술의 발전은 우리에게 많은 좋은 것들을 가져다주었다.
   (have, things, in, us, good, technology, many, advances, brought)
   ➡ _____
   _____

(2) 이 시계는 스마트폰처럼 많은 애플리케이션을 작동할 수 있다.
   (can, like, applications, this, many, watch, run, smartphones)
   ➡ _____

[05~06] 다음 대화를 읽고 물음에 답하시오.

G: Oh, I forgot to turn off the heater (A)[before / after] I left home.
B: Really? Then do you need to return home?
G: No. I can (B)[turn it off / turn off it] with my smartphone.
B: Wow, (C)나는 네가 스마트폰으로 히터를 끌 수 있다는 게 놀라워.

05 출제율 95%

위 글의 괄호 (A)~(C)에서 문맥이나 어법상 알맞은 낱말을 골라 쓰시오.

➡ (A) _____ (B) _____

06 출제율 90%

밑줄 친 (C)의 우리말에 맞게 주어진 단어를 이용해서 영작하시오.

➡ _____
_____

(can, with, surprised, that)

[07~10] 다음 대화를 읽고 물음에 답하시오.

Amy: Wow, there are so many books in this library. (①)

Hana: You're right. (②) Where can we find books about gravity?

Terry: Hi, I'm Terry, the AI librarian. Can I help you?

Amy: Hi. We're looking for books about gravity. (③)

Terry: We have fifty seven books about gravity in this library. (④) I think *The Law of Gravity* will be the best one for you.

Hana: I'm (A)_____ (surprise) that you can recommend books. (⑤)

Amy: Right. That's (B)_____ (amaze). Where is the book, Terry?

Terry: It's on the third floor. Come with me.

07 위 대화의 ①~⑤ 중 주어진 문장이 들어갈 알맞은 곳은?

> Can you recommend one, please?

①   ②   ③   ④   ⑤

08 다음 영영풀이에 해당하는 단어를 위 대화에서 찾아 쓰시오.

> to speak in favor of something

➡ _____

09 빈칸 (A)와 (B)를 괄호 안에 주어진 단어를 이용하여 채우시오.

➡ (A) _____ (B) _____

10 위 대화의 내용과 일치하지 <u>않는</u> 것을 고르시오.

① There are a lot of books about gravity in the library.

② Hana and Amy are looking for books about gravity.

③ Terry is the AI librarian.

④ Hana and Amy are in the library.

⑤ Terry is amazed that AI recommends a book.

11 다음 빈칸에 알맞은 말이 순서대로 짝지어진 것은?

> • I have known Cindy _____ a long time.
> • I have known Cindy _____ 1999.

① for – during   ② during – for

③ for – since   ④ since – for

⑤ since – during

12 다음 중 어법상 적절한 문장은?

① Koreans have played *jegichagi*, a traditional Korean game, since a long time.

② The children have yet had dinner.

③ He has left for New York last night.

④ Does he have done his homework?

⑤ My sister has been to China.

13 다음 중 어법상 바르지 <u>않은</u> 것은?

① Tony may leave early.

② The math problem is difficult. Chris must not know the answer.

③ Students may go to school only two or three times a week.

④ She may know the truth.

⑤ A lot of AI helpers may be created soon and they may help humans in lots of ways.

[14~16] 다음 글을 읽고 물음에 답하시오.

ⓐ in science and technology have caused many changes in our lives ⓑso far. In the future, science and technology will make more changes. Let's see what our lives may be ⓒlike in the near future.

출제율 85%

14 주어진 영영풀이를 참고하여 빈칸 ⓐ에 철자 A로 시작하는 단어를 쓰시오.

> changes for the better; progress in development

➡ _____

출제율 100%

15 위 글의 밑줄 친 ⓑso far와 바꿔 쓸 수 있는 말을 고르시오.

① lately
② until then
③ until now
④ for now
⑤ recently

출제율 95%

16 위 글의 밑줄 친 ⓒlike와 같은 의미로 쓰인 것을 모두 고르시오.

① She's very like her mother.
② I don't like the way he's looking at me.
③ Do you like this dress?
④ She bought a bag like yours.
⑤ I like playing tennis.

[17~19] 다음 글을 읽고 물음에 답하시오.

Sangho in the Shopping Center

ⓐShopping is much easier. There are no lines and no counters. Sangho enters a shop with his smartphone which has a special shopping app. In the shop, he takes the items he wants. ⓑ그 물건들은 자동으로 그의 스마트폰에 있는 가상 카드에 더해진다. If Sangho puts an item back, it is automatically removed from his list of purchases. When he finishes shopping, Sangho does not need to wait in line to pay. His virtual card adds up all the prices and will charge him later. Isn't that (A) ?

출제율 100%

17 위 글의 빈칸 (A)에 들어갈 알맞은 말을 고르시오.

① boring
② fancy
③ plain
④ terrible
⑤ complex

출제율 95%

18 다음 중 위 글의 밑줄 친 문장 ⓐ의 이유로 옳지 않은 것을 고르시오.

① There are no lines.
② There are many counters.
③ A shopper can purchase the items by using the smartphone which has a special shopping app.
④ If a shopper puts an item back, it is automatically removed from his or her list of purchase.
⑤ When a shopper finishes shopping, his or her virtual card adds up all the prices and will charge him or her later.

출제율 90%

19 위 글의 밑줄 친 ⓑ의 우리말에 맞게 한 단어를 보충하여, 주어진 어휘를 알맞게 배열하시오.

> a virtual card / added / on / the items / his smartphone / are / to

➡ _____
_____
_____

Sumin's 3D Printed House and Clothes

Sumin lives in a 3D printed house. (①) Building a 3D printed house is faster and cheaper than building a house with traditional methods. (②) Sumin's house looks fantastic because of its unique design. (③) A 3D printer can produce house shapes @that people cannot make with traditional building methods and materials. (④) She can choose colors and materials and can design clothes that fit her body and suit her tastes. (⑤) Sumin is now a fashion designer!

출제율 95%

20 위 글의 흐름으로 보아, 주어진 문장이 들어가기에 가장 적절한 곳은?

> Sumin also likes to make her clothes at home by using a 3D printer.

①   ②   ③   ④   ⑤

출제율 90%

21 위 글의 밑줄 친 @that과 문법적 쓰임이 같은 것을 모두 고르시오.

① The point is that you are still responsible.
② I believe that you'll succeed in the future.
③ He is the only man that I love.
④ It was beyond doubt that he was in error.
⑤ Look at the boy and the dog that are running over there.

출제율 100%

22 위 글의 요지로 알맞은 것을 고르시오.

① Building a 3D printed house is the best way to protect the environment.
② Using a 3D printer, Sumin builds her house and makes her clothes.
③ Building a 3D printed house is good because it is faster and cheaper.
④ Using a 3D printer is good for recycling resources.
⑤ 3D printed things reduce waste of resources.

Dongmin in the Hospital

Dongmin is visiting his grandfather in the hospital. An AI nurse enters the room. It moves around the room and checks the patients' conditions. When the AI nurse finds that Dongmin's grandfather has a high temperature, it gives him some medicine to lower his temperature.

Have you ever thought about these changes? Some changes @have already started to take place while others may start in the near future. Can you imagine other changes? Take some time to think about them.

출제율 95%

23 위 글을 읽고 AI 간호사가 하는 일을 우리말로 쓰시오.

➡ _____

_____

_____

출제율 90%

24 아래 〈보기〉에서 위 글의 밑줄 친 @와 현재완료의 용법이 같은 것의 개수를 고르시오.

┌─── 보기 ───┐
① She hasn't cleaned her room yet.
② My sister has gone to New York.
③ Tom has just finished his homework.
④ He has driven a car before.
⑤ He has played basketball for two hours.
└────────────┘

① 1개   ② 2개   ③ 3개   ④ 4개   ⑤ 5개

01 그림을 보고 주어진 단어를 이용하여 영작하시오.

A: Is there anything in these pictures that surprises you?

B: Yes. _____

_____

(automatic, surprise, this, itself)

[02~03] 다음 대화를 읽고 물음에 답하시오.

M: Welcome. ⓐThis is our new smart light. ⓑYou don't have to use your hands to turn it on and off.

W: Really? (A)Then can you tell me how to do it?

M: ⓒJust say, "Light on!" or "Light out!"

W: ⓓLight on or light out? ⓔThat's very difficult.

02 ⓐ~ⓔ 중 흐름상 어색한 부분을 찾아 고치시오.

➡ _____

03 밑줄 친 (A)와 같은 의미가 되도록 주어진 단어를 이용하여 영작하시오.

➡ _____ (mind)

_____ (can, ask)

04 다음 빈칸에 알맞은 단어를 〈보기〉에서 골라 쓰시오.

┌── 보기 ──┐

before ago since for

(1) I started to live in Canada five years ago. I have lived in Canada _____ five years.

(2) We became friends in 2011. We have been friends _____ 2011.

(3) Yesterday I ate African food. I have never eaten African food _____.

05 다음 우리말을 주어진 어휘를 이용하여 영작하시오.

(1) 당신은 지금 이 방을 나가서는 안 된다. (may, leave)

➡ _____

(2) 내 친구는 그 소식 때문에 슬플지도 모른다. (sad, of)

➡ _____

(3) 부모님은 내가 태어난 이후로 그 개를 길러 오셨다. (born, raise)

➡ _____

(4) 그녀는 영화를 보러 갔다. (그래서 현재 여기에 없다.) (to see the movie)

➡ _____

(5) 그녀는 강에서 수영해 본 적이 한 번 있다. (the river, once, swim)

➡ _____

(6) 그 아이들은 아직 저녁을 먹지 않았다. (have, dinner)

➡ _____

06 다음 대화의 빈칸에 철자 m으로 시작하여 알맞은 말을 쓰시오.

(1) A: Do you know where Anne is?

B: I'm not sure. She _____ be taking a walk in the park.

(2) A: What are you looking for, Son?

B: I cannot find my smartphone. _____ I lost it on my way home.

[07~09] 다음 글을 읽고 물음에 답하시오.

Sangho in the Shopping Center

ⓐShopping is much more difficult. There are no lines and no counters. Sangho enters a shop with his smartphone which has a special shopping app. In the shop, he takes the items he wants. The items are automatically added to a virtual card on his smartphone. If Sangho puts an item back, it is automatically removed from his list of purchases. ⓑWhen he finishes shopping, Sangho does not need to wait in line to pay. His virtual card adds up all the prices and will charge him later. Isn't that fancy?

07 위 글의 밑줄 친 ⓐ에서 흐름상 어색한 부분을 찾아 고치시오.

➡ _____

08 주어진 영영풀이에 해당하는 단어를 본문에서 찾아 쓰시오.

> done or seen using computers or the Internet instead of going to a place, meeting people in person, etc.

➡ _____

09 위 글의 밑줄 친 문장 ⓑ의 이유를 우리말로 쓰시오.

➡ _____

_____

[10~12] 다음 글을 읽고 물음에 답하시오.

Sumin's 3D Printed House and Clothes

Sumin lives in a 3D printed house. Building a 3D printed house is faster and cheaper than building a house with traditional methods. ⓐ Sumin's house looks like fantastic because of its unique design. A 3D printer can produce house shapes that people cannot make with traditional building methods and materials. Sumin also likes to make her clothes at home by __(A)__ a 3D printer. She can choose colors and materials and can design clothes that fit her body and suit her tastes. Sumin is now a fashion designer!

10 위 글의 빈칸 (A)에 use를 알맞은 형태로 쓰시오.

➡ _____

11 위 글의 밑줄 친 ⓐ에서 어법상 틀린 부분을 찾아 고치시오.

➡ _____

12 위 글을 읽고 3D 프린터로 집을 짓는 것의 장점 세 가지를 우리말로 쓰시오.

➡ (1) _____

(2) _____

(3) _____

_____

01 다음 대화의 밑줄 친 우리말을 영작하시오. (주어진 어휘와 조건을 이용할 것)

> A: Look! This is closing its leave.
> B: I heard about this plant. It's a fly eater.
> A: 그것이 나뭇잎 같이 생겼는데 움직여서 놀라워. (surprise, like, 놀람 표현하기, 현재진행형)
> _____

02 주어진 어휘와 현재완료 시제를 이용하여 3 문장 이상을 쓰시오.

Advances in science and technology	life in the future	to Austria
finish my homework	visit Jejudo	

(1) _____
(2) _____
(3) _____

03 다음 내용을 바탕으로 20년 후 학교의 모습을 설명하는 글을 쓰시오.

> Q1: What do students learn?
> A: They learn 3D printing.
> Q2: Who helps students at school?
> A: AI teachers help students at school.
> Q3: What new place is in every school?
> A: There is a drone station in every school.
> Q4: What other ideas do you have about future schools?
> A: Students may not carry paper textbooks anymore.

> **Schools in 20 Years**
>   Have you ever thought of how schools may change over the next 20 years? Students may learn (A)_____. (B)_____ may help students at school. There may be (C)_____ in every school. Students may not carry (D)_____ anymore.

단원별 모의고사

01 빈칸 (A)와 (B)에 들어갈 말로 알맞은 것끼리 짝지어진 것을 고르시오.

> • The jacket (A)_____ me pretty well.
> • How much are we (B)_____ for delivery for items ordered from our Web site?

	(A)	(B)
①	fits	paying
②	fits	charging
③	fits	saving
④	follow	paying
⑤	follow	charging

02 다음 주어진 우리말에 맞게 빈칸을 채우시오. (철자가 주어진 것이 있으면 그 철자로 시작할 것)

(1) 나의 과학 선생님이 중력의 법칙에 대해 가르쳐 주셨다.

➡ My science teacher taught us about the l_____ of _____.

(2) 그 환자는 위독한 상태였다.

➡ The _____ was in a critical condition.

(3) 그의 가르치는 방식은 항상 창의적이다.

➡ His teaching m_____ is always creative.

(4) 그 축제는 다음 주 목요일에 개최될 것이다.

➡ The festival will _____ place next Thursday.

03 주어진 영영풀이의 어휘를 빈칸에 써 넣으시오.

> created by computers, or appearing on computers or the Internet

> _____ reality technology needs very powerful computers.

04 다음 우리말에 맞게 주어진 단어를 바르게 배열하시오.

(1) 그들은 커피를 뽑으려고 줄을 서서 기다리고 있다.
(in, waiting, line, get, are, coffee, to, they)

➡ _____

(2) 내가 곤경에 빠졌을 때, 그녀는 나를 많이 지원해주려고 노력했다. (when으로 시작할 것)
(when, me, lot, to, in, was, a, trouble, support, she, I, tried)

➡ _____

(3) 그 여자는 자기의 구입품을 교환하려고 노력 중이다.
(exchange, purchase, woman, the, her, is, to, trying)

➡ _____

(4) 이 약을 식후에 복용해라.
(meals, medicine, this, after, take)

➡ _____

05 밑줄 친 우리말에 맞게 주어진 단어를 이용하여 영작하시오.

> M: These days, many things can work like humans. Some cars can travel without a human driver. We can make smartphones do simple work only by talking to them. 나는 우리가 이미 미래에 살고 있다는 게 놀랍다.

➡ _____

(that, future, living)

[06~08] 다음 대화를 읽고 물음에 답하시오.

Amy: Wow, there are so many books in this library. (①)

Hana: You're right. Where can we find books about gravity? (②)

Terry: Hi, I'm Terry, the AI librarian. Can I help you?

Amy: Hi. We're looking for books about gravity. (③) Can you recommend one, please?

Terry: We have fifty seven books about gravity in this library. I think The Law of Gravity will be the best one for you.

Hana: I'm surprised that you can recommend books. (④)

Amy: Right. That's amazing. (⑤)

Terry: It's on the third floor. Come with me.

06 위 대화의 ①~⑤ 중 주어진 말이 들어갈 알맞은 곳은?

> Where is the book, Terry?

①   ②   ③   ④   ⑤

07 다음 영영풀이에 해당하는 단어를 위 대화에서 찾아 쓰시오.

> a statement of fact concerning what always happens in certain circumstances; a scientific principle

➡ _____

08 위 대화를 읽고 답할 수 없는 질문을 고르시오.

① How many books are there in the library?
② Where are Amy and Hana?
③ What book was recommended by Terry?
④ After the dialogue, where are they going to go?
⑤ What floor is *The Law of Gravity* on?

[09~10] 다음 대화를 읽고 물음에 답하시오.

G: Uncle Jack! Your new drone looks cool.

M: Thanks. I designed it ⓐto saving people's lives.

G: Save people's lives?

M: Yes. It watches the ocean. If there is ⓑa person in trouble, it flies over and ⓒdrop a tube.

G: ⓓI'm surprised what drones can rescue people. Can you ⓔshow me how it works?

M: Sure. Watch this.

09 다음 영영풀이에 해당하는 단어를 위 대화에서 찾아 쓰시오.

> an unmanned aircraft or ship guided by a remote control or onboard computers

➡ _____

10 ⓐ~ⓔ 중 어법상 어색한 것의 개수를 고르시오.

① 1개   ② 2개   ③ 3개   ④ 4개   ⑤ 5개

11 다음 우리말에 맞게 주어진 단어를 바르게 배열하시오.

> A: I think shoes will change our lives in the future.
> B: 미래에 어떻게 신발이 우리의 생활을 바꿀 수 있는지 말해 줄 수 있니?
> A: I think we will run 100 meters in 5 seconds.

➡ _____

_____

12 다음 대화의 순서를 바르게 배열하시오.

> (A) Light on or light out? That's very simple.
> (B) Just say, "Light on!" or "Light out!"
> (C) Welcome. This is our new smart light. You don't have to use your hands to turn it on and off.
> (D) Really? Then can you tell me how to do it?

➡ _____

13 다음 중 어법상 어색한 것을 고르시오.

① I have never used a chatting robot before.
② I have met a famous person then.
③ Technological developments have changed our lives.
④ We have been good friends for ten years.
⑤ Advances in science and technology have caused many changes in our lives so far.

14 다음 주어진 문장의 밑줄 친 부분과 쓰임이 같은 것은?

> • You <u>may</u> leave early.

① She <u>may</u> know the truth.
② They <u>may</u> invite me to the party.
③ You <u>may</u> not read my diary.
④ All types of diseases like cancer <u>may</u> be cured.
⑤ Students <u>may</u> get help from not only human teachers but also AI teachers.

15 그림을 보고, 'may'와 주어진 단어를 이용하여 추측하는 문장을 완성하시오.

(Cindy, live, a 3D printed house, future)

➡ _____

16 다음 두 문장을 해석하고 그 차이를 설명하시오.

> (1) I lost my smartphone.
> (2) I have lost my smartphone.

➡ 해석: (1) _____
해석: (2) _____
차이: _____

_____

_____

[17~19] 다음 글을 읽고 물음에 답하시오.

Sangho in the Shopping Center

Shopping is much easier. There are no lines and no counters. Sangho enters a shop with his smartphone which has a special shopping app. In the shop, he takes the items he wants. The items are automatically added to a virtual card on his smartphone. If Sangho puts an item back, it is automatically removed from his list of purchases. When he finishes shopping, Sangho does not need to wait in line ⓐto pay. His virtual card adds up all the prices and will charge him later. Isn't that fancy?

17 아래 보기에서 위 글의 밑줄 친 ⓐto pay와 to부정사의 용법이 다른 것의 개수를 고르시오.

┌─ 보기 ────────────────────────┐
① To hear him talk, you would think him a foreigner.
② She has many children to look after.
③ He began to read the book.
④ She must be honest to say so.
⑤ I didn't know where to go.
└──────────────────────────────┘

① 1개   ② 2개   ③ 3개   ④ 4개   ⑤ 5개

18 본문의 내용과 일치하도록 다음 빈칸 (A)와 (B)에 알맞은 단어를 쓰시오.

┌──────────────────────────────┐
In the shop, the items Sangho (A)_____ are automatically added to a virtual card on his smartphone, and the items Sangho (B)_____ _____ are automatically removed from his list of purchases.
└──────────────────────────────┘

19 위 글을 읽고 대답할 수 없는 질문은?

① Are there lines or counters in the shopping center?
② Does Sangho need a special app to shop at the shopping center?
③ What operation method does the app use to automatically add the items to a virtual card on Sangho's smartphone?
④ Is the item Sangho puts back automatically removed from his list of purchases?
⑤ How does Sangho pay when he buys things at a shopping center?

[20~22] 다음 글을 읽고 물음에 답하시오.

Sumin's 3D Printed House and Clothes

Sumin lives in a 3D printed house. Building a 3D printed house is faster and cheaper than building a house with traditional methods. Sumin's house looks fantastic ⓐbecause of its unique design. A 3D printer can produce house shapes that people cannot make with traditional building methods and materials. Sumin also likes to make her clothes at home by using a 3D printer. She can choose colors and materials and can design clothes that fit her body and suit her ⓑtastes. Sumin is now __(A)__ !

20 위 글의 빈칸 (A)에 들어갈 알맞은 말을 고르시오.

① an architect   ② a fashion model
③ an engineer   ④ a fashion designer
⑤ a painter

21 위 글의 밑줄 친 ⓐbecause of와 바꿔 쓸 수 없는 말을 고르시오.

① on account of   ② thanks to
③ in spite of   ④ owing to
⑤ due to

22 위 글의 밑줄 친 ⓑtastes와 같은 의미로 쓰인 것을 고르시오.

① She has very unique taste in clothes.
② The soup tastes of onion.
③ It tastes sweet.
④ I don't like the tastes of vegetables.
⑤ She tastes with her tongue.

Special

The 100th Customer

🎣 언어 형식

- 지각동사

  Mr. Kang **watched** them **eat**.

- 'too+형용사/부사+to+동사원형' 구문

  She was **too** poor **to** pay for two bowls.

Words & Expressions

Key Words

□ **bedroom** [bédrùːm] 몡 침실

□ **bowl** [boul] 몡 (우묵한) 그릇, 통

□ **break** [breik] 몡 휴식, (학교의) 쉬는 시간

□ **chair** [tʃɛər] 몡 의자

□ **chew** [tʃuː] 동 (음식을) 씹다

□ **count** [kaunt] 동 수를 세다, 계산하다

□ **counter** [káuntər] 몡 계산대

□ **customer** [kʌ́stəmər] 몡 손님, 고객

□ **elderly** [éldərli] 혱 연세가 드신

□ **even** [íːvən] 뷰 (예상 밖의 놀라운 일을 나타내어) ~도, ~조차

□ **grandson** [grǽndsʌn] 몡 손자

□ **if** [if] 젭 만일 ~라면

□ **meal** [miːl] 몡 식사

□ **novel** [návəl] 몡 소설

□ **order** [ɔ́ːrdər] 동 (음식, 음료 등을) 주문하다

□ **owner** [óunər] 몡 주인, 소유주

□ **player** [pléiər] 몡 참가자, 선수, 배우

□ **producer** [prədjúːsər] 몡 생산자, 제작자

□ **raise** [reiz] 동 (자금 등을) 모으다

□ **single** [síŋgl] 혱 단 하나의, 단일의

□ **tap** [tæp] 동 (가볍게) 톡톡 두드리다, 치다

□ **treat** [triːt] 동 대접하다, 다루다

□ **turn** [təːrn] 몡 (무엇을 할) 차례, 순번

□ **yet** [jet] 뷰 (부정문, 의문문에서) 아직

Key Expressions

□ **be about to** 막 ~하려는 참이다

□ **can't wait to 동사원형** 빨리 ~하고 싶다, ~하는 것이 기다려지다

□ **have to 동사원형** ~해야 한다

□ **help+목적어+동사원형** (목적어)가 ~하는 것을 돕다

□ **pick up** 들어올리다, 집다, ~을 (차에) 태우러 가다

□ **say to oneself** 혼잣말을 하다

□ **think up** ~을 생각해 내다

□ **too+형용사/부사+to 동사원형** 너무 …해서 ~할 수 없다

□ **treat A(사람) to B(사물)** A에게 B를 대접하다

Word Power

※ 접미사 -er을 붙여 '〜하는 사람'이라는 뜻의 명사가 되는 동사들

□ **own** (소유하다) – **owner** (주인, 소유주)

□ **play** (경기하다, (연극 등을) 상연[공연]하다) – **player** (선수, 배우)

□ **produce** (생산하다, 만들다) – **producer** (생산자, 제작자)

□ **write** (쓰다, (작품·문서 등을) 저술하다) – **writer** (작가)

□ **teach** (가르치다) – **teacher** (교사)

□ **paint** (그림을 그리다) – **painter** (화가)

　(*cf.*) 접미사 -er을 붙여 '〜하는 것'이라는 뜻의 명사가 되는 동사

□ **clean** (청소하다) – **cleaner** (청소기)

□ **dry** (건조시키다) – **dryer** (건조기, 드라이어)

※ 비슷한 뜻을 가진 어휘들

□ **elderly** (연세가 드신) – **old** (나이든)

□ **producer** (생산자, 제작자) – **maker** (제조업자, 만드는 사람)

□ **raise** ((자금 등을) 모으다) – **collect** ((돈·기부·인원을) 모으다)

□ **single** (단 하나의, 단일의) – **only** (유일한)

□ **treat** (대접하다, 다루다) – **deal with** ((문제 등을) 다루다)

English Dictionary

□ **bedroom** 침실
→ a room that you sleep in
당신이 자는 방

□ **chair** 의자
→ a piece of furniture for one person to sit on, with a back, legs, and sometimes two arms
한 사람이 앉기 위한, 등받이와 다리, 때때로 팔걸이가 있는 가구

□ **chew** (음식을) 씹다
→ to break food etc. with the teeth before swallowing
음식을 삼키기 전에 이로 음식을 부수다

□ **counter** 계산대
→ the place where customers are served or pay in a restaurant or shop
식당이나 가게에서 손님들이 시중을 받고 돈을 지불하는 장소

□ **customer** 손님, 고객
→ a person who buys goods from a shop, etc.
가게에서 물건을 사는 사람

□ **grandson** 손자
→ a son of one's son or daughter
어떤 사람의 아들이나 딸의 아들

□ **meal** 식사
→ an occasion when you eat food such as breakfast, lunch, and dinner
아침, 점심, 저녁 같은 음식을 먹는 것

□ **novel** 소설
→ a book telling a long story in prose
산문의 형식으로 긴 이야기를 하는 책

□ **single** 단 하나의
→ comprising only one part
오직 하나의 부분으로만 이루어진

□ **think up** ~을 생각해 내다
→ to invent or to imagine something, especially an excuse
특히 변명으로 어떤 것을 지어내거나 상상해 내다

□ **treat** 대접하다
→ to buy or give someone something special
어떤 사람에게 특별한 것을 사 주거나 주다

The 100th Customer

One day, an elderly woman walked into a restaurant. She was with
_{old보다 정중한 표현, 나이가 드신}
her grandson. Quietly, the woman asked Mr. Kang, the owner of the
_{'Mr. Kang'과 'the owner of the restaurant'는 동격, 콤마(,)가 쓰였다.}
restaurant.

"How much is a bowl of Gukbap?"
_{How much ~?: 양이나 가격을 물을 때 쓰임. 여기에서는 국밥 한 그릇의 가격을 묻고 있다.}
"It's 4,000 won, ma'am," Mr. Kang answered with a smile. She
_{미소 지으며}
was too poor to pay for two bowls. She ordered a single bowl for her
_{too+형용사/부사+to+동사원형: 너무 ~해서 …할 수 없다}
grandson.

"Are you sure you are not hungry, Grandma?" the boy asked, as he
_{sure와 you 사이에 접속사 that이 생략}
ate the hot soup.

"No, I'm not hungry. Don't worry about me." She picked up some

Gimchi and chewed on it happily.
_{~을 씹었다, 입에 물었다}
Mr. Kang watched them eat, and a warm feeling came over him.
_{지각동사+목적어+동사원형: 목적격보어로 동사원형이나 현재분사가 온다.} _{come over: (격한 감정 등이) ~에게 밀려오다}
He thought up a plan to give the boy a free meal. When the woman
_{to부정사(형용사적 용법)}
was about to pay, Mr. Kang waved his hands and said, "No need,

ma'am. In my restaurant, you don't pay if you're the 100th customer
_{만일 ~라면(조건을 나타내는 접속사)}
of the day." The woman and her grandson thanked Mr. Kang and left.

owner: 주인
order: 주문하다
single: 단 하나의, 단일의
chew: ~을 씹다
meal: 식사
pick up: 집다
think up: ~을 생각해 내다
be about to: 막 ~하려는 참이다

📎 **확인문제**

● 다음 문장이 본문의 내용과 일치하면 T, 일치하지 <u>않으면</u> F를 쓰시오.

1 One day, an elderly woman walked into a restaurant with her grandson. ☐

2 She had enough money to pay for two bowls. ☐

3 Mr. Kang thought up a plan to give the boy a free meal. ☐

4 It was true that the woman was the 100th customer of the day. ☐

A month later, Mr. Kang saw the boy in the street outside the restaurant. The boy was gathering stones.

"What are you doing?" asked Mr. Kang.

"I'm counting the number of customers who enter your restaurant. Today is my grandma's birthday."

'He wants to be the 100th customer and treat his grandmother to a bowl of Gukbap!' Mr. Kang said to himself.

Mr. Kang looked down. He could see that the number of stones was not yet even fifty. He had to do something to help the boy gather 100 stones. Mr. Kang went back into the restaurant and called his friends.

"Come to my restaurant now and bring everyone who works with you. There is a boy who needs your help."

People began to arrive at the restaurant. When the 99th customer arrived, Mr. Kang heard the boy say, "It's our turn, Grandma." Mr. Kang welcomed them and served the woman a free bowl of Gukbap.

"Are you sure you're not hungry?" the woman asked the boy.

The boy chewed loudly on some Gimchi and said with a smile,

"No, I'm not hungry, Grandma. Don't worry about me. Happy birthday!"

outside: ~ 밖에

stone: 돌

treat: 대접하다

yet: 아직

even: ~도, ~조차

확인문제

● 다음 문장이 본문의 내용과 일치하면 T, 일치하지 않으면 F를 쓰시오.

1　The boy was counting the number of customers who entered Mr. Kang's restaurant.

　　☐

2　The number of stones was already over fifty. ☐

3　Mr. Kang went back into the restaurant and called his friends. ☐

4　Mr. Kang welcomed the boy and his grandmother and served them two free bowls of Gukbap. ☐

● 우리말을 참고하여 빈칸에 알맞은 말을 쓰시오.

1 The _____ Customer

2 One day, an _____ woman walked into a restaurant.

3 She was _____ _____ _____.

4 _____, the woman asked Mr. Kang, _____ _____ of the restaurant.

5 "_____ _____ is a bowl of Gukbap?"

6 "It's 4,000 won, ma'am," Mr. Kang answered _____ _____ _____.

7 She was _____ _____ _____ _____ for two bowls.

8 She ordered a single bowl _____ _____ _____.

9 "_____ _____ _____ you are not hungry, Grandma?" the boy asked, as he ate the hot soup.

10 "_____, I'm not hungry.

11 _____ _____ about me."

12 She picked up some Gimchi and _____ _____ it happily.

13 Mr. Kang watched them _____, and a warm feeling _____ _____ him.

14 He thought up a plan _____ _____ _____ _____ _____ _____.

15 When the woman _____ _____ _____ _____, Mr. Kang waved his hands and said, "No need, ma'am.

16 In my restaurant, you don't pay if you're _____ _____ _____ of the day."

17 The woman and her grandson _____ _____ _____ and left.

---

1 백 번째 손님

2 어느 날 한 할머니가 식당으로 걸어 들어왔다.

3 그녀는 손자와 함께 있었다.

4 그녀는 조용히 식당 주인인 강 씨에게 물었다.

5 "국밥 한 그릇이 얼마인가요?"

6 "4,000원입니다. 할머니." 강 씨는 미소 지으며 답했다.

7 그녀는 너무 가난해서 두 그릇 값을 지불할 수 없었다.

8 그녀는 손자를 위해 한 그릇을 주문했다.

9 "정말 배고프지 않으세요, 할머니?" 남자아이는 따뜻한 국물을 먹으며 물었다.

10 "응, 난 배고프지 않단다.

11 내 걱정하지 마라."

12 그녀는 행복하게 김치를 집어서 먹었다.

13 강 씨는 그들이 먹는 것을 지켜 보았고, 따뜻한 감정이 밀려왔 다.

14 그는 남자아이에게 무료로 식사 를 주기 위해 계획을 생각해 냈 다.

15 할머니가 돈을 내려고 할 때, 강 씨는 손을 흔들며 말했다. "필요 없습니다. 할머니.

16 저희 식당에서는 그 날의 백 번 째 손님이 되면 돈을 내지 않아 도 됩니다."

17 할머니와 손자는 강 씨에게 감 사해 하며 떠났다.

_____ _____ _____, Mr. Kang saw the boy in the street _____ the restaurant.

The boy _____ _____ stones.

"_____ are you doing?" asked Mr. Kang.

"I'm _____ the number of customers _____ enter your restaurant.

_____ _____ my grandma's birthday."

'He wants to be the 100th customer and _____ his grandmother to a bowl of Gukbap!' Mr. Kang _____ _____ _____.

Mr. Kang _____ _____.

He could see that _____ _____ of stones _____ not yet even fifty.

He had to do something _____ _____ the boy gather 100 stones.

Mr. Kang _____ _____ _____ the restaurant and called his friends.

"Come to my restaurant now and _____ _____ _____ works with you.

There is a boy _____ _____ your help."

People began _____ _____ _____ the restaurant.

When the 99th customer arrived, Mr. Kang heard the boy say, "_____ _____ _____, Grandma."

Mr. Kang _____ _____ and served the woman _____ _____ _____ _____ _____.

"_____ _____ _____ you're not hungry?" the woman asked the boy.

The boy chewed loudly on some Gimchi and said _____ _____, "No, I'm not hungry, Grandma.

_____ _____ about me. Happy birthday!"

---

18 한 달 후, 강 씨는 식당 밖 거리에서 그 남자아이를 보았다.

19 그 남자아이는 돌멩이를 모으고 있었다.

20 너 뭐 하고 있니?" 강 씨가 물었다.

21 "저는 아저씨 식당에 들어가는 손님들의 수를 세고 있어요.

22 오늘이 우리 할머니 생신이거든요."

23 '저 아이는 백 번째 손님이 되어서 할머니께 공짜 국밥 한 그릇을 대접하고 싶어 하는구나.' 강 씨는 혼잣말을 했다.

24 강 씨는 아래를 내려다보았다.

25 그는 돌멩이의 개수가 아직 오십 개도 안 되는 것을 볼 수 있었다.

26 그는 남자아이가 돌멩이 백 개를 모으는 것을 돕기 위해 무언가를 해야 했다.

27 강 씨는 식당으로 되돌아가 그의 친구들에게 전화했다.

28 "지금 내 식당으로 오고, 자네와 함께 일하는 모든 사람들을 데려와 주게.

29 자네 도움이 필요한 남자아이가 있어."

30 사람들이 식당에 도착하기 시작했다.

31 아흔아홉 번째 손님이 도착했을 때 강 씨는 남자아이가 "우리 차례예요, 할머니."라고 말하는 것을 들었다.

32 강 씨는 그들을 반기며 할머니께 공짜 국밥 한 그릇을 제공했다.

33 "너 정말 배고프지 않니?" 할머니가 남자아이에게 물었다.

34 남자아이는 큰 소리로 김치를 씹고 미소 지으며 말했다. "네, 전 배고프지 않아요, 할머니.

35 제 걱정 마세요. 생신 축하드려요!"

● 우리말을 참고하여 본문을 영작하시오.

1 ▶ 백 번째 손님
➡ _____

2 ▶ 어느 날 한 할머니가 식당으로 걸어 들어왔다.
➡ _____

3 ▶ 그녀는 손자와 함께 있었다.
➡ _____

4 ▶ 그녀는 조용히 식당 주인인 강 씨에게 물었다.
➡ _____

5 ▶ "국밥 한 그릇이 얼마인가요?"
➡ _____

6 ▶ "4,000원입니다, 할머니." 강 씨는 미소 지으며 답했다.
➡ _____

7 ▶ 그녀는 너무 가난해서 두 그릇 값을 지불할 수 없었다.
➡ _____

8 ▶ 그녀는 손자를 위해 한 그릇을 주문했다.
➡ _____

9 ▶ "정말 배고프지 않으세요, 할머니?" 남자아이는 따뜻한 국물을 먹으며 물었다.
➡ _____

10 ▶ "응, 난 배고프지 않단다.
➡ _____

11 ▶ 내 걱정하지 마라."
➡ _____

12 ▶ 그녀는 행복하게 김치를 집어서 먹었다.
➡ _____

13 ▶ 강 씨는 그들이 먹는 것을 지켜보았고, 따뜻한 감정이 밀려왔다.
➡ _____

14 ▶ 그는 남자아이에게 무료로 식사를 주기 위해 계획을 생각해 냈다.
➡ _____

15 ▶ 할머니가 돈을 내려고 할 때, 강 씨는 손을 흔들며 말했다. "필요 없습니다, 할머니.
➡ _____

16 ▶ 저희 식당에서는 그 날의 백 번째 손님이 되면 돈을 내지 않아도 됩니다."
➡ _____

17 ▶ 할머니와 손자는 강 씨에게 감사해 하며 떠났다.
➡ _____

18 한 달 후, 강 씨는 식당 밖 거리에서 그 남자아이를 보았다.

➡ _____

19 그 남자아이는 돌멩이를 모으고 있었다.

➡ _____

20 "너 뭐 하고 있니?" 강 씨가 물었다.

➡ _____

21 "저는 아저씨 식당에 들어가는 손님들의 수를 세고 있어요.

➡ _____

22 오늘이 우리 할머니 생신이거든요."

➡ _____

23 '저 아이는 백 번째 손님이 되어서 할머니께 공짜 국밥 한 그릇을 대접하고 싶어 하는구나.' 강 씨는 혼잣말을 했다.

➡ _____

➡ _____

24 강 씨는 아래를 내려다보았다.

➡ _____

25 그는 돌멩이의 개수가 아직 오십 개도 안 되는 것을 볼 수 있었다.

➡ _____

26 그는 남자아이가 돌멩이 백 개를 모으는 것을 돕기 위해 무언가를 해야 했다.

➡ _____

27 강 씨는 식당으로 되돌아가 그의 친구들에게 전화했다.

➡ _____

28 "지금 내 식당으로 오고, 자네와 함께 일하는 모든 사람들을 데려와 주게.

➡ _____

29 자네 도움이 필요한 남자아이가 있어."

➡ _____

30 사람들이 식당에 도착하기 시작했다.

➡ _____

31 아흔아홉 번째 손님이 도착했을 때 강 씨는 남자아이가 "우리 차례예요, 할머니."라고 말하는 것을 들었다.

➡ _____

32 강 씨는 그들을 반기며 할머니께 공짜 국밥 한 그릇을 제공했다.

➡ _____

33 "너 정말 배고프지 않니?" 할머니가 남자아이에게 물었다.

➡ _____

34 남자아이는 큰 소리로 김치를 씹고 미소 지으며 말했다. "네, 전 배고프지 않아요, 할머니.

➡ _____

35 제 걱정 마세요. 생신 축하드려요!"

➡ _____

01 밑줄 친 부분과 의미가 가장 가까운 단어를 주어진 철자로 시작하여 쓰시오.

(1) This is the <u>only</u> bank in the area.

➡ s_____

(2) There are new ways of <u>dealing with</u> the problem of street crime.

➡ t_____

(3) Sarah takes care of her <u>old</u> parents.

➡ e_____

02 빈칸에 공통으로 들어갈 단어를 쓰시오.

(1)
• Who thought _____ names for new products?
• Passengers are picking _____ their bags.

(2)
• I'll treat them _____ dinner tonight.
• Johnson always says _____ himself.

03 다음 빈칸에 알맞은 단어를 〈보기〉에서 골라 쓰시오.

┌─── 보기 ───┐
chew count order raise
└───────────┘

(1) They hoped to _____ one million dollars to buy land.

(2) I can't _____ my food well because of the toothache.

(3) _____ whatever you want regardless of expense.

(4) John had to _____ the number of animals.

04 주어진 문장과 비슷한 의미가 되도록 빈칸을 알맞게 채우시오.

┌─────────────────────────────────┐
I'm looking forward to taking the trip.
└─────────────────────────────────┘

➡ I _____ wait _____ _____ the trip.

05 다음 주어진 우리말에 맞게 빈칸을 채우시오.

(1) 거기는 여름에도 춥다.

➡ It is cold there _____ in summer.

(2) 식사 사이에 먹지 않도록 노력해라.

➡ Try not to eat between _____.

(3) 너의 차례가 오면, 한 칸을 움직여라.

➡ When it's your _____, move one space.

(4) 버스 운전사가 아직 안 왔다.

➡ The bus driver isn't here _____.

06 다음 영영풀이에 해당하는 말을 주어진 철자로 시작하여 쓰시오.

┌─────────────────────────────────┐
a piece of furniture for one person to sit on, with a back, legs, and sometimes two arms
└─────────────────────────────────┘

➡ c_____

┌─────────────────────────────────┐
to break food etc. with the teeth before swallowing
└─────────────────────────────────┘

➡ c_____

07 다음 문장에서 어법상 어색한 부분을 바르게 고쳐 쓰시오.

(1) I saw you to enter the museum.

➡ _____

(2) I heard my friend laughed loudly in English class.

➡ _____
_____

(3) The kid is very short to reach that book.

➡ _____

(4) I am too tired that I can't get up early.

➡ _____

08 주어진 동사를 빈칸에 알맞게 쓰시오.

(A) The cook smelled soup _____.
(burn)
(B) The chair is too heavy _____.
(carry)

09 다음 우리말을 주어진 어휘를 이용하여 영작하시오.

(1) 그 셔츠는 너무 커서 입을 수 없다. (wear, large, to)

➡ _____

(2) 나는 Tom이 나에 대해 얘기하는 것을 들었다. (talk)

➡ _____

(3) 그는 사실을 말할 만큼 정직하다. (enough, tell)

➡ _____

[10~12] 다음 글을 읽고 물음에 답하시오.

One day, an elderly woman walked into a restaurant. She was ⓐ her grandson. Quietly, the woman asked Mr. Kang, the owner of the restaurant.

"ⓑHow much is a bowl of Gukbap?"

"It's 4,000 won, ma'am," Mr. Kang answered ⓒ a smile. ⓓShe was too poor to pay for two bowls. She ordered a single bowl for her grandson.

10 위 글의 빈칸 ⓐ와 ⓒ에 공통으로 들어갈 알맞은 전치사를 쓰시오.

➡ _____

11 위 글의 밑줄 친 ⓑ를 다음과 같이 바꿔 쓸 때 빈칸에 들어갈 알맞은 말을 쓰시오.

➡ What's the _____ of a bowl of Gukbap?

12 위 글의 밑줄 친 ⓓ를 다음과 같이 바꿔 쓸 때 빈칸에 들어갈 알맞은 말을 쓰시오.

➡ She was _____ poor _____ she _____ pay for two bowls.

[13~15] 다음 글을 읽고 물음에 답하시오.

"Are you sure you are not hungry, Grandma?" the boy asked, as he ate the hot soup.

"(A)[Yes / No], I'm not hungry. Don't worry about me." She picked up some Gimchi and chewed on it happily. ⓐMr. Kang watched them to eat, and a warm feeling came over him. He thought up ⓑa plan to give the boy a free meal. When the woman was about (B)[to pay / paying], Mr. Kang waved his hands and said, "No need, ma'am. In my restaurant, you don't pay if you're the 100th (C)[customer / guest] of the day." The woman and her grandson thanked Mr. Kang and left.

13 위 글의 괄호 (A)~(C)에서 문맥이나 어법상 알맞은 낱말을 골라 쓰시오.

➡ (A) _____ (B) _____ (C) _____

14 위 글의 밑줄 친 ⓐ에서 어법상 **틀린** 부분을 찾아 고치시오.

➡ _____

15 위 글의 밑줄 친 ⓑ a plan의 구체적인 내용을 우리말로 쓰시오.

➡ _____

_____

[16~18] 다음 글을 읽고 물음에 답하시오.

A month later, Mr. Kang saw the boy in the street outside the restaurant. The boy was gathering stones.

"What are you doing?" asked Mr. Kang.

"I'm counting the number of customers ⓐ _____ enter your restaurant. Today is my grandma's birthday."

'He wants to be the 100th customer and treat his grandmother to a bowl of Gukbap!' Mr. Kang said to himself.

Mr. Kang looked down. He could see ⓑ _____ the number of stones was not yet even fifty. He had to do ⓒunderline{something} to help the boy gather 100 stones. Mr. Kang went back into the restaurant and called his friends.

"Come to my restaurant now and bring everyone who works with you. There is a boy ⓓ _____ needs your help."

16 빈칸 ⓐ, ⓑ, ⓓ에 공통으로 들어갈 알맞은 말을 쓰시오.

➡ _____

17 밑줄 친 ⓒ가 구체적으로 가리키는 내용을 우리말로 쓰시오.

➡ _____

_____

18 Why did Mr. Kang call his friends and ask them to come to his restaurant? Fill in the blanks with suitable words.

➡ Because he wanted to make the boy

_____ _____ of the day.

[19~21] 다음 글을 읽고 물음에 답하시오.

People began to ⓐarrive at the restaurant. When the 99th customer arrived, Mr. Kang heard the boy _(A)_ , "It's our turn, Grandma." Mr. Kang welcomed them and ⓑserved the woman a free bowl of Gukbap.

19 빈칸 (A)에 say를 알맞은 형태로 쓰시오.

➡ _____

20 밑줄 친 ⓐarrive at과 바꿔 쓸 수 있는 단어를 쓰시오.

➡ _____

21 밑줄 친 ⓑ를 3형식으로 고치시오.

➡ _____

출제율 95%

01 다음 중 단어의 관계가 나머지 넷과 <u>다른</u> 하나는?

① own – owner
② dry – dryer
③ write – writer
④ teach – teacher
⑤ produce – producer

출제율 95%

02 다음 빈칸에 공통으로 들어갈 말로 알맞은 것을 주어진 철자로 시작하여 쓰시오.

(1)
- I will p_____ my sister at the airport.
- We have to p_____ the trash on the street.

(2)
- R_____ your hand if you know the right answer.
- They r_____d funds to help the flood victim.

출제율 90%

03 다음 우리말에 맞게 주어진 단어를 바르게 배열하시오.

(1) 그녀는 그에게 점심을 대접했다. (to, she, him, lunch, treated)

➡ _____

(2) 그가 나한테 전화했을 때, 나는 막 나가려는 참이었다. (I, about, he, was, me, leave, when, to, called) (when으로 시작할 것)

➡ _____

(3) 소녀는 여동생이 케이크 만드는 것을 도왔다. (a cake, helped, make, her, the girl, sister)

➡ _____

(4) 나는 그것을 정말 보고 싶어. (can't, to, I, it, wait, watch)

➡ _____

출제율 90%

04 다음 중 밑줄 친 부분의 뜻풀이가 바르지 <u>않은</u> 것은?

① Put the vegetables in the salad <u>bowl</u>. (그릇)
② We had a very warm welcome from the <u>owner</u> of the house. (주인)
③ I had to <u>think up</u> a better excuse. (추측하다)
④ I <u>ordered</u> a cup of coffee and a sandwich. (주문했다)
⑤ He sent her a <u>single</u> red rose. (하나의)

출제율 95%

05 다음 두 문장에 공통으로 알맞은 것은?

- The plane was _____ to take off.
- What _____ going on a picnic?

① of
② with
③ from
④ along
⑤ about

출제율 100%

06 밑줄 친 부분과 의미가 가장 가까운 것을 고르시오.

He held a concert to <u>collect</u> money for charity.

① protect
② carry
③ raise
④ drop
⑤ create

07 다음 중 어법상 바른 것은?

① It is so hot to go out today.

② He was too poor that he couldn't buy a car.

③ The problem is so easy that he can solve.

④ Mike felt someone tapped him on the shoulder.

⑤ Harry heard his friend speak on the phone.

08 다음 중 어법상 <u>어색한</u> 것은?

① It was too late to save the man.

② Sarah is so sick that she can't go to school today.

③ I felt the ground shook once.

④ He listened to the teacher talk.

⑤ When I arrived there, I saw him leaving the room.

09 주어진 두 문장을 한 문장으로 바꿔 쓰시오. (접속사나 관계대명사 사용 금지)

(1) • I felt something.

　• It was biting my leg.

　➡ _____

(2) • We enjoyed listening to the bird.

　• The bird sang.

　➡ _____

(3) • Did you see the children?

　• The children were playing soccer on the ground.

　➡ _____

10 다음 우리말에 맞게 주어진 어휘를 이용하여 영작하시오.

(1) Kate는 누군가가 그녀의 가방을 만지는 것을 느꼈다. (feel, touch, someone)

　➡ _____

(2) 나는 네가 나를 부르는 것을 듣지 못했다. (hear, call)

　➡ _____

(3) 나는 해변에서 그 소년이 모래성을 쌓고 있는 것을 보았다. (watch, a sandcastle, build)

　➡ _____

(4) 나는 너무 어려서 그 영화를 볼 수 없었다. (so, young, watch the movie)

　➡ _____

(5) 그녀는 첫 기차를 탈 만큼 충분히 일찍 일어났다. (get, early, enough, catch)

　➡ _____

(6) 차가 너무 뜨거워서 마실 수가 없다. (the tea, hot, too)

　➡ _____

11 다음 문장을 같은 뜻을 갖는 문장으로 바꿔 쓰시오.

(1) She is too shy to ask for help.

　➡ _____

(2) The stars in the sky are too many to count.

　➡ _____

(3) The problem is easy enough for him to solve.

　➡ _____

[12~15] 다음 글을 읽고 물음에 답하시오.

"Are you sure you are not hungry, Grandma?" the boy asked, ⓐas he ate the hot soup.

"No, I'm not hungry. Don't worry about me." She picked up some Gimchi and chewed on it happily.

Mr. Kang watched them ___(A)___, and a warm feeling came over him. He thought up a plan ⓑto give the boy a free meal. When the woman was about to pay, Mr. Kang waved his hands and said, "No need, ma'am. In my restaurant, you don't pay if you're the 100th customer of the day." The woman and her grandson thanked Mr. Kang and left.

출제율 90%

12 위 글의 빈칸 (A)에 들어갈 말을 <u>모두</u> 고르시오.

① eaten   ② eat

③ ate   ④ to eat

⑤ eating

출제율 95%

13 위 글의 밑줄 친 ⓐas와 같은 의미로 쓰인 것을 고르시오.

① Do as you are told.

② It can be used as a chair.

③ She came up as I was speaking.

④ I regard him as a fool.

⑤ I love you as much as she does.

출제율 85%

14 위 글의 밑줄 친 ⓑ를 3형식으로 고치시오.

➡ _____

출제율 90%

15 위 글에서 할머니와 Mr. Kang이 보여준 배려의 행동을 각각 우리말로 쓰시오.

➡ 할머니 : _____

    Mr. Kang : _____

_____

[16~18] 다음 글을 읽고 물음에 답하시오.

A month later, Mr. Kang saw the boy in the street outside the restaurant. The boy was gathering stones.

"What are you doing?" asked Mr. Kang.

"I'm counting the number of customers who enter your restaurant. (①) Today is my grandma's birthday."

(②) 'He wants to be the 100th customer and treat his grandmother ⓐ a bowl of Gukbap!' Mr. Kang said ⓑ himself.

(③) Mr. Kang looked down. (④) He could see that the number of stones was not yet even fifty. (⑤) Mr. Kang went back into the restaurant and called his friends.

"Come to my restaurant now and bring everyone who works with you. There is a boy who needs your help."

출제율 90%

16 위 글의 빈칸 ⓐ와 ⓑ에 공통으로 들어갈 전치사를 쓰시오.

➡ _____

출제율 100%

17 위 글의 흐름으로 보아, 주어진 문장이 들어가기에 가장 적절한 곳은?

He had to do something to help the boy gather 100 stones.

①   ②   ③   ④   ⑤

18 위 글에서 알 수 있는 'Mr. Kang'의 성격으로 가장 알맞은 것을 고르시오.

① patient
② considerate
③ funny
④ curious
⑤ outgoing

[19~21] 다음 글을 읽고 물음에 답하시오.

People began to arrive at the restaurant. When the 99th customer arrived, Mr. Kang heard the boy say, "It's our ⓐturn, Grandma." Mr. Kang welcomed them and ⓑ할머니께 공짜 국밥 한 그릇을 제공했다.

19 위 글의 밑줄 친 ⓐturn과 같은 의미로 쓰인 것을 고르시오.

① The wheels of the car began to turn.
② Ann and Jane turn 21 in June.
③ Please wait your turn.
④ Why did she turn the wheel to the left?
⑤ The car made a turn to the right.

20 위 글의 밑줄 친 ⓑ의 우리말에 맞게 한 단어를 보충하여, 주어진 어휘를 알맞게 배열하시오.

Gukbap / a / served / bowl / woman / of / the

➡ _____

21 위 글의 분위기로 가장 알맞은 것을 고르시오.

① moving
② depressing
③ comical
④ miserable
⑤ boring

[22~24] 다음 글을 읽고 물음에 답하시오.

ⓐMr. Kang watched them eat, and a warm feeling came over him. He thought up a plan to give the boy a ⓑfree meal. When the woman was about to pay, Mr. Kang waved his hands and said, "No need, ma'am. In my restaurant, you don't pay ⓒ그 날의 백 번째 손님이 되면." The woman and her grandson thanked Mr. Kang and left.

22 위 글의 밑줄 친 문장 ⓐ에서 알 수 있는 'Mr. Kang'의 심경으로 가장 알맞은 것을 고르시오.

① ashamed
② excited
③ disappointed
④ bored
⑤ touched

23 위 글의 밑줄 친 ⓑfree와 같은 의미로 쓰인 것을 고르시오.

① You are free to come and go.
② Keep Friday night free for my party.
③ She struggled to free herself.
④ Admission is free.
⑤ The researchers set the birds free.

24 위 글의 밑줄 친 ⓒ의 우리말에 맞게 주어진 어휘를 이용하여 8단어로 영작하시오.

you're, 100th, the day

➡ _____

[25~27] 다음 글을 읽고 물음에 답하시오.

A month later, Mr. Kang saw the boy in the street outside the restaurant. The boy was gathering stones.

"What are ①you doing?" asked Mr. Kang.

"I'm counting the number of customers who enter your restaurant. Today is ②my grandma's birthday."

'③He wants to be the 100th customer and treat ④his grandmother to a bowl of Gukbap!' Mr. Kang said to (A)[him / himself].

Mr. Kang looked down. He could see that the number of stones (B)[was / were] not yet even fifty. He had to do something to help the boy (C)[gather / gathering] 100 stones. Mr. Kang went back into the restaurant and called ⑤his friends.

"Come to my restaurant now and bring everyone who works with you. There is a boy who needs your help."

25 밑줄 친 ①~⑤ 중에서 가리키는 대상이 나머지 넷과 <u>다른</u> 것은?

①   ②   ③   ④   ⑤

26 위 글의 괄호 (A)~(C)에서 어법상 알맞은 낱말을 골라 쓰시오.

➡ (A) _____ (B) _____ (C) _____

27 위 글의 내용과 일치하지 <u>않는</u> 것은?

① 한 달 후, 강 씨는 식당 밖 거리에서 그 남자아이를 보았다.
② 그 남자아이는 돌멩이를 모으고 있었다.
③ 그 남자아이는 식당에 들어가는 손님들의 수를 세고 있었다.
④ 식당의 손님은 이미 오십 명을 넘었다.
⑤ 강 씨는 남자아이가 돌멩이 백 개를 모으는 것을 돕기 위해 식당으로 되돌아가 그의 친구들에게 전화했다.

[28~30] 다음 글을 읽고 물음에 답하시오.

People began ⓐto arrive at the restaurant. When the 99th customer arrived, Mr. Kang heard the boy say, "It's our turn, Grandma." Mr. Kang welcomed ⓑthem and served the woman a __(A)__ bowl of Gukbap.

"Are you sure you're not hungry?" the woman asked the boy. The boy chewed loudly on some Gimchi and said with a smile, "No, I'm not hungry, Grandma. Don't worry about me. Happy birthday!"

28 아래 〈보기〉에서 위 글의 밑줄 친 ⓐto arrive와 문법적 쓰임이 같은 것의 개수를 고르시오.

┌──── 보기 ────┐
① There is no water <u>to drink</u>.
② <u>To see</u> is <u>to believe</u>.
③ <u>To tell</u> a lie again, you will be punished.
④ He must be foolish <u>to say</u> such a thing.
⑤ He promised <u>to buy</u> me new shoes.
└────────────┘

① 1개   ② 2개   ③ 3개   ④ 4개   ⑤ 5개

29 위 글의 밑줄 친 ⓑthem이 가리키는 것을 영어로 쓰시오.

➡ _____

30 주어진 영영풀이를 참고하여 빈칸 (A)에 철자 f로 시작하는 단어를 쓰시오.

costing nothing

➡ _____

31 위 글의 종류로 알맞은 것을 고르시오.

① e-mail
② article
③ essay
④ diary
⑤ review

32 위 글의 내용과 일치하지 <u>않는</u> 것은?

① 한 달 전에 한 부인이 그녀의 손자에게 줄 국밥 한 그릇을 주문했다.
② Mr. Kang은 그 부인이 그 날의 백 번째 손님이기 때문에 돈을 내지 않아도 된다고 말했다.
③ 오늘 소년은 국밥을 먹고 싶다고 Mr. Kang에게 말했다.
④ Mr. Kang은 소년을 그 날의 백 번째 손님으로 만들기 위해 친구들에게 전화했다.
⑤ 아흔아홉 번째 손님이 도착했을 때 소년과 할머니가 들어왔다.

[31~32] 다음 글을 읽고 물음에 답하시오.

20XX. 10. 15.

A month ago, a woman ordered a bowl of Gukbap for her grandson. She was too poor to pay for two bowls. A warm feeling came over me. I told her not to pay because she was the 100th customer of the day.

Today I saw the boy count the number of customers who entered my restaurant. He wanted to treat his grandmother to a free bowl of Gukbap. I called my friends to make the boy the 100th customer of the day. When the 99th customer arrived, the boy and his grandmother came in. I welcomed them and served them a free bowl of Gukbap.

I= Mr. Kang

[33~34] 다음 글을 읽고 물음에 답하시오.

Mr. Kang was ⓐmoved and wanted to give the boy ⓑ공짜 국밥 한 그릇. He said to the boy, "You don't pay if today is someone's birthday," and served the boy ⓑ공짜 국밥 한 그릇.

33 위 글의 밑줄 친 ⓐmoved와 바꿔 쓸 수 있는 단어를 쓰시오.

➡ _____

34 위 글의 밑줄 친 ⓑ의 우리말을 다섯 단어로 쓰시오.

➡ _____

INSIGHT
on the textbook

교과서 파헤치기

※ 다음 영어를 우리말로 쓰시오.

01	teammate	
02	perfect	
03	calm	
04	achieve	
05	difficulty	
06	face	
07	award	
08	terrible	
09	fail	
10	finally	
11	positive	
12	gentle	
13	base	
14	recognize	
15	sentence	
16	although	
17	recycle	
18	overcome	
19	earn	
20	excellence	
21	pain	

22	present	
23	effort	
24	honor	
25	lend	
26	major	
27	excellent	
28	respect	
29	solve	
30	rudely	
31	support	
32	talented	
33	phrase	
34	color line	
35	think to oneself	
36	no longer	
37	win first place	
38	turn down	
39	give up	
40	over and over	
41	present A with B	
42	at bat	
43	cannot believe one's eyes	

※ 다음 우리말을 영어로 쓰시오.

01 이루다, 달성하다		
02 침착한		
03 인정하다, 알아보다		
04 어려움, 곤경, 장애		
05 완벽한		
06 얻다, 획득하다		
07 비록 ~일지라도		
08 우수, 탁월, 뛰어남		
09 아픔, 고통		
10 상		
11 뛰어난		
12 긍정적인		
13 직면하다, 직시하다		
14 재활용하다		
15 존경		
16 예우하다, ~을 공경하다		
17 실패하다		
18 풀다, 해결하다		
19 재능이 있는		
20 지지		
21 마침내		

22 점잖은		
23 수여하다, 증정하다		
24 무례하게		
25 팀 동료		
26 문장		
27 (공을) 치다		
28 노력		
29 빌려주다		
30 주요한		
31 극복하다		
32 무서운		
33 경기장, 스타디움		
34 야구의 루		
35 포기하다		
36 마음속으로 생각하다		
37 더 이상 ~ 아닌		
38 ~ 덕분에		
39 반복해서		
40 1등을 하다, 우승하다		
41 ~을 거절하다, 소리를 줄이다		
42 A에게 B를 수여하다		
43 수업을 듣다		

※ 다음 영영풀이에 알맞은 단어를 <보기>에서 골라 쓴 후, 우리말 뜻을 쓰시오.

1 _____ : unusually or extremely good: _____

2 _____ : a person who is in the same team: _____

3 _____ : a player stationed at a base: _____

4 _____ : to be unable to do something: _____

5 _____ : in a way that shows no respect for others: _____

6 _____ : relating to classical music: _____

7 _____ : a feeling that you have in a part of your body when you are hurt or ill :
_____

8 _____ : to give someone the use of something for a limited time: _____

9 _____ : greater or more important than other people or things in a group:
_____

10 _____ : to succeed in dealing with or controlling a problem: _____

11 _____ : to hit the ball with a bat in a game such as baseball or cricket:
_____

12 _____ : believing that good things will happen rather than bad ones: _____

13 _____ : to see and know what someone or something is: _____

14 _____ : a prize or other reward that is given to someone who has achieved something:
_____

15 _____ : not affected by strong emotions such as excitement, anger, shock, or
fear: _____

16 _____ : help and kindness that you give to someone who is having a difficult
time: _____

보기			
bat	lend	baseman	teammate
support	excellent	positive	calm
fail	award	pain	overcome
recognize	classical	rudely	major

※ 다음 우리말과 일치하도록 빈칸에 알맞은 말을 쓰시오.

Listen & Speak 1 A

1. G: Hey, Minho. Did you _____ the answer to the _____ _____?

   B: No. It's _____ _____ for me. _____ _____ _____

   _____ _____.

   G: _____ me _____. _____ _____ _____ you use this

   math rule _____ _____ the problem.

   B: Oh, I see. I'll _____ it.

2. G: Your poster _____ _____.

   B: Thanks, Kate. Did you _____ _____?

   G: Not yet. I can't _____ well. _____ can I become _____

   _____ _____?

   B: It _____ time. It's _____ that you draw _____ _____

   _____ _____.

   G: You _____ I should _____ _____?

   B: That's _____.

Listen & Speak 1 B

1. A: It's _____ _____ a good dancer. _____ should

   I do?

   B: It's _____ that you _____ _____ _____.

   A: Okay. I will _____ _____ that.

2. A: It's _____ _____ write a good story. What _____ I do?

   B: _____ _____ _____ you read many books.

   A: Okay. I _____ _____ _____ that.

Listen & Talk 2 A

1. G: Oh, this is _____ _____ _____.

   B: What's the _____?

   G: Can you teach me _____ _____ _____ cookies?

   B: Sure. It's a walk in the park.

   G: _____ _____ _____ _____ _____ that?

   B: I _____ it's _____ _____ _____.

---

1. G: 이봐, 민호야. 이 수학 문제의 정답을 찾았니?
   B: 아니. 그건 나에게 너무 어려워. 나는 수학을 잘하지 못 해.
   G: 내가 한 번 볼게. 네가 그 문제를 풀기 위해선 이 수학 공식을 이용하는 것이 중요해.
   B: 오, 알겠어. 그걸 사용해 볼게.

2. G: 네 포스터가 멋져 보여.
   B: 고마워, Kate. 네 것은 끝냈니?
   G: 아직 못 끝냈어. 나는 그림을 잘 그리지 못 해. 어떻게 하면 내가 그림을 잘 그릴 수 있을까?
   B: 시간이 필요해. 네가 가능한 자주 그림을 그리는 것이 중요해.
   G: 내가 계속 연습해야 한다는 뜻이니?
   B: 맞아.

1. A: 훌륭한 댄서가 되는 것은 어려워. 내가 무엇을 해야 할까?
   B: 절대 포기하지 않는 것이 중요해.
   A: 알겠어. 그것을 잊지 않을게.

2. A: 좋은 이야기를 쓰는 것은 어려워. 내가 무엇을 해야 할까?
   B: 책을 많이 읽는 것이 중요해.
   A: 알겠어. 그것을 잊지 않을게.

1. G: 오, 이것은 하기 어렵구나.
   B: 무슨 일이야?
   G: 쿠키를 만드는 방법을 나에게 가르쳐 줄 수 있니?
   B: 물론이지. 그건 'a walk in the park'야.
   G: 그게 무슨 뜻이니?
   B: 하기 쉽다는 뜻이야.

2. B: I _____ a singing contest tomorrow. I really _____ _____ _____

_____ _____ _____ .

G: I'll keep my fingers _____ for you.

B: _____ _____ _____ _____ _____ _____ "keep my fingers

crossed"?

G: It _____ I _____ you _____ _____ .

B: Thank you.

Listen & Talk 2 B

1. A: Two heads _____ _____ _____ one.

B: _____ do you _____ _____ "Two heads are better than

one"?

A: I _____ working _____ is better _____ _____ _____ .

2. A: _____ makes _____ .

B: What do you _____ _____ "Practice makes perfect"?

A: I _____ you learn something _____ _____ it _____

_____ .

Conversation A

M: _____ _____ my dream, I went to many auditions, but I often

_____ . _____ , I never _____ _____ . I _____ acting

and dancing _____ . _____ , I _____ my goal. It's important

_____ you _____ _____ _____ _____ .

Conversation B

Hana: You _____ sad, Jiho. What's _____ ?

Jiho: I _____ _____ I can _____ my dream.

Amy: _____ _____ _____ _____ _____ _____ _____ _____ ?

Jiho: I want to be an actor, but I always _____ _____ . Maybe I

_____ _____ _____ _____ _____ .

Amy: Do you know this _____ ?

Jiho: Sure. He's a _____ movie star.

Amy: He _____ _____ _____ _____ 100 auditions.

Jiho: Really? Maybe I _____ _____ _____ _____ . I will _____

more for my next audition.

Hana: That's right! _____ _____ _____ _____ _____

_____ .

2. B: 나 내일 노래 경연 대회가 있어.
나는 정말 1등을 하고 싶어.
G: 너에게 'keep my fingers crossed'할게.
B: 'keep my fingers crossed'가 무슨 뜻이니?
G: 그건 내가 너에게 행운을 빈다는 뜻이야.
B: 고마워.

1. A: 두 개의 머리가 머리 하나보다 낫다.
B: "두 개의 머리가 머리 하나보다 낫다."가 무슨 뜻이니?
A: 함께 일하는 것이 혼자 일하는 것보다 낫다는 뜻이야.

2. A: 연습이 완벽함을 만든다.
B: "연습이 완벽함을 만든다."가 무슨 뜻이니?
A: 반복해서 무언가를 하면 배우게 된다는 뜻이야.

M: 내 꿈을 이루기 위해 나는 많은 오디션에 갔지만 자주 떨어졌다. 하지만 나는 절대 포기하지 않았다. 나는 연기와 춤 수업을 들었다. 마침내 나는 내 목표를 이뤘다. 절대 포기하지 않는 것이 중요하다.

하나: 너 슬퍼 보여, 지호야. 무슨 일이니?
지호: 내 생각에 나는 꿈을 이룰 수 없을 것 같아.
Amy: 그게 무슨 말이니?
지호: 나는 배우가 되고 싶지만 항상 오디션에서 떨어져. 어쩌면 나는 포기해야 할 거 같아.
Amy: 너 이 배우를 아니?
지호: 당연하지. 그는 유명한 영화배우잖아.
Amy: 그는 백 번 이상 오디션에서 떨어졌대.
지호: 정말? 그러면 나도 계속 노력해야겠구나. 나는 다음 오디션을 위해서 더 연습할 거야.
하나: 바로 그거야! 절대 포기하지 않는 것이 중요해.

※ 다음 우리말에 맞도록 대화를 영어로 쓰시오.

Listen & Speak 1 A

1. G: _____
   B: _____
   G: _____
   B: _____

2. G: _____
   B: _____
   G: _____
   B: _____
   G: _____
   B: _____

1. G: 이봐, 민호야. 이 수학 문제의 정답을 찾았니?
   B: 아니. 그건 나에게 너무 어려워. 나는 수학을 잘하지 못 해.
   G: 내가 한 번 볼게. 네가 그 문제를 풀기 위해선 이 수학 공식을 이용하는 것이 중요해.
   B: 오, 알겠어. 그걸 사용해 볼게.

2. G: 네 포스터가 멋져 보여.
   B: 고마워, Kate. 네 것은 끝냈니?
   G: 아직 못 끝냈어. 나는 그림을 잘 그리지 못 해. 어떻게 하면 내가 그림을 잘 그릴 수 있을까?
   B: 시간이 필요해. 네가 가능한 자주 그림을 그리는 것이 중요해.
   G: 내가 계속 연습해야 한다는 뜻이니?
   B: 맞아.

Listen & Speak 1 B

1. A: _____
   B: _____
   A: _____

2. A: _____
   B: _____
   A: _____

1. A: 훌륭한 댄서가 되는 것은 어려워. 내가 무엇을 해야 할까?
   B: 절대 포기하지 않는 것이 중요해.
   A: 알겠어. 그것을 잊지 않을게.

2. A: 좋은 이야기를 쓰는 것은 어려워. 내가 무엇을 해야 할까?
   B: 책을 많이 읽는 것이 중요해.
   A: 알겠어. 그것을 잊지 않을게.

Listen & Talk 2 A

1. G: _____
   B: _____
   G: _____
   B: _____
   G: _____
   B: _____

1. G: 오, 이것은 하기 어렵구나.
   B: 무슨 일이야?
   G: 쿠키를 만드는 방법을 나에게 가르쳐 줄 수 있니?
   B: 물론이지. 그건 'a walk in the park'야.
   G: 그게 무슨 뜻이니?
   B: 하기 쉽다는 뜻이야.

2. B: _____
   G: _____
   B: _____
   G: _____
   B: _____

2. B: 나 내일 노래 경연 대회가 있어. 나는 정말 1등을 하고 싶어.
   G: 너에게 'keep my fingers crossed'할게.
   B: 'keep my fingers crossed'가 무슨 뜻이니?
   G: 그건 내가 너에게 행운을 빈다는 뜻이야.
   B: 고마워.

Listen & Talk 2 B

1. A: _____
   B: _____
   A: _____
2. A: _____
   B: _____
   A: _____

1. A: 두 개의 머리가 머리 하나보다 낫다.
   B: "두 개의 머리가 머리 하나보다 낫다."가 무슨 뜻이니?
   A: 함께 일하는 것이 혼자 일하는 것보다 낫다는 뜻이야.

2. A: 연습이 완벽함을 만든다.
   B: "연습이 완벽함을 만든다."가 무슨 뜻이니?
   A: 반복해서 무언가를 하면 배우게 된다는 뜻이야.

Conversation A

M: _____
   _____
   _____

M: 내 꿈을 이루기 위해 나는 많은 오디션에 갔지만 자주 떨어졌다. 하지만 나는 절대 포기하지 않았다. 나는 연기와 춤 수업을 들었다. 마침내 나는 내 목표를 이뤘다. 절대 포기하지 않는 것이 중요하다.

Conversation B

Hana: _____
Jiho: _____
Amy: _____
Jiho: _____
Amy: _____
Jiho: _____
Amy: _____
Jiho: _____
Hana: _____

하나: 너 슬퍼 보여, 지호야. 무슨 일이니?
지호: 내 생각에 나는 꿈을 이룰 수 없을 것 같아.
Amy: 그게 무슨 말이니?
지호: 나는 배우가 되고 싶지만 항상 오디션에서 떨어져. 어쩌면 나는 포기해야 할 거 같아.
Amy: 너 이 배우를 아니?
지호: 당연하지. 그는 유명한 영화배우잖아.
Amy: 그는 백 번 이상 오디션에서 떨어졌대.
지호: 정말? 그러면 나도 계속 노력해야겠구나. 나는 다음 오디션을 위해서 더 연습할 거야.
하나: 바로 그거야! 절대 포기하지 않는 것이 중요해.

※ 다음 우리말과 일치하도록 빈칸에 알맞은 것을 골라 쓰시오.

1 Jackie Robinson _____ the _____ _____
　　A. Color　　　　　B. Breaks　　　　C. Line

2 _____ was New York City _____ _____ 15, 1947.
　　A. April　　　　　B. it　　　　　　C. on

3 Jackie Robinson, an African American, _____ _____ the field _____ second baseman _____ the Brooklyn Dodgers.
　　A. on　　　　　　B. for　　　　　C. went　　　　D. as

4 People _____ _____ their _____.
　　A. believe　　　　B. couldn't　　　C. eyes

5 He was the _____ African _____ player to _____ _____ a Major League team.
　　A. American　　　B. play　　　　C. first　　　D. on

6 That day, the _____ _____ was _____.
　　A. line　　　　　B. broken　　　　C. color

7 Robinson _____ _____ _____.
　　A. difficulties　　B. faced　　　　C. many

8 _____ Robinson was a _____ player and a _____ person, his teammates did not want to play _____ him.
　　A. gentle　　　　B. although　　　C. talented　　D. with

9 _____ hotel _____ the team _____ _____ Robinson was on the team.
　　A. because　　　B. turned　　　　C. down　　　D. every

10 When he was at _____, people in the stands _____ shouted _____ him.
　　A. rudely　　　　B. at　　　　　　C. bat

11 Robinson _____ to _____, 'I need to _____ calm and _____ on baseball.
　　A. keep　　　　　B. thought　　·　C. focus　　　D. himself

12 I will _____ and _____ a player who people _____.
　　A. like　　　　　B. try　　　　　C. become

13 Then, next season, _____ will _____ _____ African American players in the _____.'
　　A. there　　　　　B. more　　　　C. league　　　D. be

14 Robinson _____ all his time and _____ baseball.
　　A. into　　　　　B. put　　　　　C. energy

---

1 Jackie Robinson 인종 차별을 깨다

2 1947년 4월 15일 뉴욕시에 서였다.

3 아프리카계 미국인 Jackie Robinson은 브루클린 다저스의 2루수로 경기장에 나갔다.

4 사람들은 자신들의 눈을 의심했다.

5 그는 메이저리그 팀에서 경기한 최초의 아프리카계 미국인 선수였다.

6 그날 인종 차별이 깨졌다.

7 Robinson은 많은 어려움에 직면했다.

8 Robinson은 재능 있는 선수이고 온화한 사람이었지만 그의 팀원들은 그와 함께 경기하기를 원하지 않았다.

9 Robinson이 팀에 있었기 때문에 모든 호텔에서 그 팀을 거절했다.

10 그가 타석에 있을 때, 관중석에 있는 사람들이 그에게 무례하게 소리치기도 했다.

11 Robinson은 마음속으로 생각했다. '나는 평정심을 유지하고 야구에 집중해야 해.

12 나는 노력해서 사람들이 좋아하는 선수가 될 거야.

13 그러면 다음 시즌에는 아프리카계 미국인 선수가 리그에 더 많이 생길 거야.'

14 Robinson은 자신의 모든 시간과 에너지를 야구에 집중했다.

15 _____ _____, he became great at _____ and base _____.

    A. batting   B. with   C. running   D. practice

16 Robinson's _____ _____ his _____.

    A. moved   B. effort   C. teammates

17 When people shouted at Robinson, _____ of his teammates walked _____ to Robinson and _____ him _____ the shoulder.

    A. on   B. up   C. one   D. tapped

18 "_____ not _____ _____ them.

    A. to   B. do   C. listen

19 You're _____ _____," he said.

    A. fine   B. doing

20 His _____ _____ Robinson _____ play _____.

    A. harder   B. helped   C. support   D. to

21 _____, Robinson _____ the _____ of _____ players and fans.

    A. other   B. earned   C. finally   D. respect

22 _____ _____ Robinson, the Dodgers _____ the National League Championship _____ 1947.

    A. won   B. to   C. thanks   D. in

23 The league _____ Robinson's excellence and _____ him _____ the Rookie of the Year Award in the _____ year.

    A. presented   B. recognized   C. same   D. with

24 After that season, _____ teams _____ African American players _____ _____ them.

    A. join   B. asked   C. other   D. to

25 Robinson's _____ _____ was 42.

    A. number   B. uniform

26 Baseball players in Major League teams _____ _____ wear the number 42 _____ _____ him.

    A. honor   B. longer   C. to   D. no

27 Every year, _____, on April 15, _____ player _____ the number that Robinson _____.

    A. wears   B. however   C. wore   D. every

28 The day _____ _____ "Jackie Robinson Day."

    A. called   B. is

---

15 연습을 함으로써 그는 타격과 주루를 잘하게 되었다.

16 Robinson의 노력은 그의 팀원들을 감동시켰다.

17 사람들이 Robinson에게 소리쳤을 때, 그의 팀 동료 중 한 명이 Robinson에게 다가가 어깨를 두드렸다.

18 "그들 말을 듣지 마.

19 너는 잘하고 있어."라고 그가 말했다.

20 그의 지지는 Robinson이 더 열심히 경기하는 데 도움이 됐다.

21 마침내, Robinson은 다른 선수들과 팬들의 존경을 받았다.

22 Robinson 덕분에 다저스는 1947년에 내셔널리그 챔피언십에서 우승하게 되었다.

23 리그에서는 Robinson의 탁월함을 인정했고, 같은 해에 그에게 신인상을 수여했다.

24 그 시즌 이후, 다른 팀들은 아프리카계 미국인 선수들에게 자신들의 팀에 합류할 것을 요청했다.

25 Robinson의 등 번호는 42번이었다.

26 메이저리그 팀의 야구 선수들은 그에 대한 존경을 보여 주기 위해 더 이상 42번을 달지 않는다.

27 하지만 매년 4월 15일, 모든 선수들은 Robinson이 달았던 번호를 단다.

28 이 날을 '재키 로빈슨 데이'라고 부른다.

※ 다음 우리말과 일치하도록 빈칸에 알맞은 말을 쓰시오.

1 Jackie Robinson _____

2 It was New York City _____ _____ _____ , _____.

3 Jackie Robinson, an _____ _____, went on the field _____ second baseman _____ the Brooklyn Dodgers.

4 People _____.

5 He was _____ to play on a Major League team.

6 That day, _____.

7 Robinson _____.

8 _____ Robinson was a _____ _____ and a gentle person, his teammates did not want _____ _____ _____.

9 Every hotel _____ _____ _____ _____ because Robinson was on the team.

10 When he _____ _____ _____, people in the stands _____ _____ _____ him.

11 Robinson _____ _____ _____, 'I need to _____ _____ and _____ _____ baseball.

12 I will try and _____ a player _____.

13 Then, next season, _____ _____ _____ African American players in the league.'

14 Robinson _____ all his time and energy _____ baseball.

1 Jackie Robinson 인종 차별을 깨다

2 1947년 4월 15일 뉴욕시에서였다.

3 아프리카계 미국인 Jackie Robinson은 브루클린 다저스의 2루수로 경기장에 나갔다.

4 사람들은 자신들의 눈을 의심했다.

5 그는 메이저리그 팀에서 경기한 최초의 아프리카계 미국인 선수였다.

6 그날 인종 차별이 깨졌다.

7 Robinson은 많은 어려움에 직면했다.

8 Robinson은 재능 있는 선수이고 온화한 사람이었지만 그의 팀원들은 그와 함께 경기하기를 원하지 않았다.

9 Robinson이 팀에 있었기 때문에 모든 호텔에서 그 팀을 거절했다.

10 그가 타석에 있을 때, 관중석에 있는 사람들이 그에게 무례하게 소리치기도 했다.

11 Robinson은 마음속으로 생각했다. '나는 평정심을 유지하고 야구에 집중해야 해.

12 나는 노력해서 사람들이 좋아하는 선수가 될 거야.

13 그러면 다음 시즌에는 아프리카계 미국인 선수가 리그에 더 많이 생길 거야.'

14 Robinson은 자신의 모든 시간과 에너지를 야구에 집중했다.

15 _____ _____, he became great _____ _____ and _____ _____.

16 Robinson's _____ _____ his _____.

17 When people _____ _____ Robinson, _____ _____ _____ _____ walked _____ _____ Robinson and _____ _____ _____ _____.

18 " _____ _____ _____ _____ them.

19 You're _____ _____," he said.

20 His support _____ Robinson _____ _____ _____.

21 Finally, Robinson _____ _____ _____ of other players and fans.

22 _____ _____ Robinson, the Dodgers _____ the National League Championship in 1947.

23 The league _____ Robinson's excellence and _____ him _____ the Rookie of the Year Award in the _____ _____.

24 After that season, _____ teams _____ African American players _____ _____ them.

25 Robinson's _____ _____ was 42.

26 Baseball players in Major League teams _____ _____ _____ the number 42 _____ _____ _____.

27 _____ year, _____, on April 15, every player _____ the number that Robinson _____.

28 The day _____ _____ "Jackie Robinson Day."

15 연습을 함으로써 그는 타격과 주루를 잘하게 되었다.

16 Robinson의 노력은 그의 팀원들을 감동시켰다.

17 사람들이 Robinson에게 소리쳤을 때, 그의 팀 동료 중 한 명이 Robinson에게 다가가 어깨를 두드렸다.

18 "그들 말을 듣지 마.

19 너는 잘하고 있어."라고 그가 말했다.

20 그의 지지는 Robinson이 더 열심히 경기하는 데 도움이 됐다.

21 마침내, Robinson은 다른 선수들과 팬들의 존경을 받았다.

22 Robinson 덕분에 다저스는 1947년에 내셔널리그 챔피언십에서 우승하게 되었다.

23 리그에서는 Robinson의 탁월함을 인정했고, 같은 해에 그에게 신인상을 수여했다.

24 그 시즌 이후, 다른 팀들은 아프리카계 미국인 선수들에게 자신들의 팀에 합류할 것을 요청했다.

25 Robinson의 등 번호는 42번이었다.

26 메이저리그 팀의 야구 선수들은 그에 대한 존경을 보여 주기 위해 더 이상 42번을 달지 않는다.

27 하지만 매년 4월 15일, 모든 선수들은 Robinson이 달았던 번호를 단다.

28 이 날을 '재키 로빈슨 데이'라고 부른다.

※ 다음 문장을 우리말로 쓰시오.

1 Jackie Robinson Breaks the Color Line

➡ _____

2 It was New York City on April 15, 1947.

➡ _____

3 Jackie Robinson, an African American, went on the field as second baseman for the Brooklyn Dodgers.

➡ _____

4 People couldn't believe their eyes.

➡ _____

5 He was the first African American player to play on a Major League team.

➡ _____

6 That day, the color line was broken.

➡ _____

7 Robinson faced many difficulties.

➡ _____

8 Although Robinson was a talented player and a gentle person, his teammates did not want to play with him.

➡ _____

9 Every hotel turned the team down because Robinson was on the team.

➡ _____

10 When he was at bat, people in the stands rudely shouted at him.

➡ _____

11 Robinson thought to himself, 'I need to keep calm and focus on baseball.

➡ _____

12 I will try and become a player who people like.

➡ _____

13 Then, next season, there will be more African American players in the league.'

➡ _____

14 Robinson put all his time and energy into baseball.

➡ _____

15 With practice, he became great at batting and base running.

➡ _____

16 ▶ Robinson's effort moved his teammates.

➡ _____

17 ▶ When people shouted at Robinson, one of his teammates walked up to Robinson and tapped him on the shoulder.

➡ _____

18 ▶ "Do not listen to them.

➡ _____

19 ▶ You're doing fine," he said.

➡ _____

20 ▶ His support helped Robinson to play harder.

➡ _____

21 ▶ Finally, Robinson earned the respect of other players and fans.

➡ _____

22 ▶ Thanks to Robinson, the Dodgers won the National League Championship in 1947.

➡ _____

23 ▶ The league recognized Robinson's excellence and presented him with the Rookie of the Year Award in the same year.

➡ _____

24 ▶ After that season, other teams asked African American players to join them.

➡ _____

25 ▶ Robinson's uniform number was 42.

➡ _____

26 ▶ Baseball players in Major League teams no longer wear the number 42 to honor him.

➡ _____

27 ▶ Every year, however, on April 15, every player wears the number that Robinson wore.

➡ _____

28 ▶ The day is called "Jackie Robinson Day."

➡ _____

Step4

※ 다음 괄호 안의 단어들을 우리말에 맞도록 바르게 배열하시오.

1 (Robinson / Jackie / Breaks / Color / the / Line)
➡ _____

2 (was / it / York / New / City / April / on / 1947. / 15,)
➡ _____

3 (Robinson, / Jackie / African / an / American, / on / went / field / the / second / as / baseman / the / for / Dodgers. / Brooklyn)
➡ _____
_____

4 (couldn't / people / their / believe / eyes.)
➡ _____

5 (was / he / first / the / American / African / to / player / on / play / a / League / Major / team.)
➡ _____

6 (day, / that / color / the / was / broken. / line)
➡ _____

7 (faced / Robinson / difficulties. / many)
➡ _____

8 (Robinson / although / a / was / player / talented / and / gentle / a / person, / teammates / his / not / did / to / want / him. / with / play)
➡ _____

9 (hotel / every / the / turned / team / down / because / was / Robinson / on / team. / the)
➡ _____

10 (he / when / at / was / bat, / in / people / the / stands / shouted / rudely / him. / at)
➡ _____

11 (thought / Robinson / himself, / to / 'I / to / need / calm / keep / and / on / focus / baseball.)
➡ _____

12 (I / try / will / and / a / become / player / people / who / like.)
➡ _____

13 (next / then, / season, / will / there / more / be / American / African / players / in / league.' / the)
➡ _____

14 (put / Robinson / all / time / his / and / into / baseball. / energy)
➡ _____

1 Jackie Robinson 인종 차별을 깨다

2 1947년 4월 15일 뉴욕시에 서였다.

3 아프리카계 미국인 Jackie Robinson은 브루클린 다저스의 2루수로 경기장에 나갔다.

4 사람들은 자신들의 눈을 의심했다.

5 그는 메이저리그 팀에서 경기한 최초의 아프리카계 미국인 선수였다.

6 그날 인종 차별이 깨졌다.

7 Robinson은 많은 어려움에 직면했다.

8 Robinson은 재능 있는 선수이고 온화한 사람이었지만 그의 팀원들은 그와 함께 경기하기를 원하지 않았다.

9 Robinson이 팀에 있었기 때문에 모든 호텔에서 그 팀을 거절했다.

10 그가 타석에 있을 때, 관중석에 있는 사람들이 그에게 무례하게 소리치기도 했다.

11 Robinson은 마음속으로 생각했다. '나는 평정심을 유지하고 야구에 집중해야 해.

12 나는 노력해서 사람들이 좋아하는 선수가 될 거야.

13 그러면 다음 시즌에는 아프리카계 미국인 선수가 리그에 더 많이 생길 거야.'

14 Robinson은 자신의 모든 시간과 에너지를 야구에 집중했다.

15 (practice, / with / became / he / at / great / batting / and / running. / base)

➡ _____

16 (effort / Robinson's / moved / teammates. / his)

➡ _____

17 (people / when / at / shouted / Robinson, / of / one / teammates / his / up / walked / to / Robinson / and / him / tapped / the / on / shoulder.)

➡ _____

_____

18 (not / "do / to / listen / them.)

➡ _____

19 (doing / you're / fine," / said. / he)

➡ _____

20 (support / his / Robinson / helped / play / harder. / to)

➡ _____

21 (Robinson / finally, / the / earned / respect / other / of / fans. / and / players)

➡ _____

22 (to / thanks / Robinson, / Dodgers / the / the / won / National / Championship / League / 1947. / in)

➡ _____

_____

23 (league / the / Robinson's / recognized / presented / and / excellence / with / him Rookie / the / of / the / Award / Year / the / in / year. / same)

➡ _____

24 (that / after / season, / teams / other / African / asked / players / American / to / them. / join)

➡ _____

_____

25 (uniform / Robinson's / was / number / 42.)

➡ _____

26 (players / baseball / Major / in / League / no / teams / wear / longer / number / the / to / 42 / him. / honor)

➡ _____

_____

27 (year, / every / on / however, / 15, / April / player / every / the / wears / that / number / wore. / Robinson)

➡ _____

_____

28 (day / the / called / is / "Jackie / Day." / Robinson)

➡ _____

15 연습을 함으로써 그는 타격과 주루를 잘하게 되었다.

16 Robinson의 노력은 그의 팀원들을 감동시켰다.

17 사람들이 Robinson에게 소리쳤을 때, 그의 팀 동료 중 한 명이 Robinson에게 다가가 어깨를 두드렸다.

18 "그들 말을 듣지 마.

19 너는 잘하고 있어."라고 그가 말했다.

20 그의 지지는 Robinson이 더 열심히 경기하는 데 도움이 됐다.

21 마침내, Robinson은 다른 선수들과 팬들의 존경을 받았다.

22 Robinson 덕분에 다저스는 1947년에 내셔널리그 챔피언십에서 우승하게 되었다.

23 리그에서는 Robinson의 탁월함을 인정했고, 같은 해에 그에게 신인상을 수여했다.

24 그 시즌 이후, 다른 팀들은 아프리카계 미국인 선수들에게 자신들의 팀에 합류할 것을 요청했다.

25 Robinson의 등 번호는 42번이었다.

26 메이저리그 팀의 야구 선수들은 그에 대한 존경을 보여 주기 위해 더 이상 42번을 달지 않는다.

27 하지만 매년 4월 15일, 모든 선수들은 Robinson이 달았던 번호를 단다.

28 이 날을 '재키 로빈슨 데이'라고 부른다.

※ 다음 우리말을 영어로 쓰시오.

1   Jackie Robinson 인종 차별을 깨다

➡ _____

2   1947년 4월 15일 뉴욕시에서였다.

➡ _____

3   아프리카계 미국인 Jackie Robinson은 브루클린 다저스의 2루수로 경기장에 나갔다.

➡ _____

4   사람들은 자신들의 눈을 의심했다.

➡ _____

5   그는 메이저리그 팀에서 경기한 최초의 아프리카계 미국인 선수였다.

➡ _____

6   그날 인종 차별이 깨졌다.

➡ _____

7   Robinson은 많은 어려움에 직면했다.

➡ _____

8   Robinson은 재능 있는 선수이고 온화한 사람이었지만 그의 팀원들은 그와 함께 경기하기를 원하지 않았다.

➡ _____

9   Robinson이 팀에 있었기 때문에 모든 호텔에서 그 팀을 거절했다.

➡ _____

10   그가 타석에 있을 때, 관중석에 있는 사람들이 그에게 무례하게 소리치기도 했다.

➡ _____

11   Robinson은 마음속으로 생각했다. '나는 평정심을 유지하고 야구에 집중해야 해.

➡ _____

12   나는 노력해서 사람들이 좋아하는 선수가 될 거야.

➡ _____

13   그러면 다음 시즌에는 아프리카계 미국인 선수가 리그에 더 많이 생길 거야.'

➡ _____

14   Robinson은 자신의 모든 시간과 에너지를 야구에 집중했다.

➡ _____

15   연습을 함으로써 그는 타격과 주루를 잘하게 되었다.

➡ _____

16 Robinson의 노력은 그의 팀원들을 감동시켰다.

➡ _____

17 사람들이 Robinson에게 소리쳤을 때, 그의 팀 동료 중 한 명이 Robinson에게 다가가 어깨를 두드렸다.

➡ _____

18 "그들 말을 듣지 마.

➡ _____

19 너는 잘하고 있어."라고 그가 말했다.

➡ _____

20 그의 지지는 Robinson이 더 열심히 경기하는 데 도움이 됐다.

➡ _____

21 마침내, Robinson은 다른 선수들과 팬들의 존경을 받았다.

➡ _____

22 Robinson 덕분에 다저스는 1947년에 내셔널리그 챔피언십에서 우승하게 되었다.

➡ _____

23 리그에서는 Robinson의 탁월함을 인정했고, 같은 해에 그에게 신인상을 수여했다.

➡ _____

24 그 시즌 이후, 다른 팀들은 아프리카계 미국인 선수들에게 자신들의 팀에 합류할 것을 요청했다.

➡ _____

25 Robinson의 등 번호는 42번이었다.

➡ _____

26 메이저리그 팀의 야구 선수들은 그에 대한 존경을 보여 주기 위해 더 이상 42번을 달지 않는다.

➡ _____

27 하지만 매년 4월 15일, 모든 선수들은 Robinson이 달았던 번호를 단다.

➡ _____

28 이 날을 '재키 로빈슨 데이'라고 부른다.

➡ _____

※ 다음 우리말과 일치하도록 빈칸에 알맞은 말을 쓰시오.

Language in Use

1. I visited three countries _____ _____.

2. France was _____ _____ _____ _____ I _____.

3. Mary is the girl _____ I _____ in Paris.

4. The blue watch is the _____ _____ _____ _____ there _____ my brother.

1. 작년에 나는 3개국을 방문했다.
2. 프랑스가 내가 방문한 첫 번째 국가였다.
3. Mary는 내가 파리에서 만났던 소녀이다.
4. 그 파란 시계는 그곳에서 내 동생을 위해 산 선물이다.

Enjoy Writing B

1. _____ I Will _____ My Dream

2. I _____ _____ _____ a designer.

3. There are three things _____ I _____ _____ do _____ _____ my dream.

4. I need to be _____, be _____, and never _____ _____.

5. _____ healthy will _____ me _____ for my dream.

6. Being creative will _____ _____ something different.

7. Plus, I will always tell _____ never _____ because it will _____ _____ harder.

1. 어떻게 나의 꿈을 성취할 것인가
2. 나는 디자이너가 되기를 원한다.
3. 나의 꿈을 성취하기 위해 내가 할 필요가 있는 세 가지가 있다.
4. 나는 건강해야 하고, 창의적이어야 하고, 그리고 결코 포기하지 말아야 한다.
5. 건강한 것은 나의 꿈을 계속 유지하도록 도와줄 것이다.
6. 창의적인 것은 내가 무언가 다른 것을 하도록 도와줄 것이다.
7. 더하여, 내 스스로에게 결코 포기하지 말라고 항상 말할 것인데, 이는 내가 더 열심히 노력하도록 해 줄 것이기 때문이다.

Wrap Up 2

1. B: _____ difficult _____ _____ English.

2. G: Rome _____ _____ _____ in a day.

3. B: _____ do you _____ that?

4. G: I mean it _____ time _____ _____ _____.

5. B: I _____.

1. B: 영어를 배우는 것은 어려워.
2. G: 로마는 하루아침에 이루어지지 않았어.
3. B: 그게 무슨 뜻이니?
4. G: 무언가를 이루는 데 시간이 걸린다는 뜻이야.
5. B: 알겠어.

구석구석 지문 Test

※ 다음 우리말을 영어로 쓰시오.

Language in Use

1. 작년에 나는 3개국을 방문했다.
   ➡ _____

2. 프랑스가 내가 방문한 첫 번째 국가였다.
   ➡ _____

3. Mary는 내가 파리에서 만났던 소녀이다.
   ➡ _____

4. 그 파란 시계는 그곳에서 내 동생을 위해 산 선물이다.
   ➡ _____

Enjoy Writing B

1. 어떻게 나의 꿈을 성취할 것인가
   ➡ _____

2. 나는 디자이너가 되기를 원한다.
   ➡ _____

3. 나의 꿈을 성취하기 위해 내가 할 필요가 있는 세 가지가 있다.
   ➡ _____

4. 나는 건강해야 하고, 창의적이어야 하고, 그리고 결코 포기하지 말아야 한다.
   ➡ _____

5. 건강한 것은 나의 꿈을 계속 유지하도록 도와줄 것이다.
   ➡ _____

6. 창의적인 것은 내가 무언가 다른 것을 하도록 도와줄 것이다.
   ➡ _____

7. 더하여, 내 스스로에게 결코 포기하지 말라고 항상 말할 것인데, 이는 내가 더 열심히 노력하도록 해 줄 것이기 때문이다.
   ➡ _____

Wrap Up 2

1. B: 영어를 배우는 것은 어려워.
   ➡ _____

2. G: 로마는 하루아침에 이루어지지 않았어.
   ➡ _____

3. B: 그게 무슨 뜻이니?
   ➡ _____

4. G: 무언가를 이루는 데 시간이 걸린다는 뜻이야.
   ➡ _____

5. B: 알겠어.
   ➡ _____

※ 다음 영어를 우리말로 쓰시오.

01	counter	
02	automatically	
03	condition	
04	price	
05	recommend	
06	decorate	
07	medicine	
08	material	
09	society	
10	rescue	
11	technology	
12	fit	
13	advance	
14	temperature	
15	experience	
16	charge	
17	fancy	
18	lower	
19	skill	
20	purchase	
21	huge	

22	later	
23	virtual	
24	difference	
25	heavily	
26	law	
27	since	
28	gravity	
29	deliver	
30	pay	
31	method	
32	work	
33	patient	
34	real	
35	forget to 동사원형	
36	in space	
37	take care of	
38	be ready for	
39	put on	
40	move around	
41	take place	
42	in the future	
43	would like to 동사원형	

※ 다음 우리말을 영어로 쓰시오.

01	심하게, 아주 많이	
02	자동적으로	
03	(지불, 대금 등을) 청구하다	
04	사서	
05	상태, 조건	
06	작동하다	
07	경험	
08	구하다	
09	발전	
10	(치수·모양 등이) 꼭 맞다	
11	중력	
12	거대한	
13	~ 이후로	
14	가격	
15	배달하다	
16	장식하다, 꾸미다	
17	낮추다	
18	구조하다	
19	기술	
20	온도	
21	~을 추천하다	

22	약	
23	환자	
24	차이, 차이점	
25	가상의	
26	구입(품)	
27	방법, 방식	
28	사회	
29	맛보다	
30	재료	
31	~을 제공하다	
32	추측하다	
33	(돈을) 지불하다	
34	과학 기술, 생산 기술	
35	일어나다, 개최되다	
36	~할 준비가 되다	
37	입다, 쓰다, 신다	
38	합산하다	
39	~을 돌보다	
40	~할 필요가 없다	
41	돌아다니다	
42	~에 대해 걱정하다	
43	곤경에 빠져서, 난처하여	

Step3

※ 다음 영영풀이에 알맞은 단어를 <보기>에서 골라 쓴 후, 우리말 뜻을 쓰시오.

1 _____ : a substance that you take to cure an illness: _____

2 _____ : to save someone or something from danger or harm: _____

3 _____ : with operating by itself: _____

4 _____ : someone who is receiving medical treatment: _____

5 _____ : a substance that is used for a particular purpose: _____

6 _____ : to speak in favor of something: _____

7 _____ : a way of doing something, especially a planned way: _____

8 _____ : to take something to somewhere to give it to someone: _____

9 _____ : to add ornaments, etc. to something to make it more attractive: _____

10 _____ : a piece of computer software that is designed to do a particular job: _____

11 _____ : created by computers, or appearing on computers or the Internet: _____

12 _____ : a place where a bus or train stops to allow passengers to get on and off: _____

13 _____ : progress or an instance of progress in science, technology, human knowledge, etc.: _____

14 _____ : an unmanned aircraft or ship guided by remote control or onboard computers: _____

15 _____ : a statement of fact concerning what always happens in certain circumstances; a scientific principle: _____

16 _____ : to ask someone to pay an amount of money for something that you are selling to them or doing for them: _____

보기

law	station	advance	recommend
automatically	charge	patient	medicine
deliver	rescue	method	app
material	drone	decorate	virtual

※ 다음 우리말과 일치하도록 빈칸에 알맞은 말을 쓰시오.

Listen & Speak 1 A

1. G: Oh, I _____ _____ _____ _____ the heater before I
   left home.
   B: Really? Then do you _____ _____ _____ home?
   G: No. I can _____ it _____ with my smartphone.
   B: Wow, I'm _____ _____ you can turn _____ the heater
   _____ your smartphone.

2. W: _____ _____ VR World. Would you _____ _____
   _____ Niagara Falls?
   B: Sure.
   W: Okay, _____ this _____.
   B: All _____. Wow, it _____ so real.
   W: It is huge, _____ _____?
   B: Yes, and _____ _____ that I feel water on my face.

Listen & Speak 1 B

1. A: Is _____ anything in these pictures that _____ you?
   B: Yes. I'm _____ that this drone can _____ a dog.

2. A: Is _____ _____ in these pictures _____ _____ you?
   B: Yes. _____ _____ _____ this car can drive _____
   _____.

Listen & Speak 2 A

1. W: May I _____ you?
   B: Hi, I'm _____ _____ a smart watch. Can you _____
   _____ _____?
   W: Sure. _____ _____ this one. It can play music _____ you.
   B: _____ cool.
   W: Also, you can _____ _____ anything just _____ _____
   to it.
   B: That's great. I _____ _____ it.

1. G: 아, 나는 집에서 나오기 전에 히터
      끄는 것을 잊어버렸어.
   B: 정말? 그러면 넌 집으로 돌아가야
      하니?
   G: 아니. 나는 내 스마트폰으로 히터
      를 끌 수 있어.
   B: 우와, 나는 네가 스마트폰으로 히
      터를 끌 수 있다는 게 놀라워.

2. W: VR 세계에 오신 것을 환영해요.
       나이아가라 폭포를 방문하고 싶은
       가요?
   B: 물론이죠.
   W: 좋아요, 이걸 쓰세요.
   B: 알겠어요. 우와, 이것은 정말 진짜
      처럼 보여요.
   W: 거대하죠, 그렇지 않아요?
   B: 네, 그리고 얼굴에서 물이 느껴진
      다는 게 놀라워요.

1. A: 이 사진들에서 너를 놀라게 한 것
      이 있니?
   B: 응, 나는 이 드론이 개를 산책시킬
      수 있는 게 놀라워.

2. A: 이 사진들에서 너를 놀라게 한 것
      이 있니?
   B: 응, 나는 이 차가 자동으로 운전할
      수 있는 게 놀라워.

1. W: 도와드릴까요?
   B: 안녕하세요, 저는 스마트 워치를
      찾고 있어요. 하나 보여 주실래요?
   W: 물론이죠. 이것을 보세요. 그것은
      당신을 위해 음악을 연주할 수 있
      어요.
   B: 멋지네요.
   W: 또한 그것에게 말만 하면 어떤 것
      이든 검색할 수 있어요.
   B: 멋지네요. 저 그거 살게요.

2. **M:** Welcome. This is our new smart light. You _____ _____ your hands to _____ it _____ and _____.

W: Really? Then can you _____ me _____ do it?

M: Just say, "Light _____!" or "Light _____!"

W: Light _____ or light out? That's very _____.

Listen & Speak 2 B

1. **A:** I want to _____ go. Can you _____ go with me, please?

B: _____.

2. **A:** My room is _____. Can you _____ it, please?

B: Sure.

3. **A:** The dog wants _____ _____ _____. Can you _____ the dog, please?

B: Sure.

Conversation A

M: These days, many things can _____ _____ humans. Some cars can _____ _____ a human driver. We can make smartphones do _____ work only _____ _____ _____ them. _____ _____ _____ we're _____ _____ in the future.

Conversation B

Amy: Wow, there _____ so many _____ in this library.

Hana: You're right. _____ _____ we find books about _____?

Terry: Hi, I'm Terry, the AI _____. Can I help you?

Amy: Hi. We're _____ _____ books about _____. Can you _____ one, please?

Terry: We have _____ _____ _____ about gravity in this library. I think *The Law of Gravity* will be the best one for you.

Hana: I'm surprised _____ _____ _____ _____ _____ _____.

Amy: Right. That's _____. Where is the book, Terry?

Terry: It's _____ the _____ _____. Come with me.

2. **M:** 환영해요. 이것은 우리의 새로운 스마트 전등이에요. 그것을 켜고 끄기 위해 손을 사용할 필요가 없어요.

W: 정말로요? 그러면 그것을 켜고 끄는 방법을 나에게 말해 줄 수 있나요?

M: "불 켜!" 또는 "불 꺼!"라고 말해요.

W: 불 켜 또는 불 꺼? 정말 간단하네요.

1. **A:** 나는 바둑을 두고 싶어. 나와 함께 바둑을 둘 수 있니?

B: 물론이지.

2. **A:** 나의 방은 지저분해. 청소해 줄 수 있니?

B: 물론이지.

3. **A:** 개가 나가고 싶어 해. 개를 산책시켜 줄 수 있니?

B: 물론이지.

M: 오늘날, 많은 것들이 인간처럼 작동한다. 어떤 차들은 인간 운전자 없이 이동할 수 있다. 우리는 스마트폰에 말하는 것만으로 스마트폰이 간단한 일을 하게 할 수 있다. 나는 우리가 이미 미래에 살고 있다는 게 놀랍다.

Amy: 와, 이 도서관에는 책이 아주 많구나.

하나: 네 말이 맞아. 우리가 중력에 관한 책들을 어디에서 찾을 수 있을까?

Terry: 안녕, 나는 AI 사서인 Terry라고 해. 내가 도와줄까?

Amy: 안녕, 우리는 중력에 관한 책들을 찾고 있어. 추천해 줄 수 있니?

Terry: 이 도서관에는 중력에 관한 책이 57권 있단다. 나는 'The Law of Gravity'라는 책이 너희들에게 가장 좋은 책일 거라고 생각해.

하나: 나는 네가 책을 추천해 줄 수 있다니 놀라워.

Amy: 맞아. 놀랍다. Terry야, 그 책은 어디에 있니?

Terry: 그건 3층에 있어. 나를 따라와.

※ 다음 우리말에 맞도록 대화를 영어로 쓰시오.

Listen & Speak 1 A

1. G: _____
   B: _____
   G: _____
   B: _____

2. W: _____
   B: _____
   W: _____
   B: _____
   W: _____
   B: _____

Listen & Speak 1 B

1. A: _____
   B: _____

2. A: _____
   B: _____

Listen & Speak 2 A

1. W: _____
   B: _____
   W: _____
   B: _____
   W: _____
   B: _____

1. G: 아, 나는 집에서 나오기 전에 히터 끄는 것을 잊어버렸어.
   B: 정말? 그러면 넌 집으로 돌아가야 하니?
   G: 아니. 나는 내 스마트폰으로 히터를 끌 수 있어.
   B: 우와, 나는 네가 스마트폰으로 히터를 끌 수 있다는 게 놀라워.

2. W: VR 세계에 오신 것을 환영해요. 나이아가라 폭포를 방문하고 싶은가요?
   B: 물론이죠.
   W: 좋아요, 이걸 쓰세요.
   B: 알겠어요. 우와, 이것은 정말 진짜처럼 보여요.
   W: 거대하죠, 그렇지 않아요?
   B: 네, 그리고 얼굴에서 물이 느껴진다는 게 놀라워요.

1. A: 이 사진들에서 너를 놀라게 한 것이 있니?
   B: 응, 나는 이 드론이 개를 산책시킬 수 있는 게 놀라워.

2. A: 이 사진들에서 너를 놀라게 한 것이 있니?
   B: 응, 나는 이 차가 자동으로 운전할 수 있는 게 놀라워.

1. W: 도와드릴까요?
   B: 안녕하세요, 저는 스마트 워치를 찾고 있어요. 하나 보여 주실래요?
   W: 물론이죠. 이것을 보세요. 그것은 당신을 위해 음악을 연주할 수 있어요.
   B: 멋지네요.
   W: 또한 그것에게 말만 하면 어떤 것이든 검색할 수 있어요.
   B: 멋지네요. 저 그거 살게요.

2. M: _____
   _____

   W: _____

   M: _____

   W: _____

2. M: 환영해요. 이것은 우리의 새로운 스마트 전등이에요. 그것을 켜고 끄기 위해 손을 사용할 필요가 없어요.

   W: 정말로요? 그러면 그것을 켜고 끄는 방법을 나에게 말해 줄 수 있나요?

   M: "불 켜!" 또는 "불 꺼!"라고 말해요.

   W: 불 켜 또는 불 꺼? 정말 간단하네요.

Listen & Speak 2 B

1. A: _____
   B: _____

2. A: _____
   B: _____

3. A: _____
   B: _____

1. A: 나는 바둑을 두고 싶어. 나와 함께 바둑을 둘 수 있니?
   B: 물론이지.

2. A: 나의 방은 지저분해. 청소해 줄 수 있니?
   B: 물론이지.

3. A: 개가 나가고 싶어 해. 개를 산책시켜 줄 수 있니?
   B: 물론이지.

Conversation A

M: _____
   _____
   _____

M: 오늘날, 많은 것들이 인간처럼 작동한다. 어떤 차들은 인간 운전자 없이 이동할 수 있다. 우리는 스마트폰에 말하는 것만으로 스마트폰이 간단한 일을 하게 할 수 있다. 나는 우리가 이미 미래에 살고 있다는 게 놀랍다.

Conversation B

Amy: _____

Hana: _____

Terry: _____

Amy: _____

Terry: _____
   _____

Hana: _____

Amy: _____

Terry: _____

Amy: 와, 이 도서관에는 책이 아주 많구나.

하나: 네 말이 맞아. 우리가 중력에 관한 책들을 어디에서 찾을 수 있을까?

Terry: 안녕, 나는 AI 사서인 Terry라고 해. 내가 도와줄까?

Amy: 안녕, 우리는 중력에 관한 책들을 찾고 있어. 추천해 줄 수 있니?

Terry: 이 도서관에는 중력에 관한 책이 57권 있단다. 나는 'The Law of Gravity'라는 책이 너희들에게 가장 좋은 책일 거라고 생각해.

하나: 나는 네가 책을 추천해 줄 수 있다니 놀라워.

Amy: 맞아. 놀랍다. Terry야, 그 책은 어디에 있니?

Terry: 그건 3층에 있어. 나를 따라와.

※ 다음 우리말과 일치하도록 빈칸에 알맞은 것을 골라 쓰시오.

1 _____ _____
A. Society　　　B. Changing

2 _____ in science and technology have _____ many changes in our lives _____ _____.
A. far　　　B. advances　　　C. so　　　D. caused

3 In the _____, science and technology will _____ more _____.
A. make　　　B. future　　　C. changes

4 Let's see _____ our lives may be _____ in the _____ future.
A. like　　　B. what　　　C. near

5 Sangho in the _____ _____
A. Center　　　B. Shopping

6 Shopping is _____ _____.
A. easier　　　B. much

7 _____ are no _____ and no _____.
A. lines　　　B. there　　　C. counters

8 Sangho _____ a shop _____ his smartphone which has a _____ shopping _____.
A. with　　　B. special　　　C. app　　　D. enters

9 In the _____, he _____ the _____ he wants.
A. items　　　B. shop　　　C. takes

10 The _____ are _____ _____ to a _____ card on his smartphone.
A. virtual　　　B. automatically　　　C. items　　　D. added

11 If Sangho _____ an item _____, it is _____ _____ from his list of purchases.
A. removed　　　B. back　　　C. puts　　　D. automatically

12 When he finishes _____, Sangho does not _____ to wait in _____ to _____.
A. line　　　B. shopping　　　C. pay　　　D. need

13 His virtual card _____ _____ all the prices and will _____ him _____.
A. up　　　B. later　　　C. charge　　　D. adds

14 _____ that _____?
A. fancy　　　B. isn't

1 변화하는 사회

2 과학과 기술의 발전은 지금까 우리의 삶에 많은 변화를 초 해 왔다.

3 미래에 과학 기술은 더 많은 화를 만들 것이다.

4 가까운 미래에 우리의 삶이 떻게 될지 살펴보자.

5 쇼핑 센터에 있는 상호

6 쇼핑이 훨씬 쉽다.

7 줄도 없고 계산대도 없다.

8 상호는 특별한 쇼핑 앱이 있 스마트폰을 가지고 가게로 들 간다.

9 가게에서 그는 그가 원하는 건들을 집는다.

10 그 물건들은 자동으로 그의 마트폰에 있는 가상 카드에 해진다.

11 만약 상호가 물건을 되돌려 으면 그것은 자동으로 그의 매 목록에서 제거된다.

12 쇼핑을 끝냈을 때 상호는 돈 지불하기 위해 줄을 설 필요 없다.

13 그의 가상 카드가 모든 가 더해서 나중에 그에게 청구 것이다.

14 정말 멋지지 않은가?

15 Sumin's 3D _____ _____ and _____
A. Clothes   B. House   C. Printed

16 Sumin _____ in a _____ _____ house.
A. lives   B. printed   C. 3D

17 _____ a 3D printed house is faster and _____ than building a house _____ traditional _____.
A. cheaper   B. building   C. methods   D. with

18 Sumin's house _____ _____ because of its _____ design.
A. unique   B. fantastic   C. looks

19 A 3D printer can _____ house _____ that people cannot make with _____ building methods and _____.
A. traditional   B. shapes   C. materials   D. produce

20 Sumin _____ likes to make her _____ at home _____ a 3D printer.
A. clothes   B. using   C. by   D. also

21 She can _____ colors and materials and can design clothes that _____ her body and _____ her _____.
A. fit   B. suit   C. choose   D. tastes

22 Sumin is now a _____ _____!
A. designer   B. fashion

23 Dongmin _____ the _____
A. Hospital   B. in

24 Dongmin is _____ his _____ in the _____.
A. grandfather   B. hospital   C. visiting

25 An _____ _____ _____ the room.
A. enters   B. nurse   C. AI

26 It _____ _____ the room and _____ the patients' _____.
A. checks   B. around   C. conditions   D. moves

27 When the AI nurse finds that Dongmin's grandfather has a _____ _____, it gives him some _____ to _____ his temperature.
A. temperature   B. lower   C. medicine   D. high

28 _____ you ever _____ about these _____?
A. changes   B. have   C. thought

29 Some changes have already started to _____ _____ while _____ may start in the _____ future.
A. place   B. near   C. others   D. take

30 Can you _____ _____ _____?
A. other   B. changes   C. imagine

31 _____ some time to _____ _____ them.
A. think   B. take   C. about

15 수민이의 3D 프린터로 만든 집과 옷

16 수민이는 3D 프린터로 만든 집에 산다.

17 3D 프린터로 집을 짓는 것은 전통적인 방법으로 집을 짓는 것보다 더 빠르고 저렴하다.

18 수민이의 집은 독특한 디자인 때문에 멋져 보인다.

19 3D 프린터는 사람들이 전통 건축 방법과 재료들로 만들 수 없는 집 모양을 만들어 낼 수 있다.

20 수민이는 또한 집에서 3D 프린터를 사용해 옷을 만드는 것을 좋아한다.

21 그녀는 색깔과 재료를 고를 수 있고 자신의 몸과 취향에 맞는 옷을 디자인할 수 있다.

22 수민이는 이제 패션 디자이너이다!

23 병원에 있는 동민

24 동민이는 병원에 계시는 그의 할아버지를 방문하고 있다.

25 AI 간호사가 병실로 들어온다.

26 그것은 병실을 돌아다니고, 환자들의 상태를 확인한다.

27 AI 간호사가 동민이 할아버지가 열이 높다는 것을 알았을 때 그것은 그의 체온을 낮추기 위해 그에게 약을 준다.

28 여러분은 이러한 변화에 대해 생각해 본 적 있는가?

29 어떤 변화는 이미 일어나기 시작했고 반면 다른 것들은 가까운 미래에 일어날지도 모른다.

30 여러분은 다른 변화들을 상상할 수 있는가?

31 그것들에 대해 잠깐 생각해 보자.

※ 다음 우리말과 일치하도록 빈칸에 알맞은 말을 쓰시오.

1 _____ Society

2 _____ in science and _____ _____ _____ many _____ in our lives _____ _____.

3 _____ _____ _____, science and technology will _____ _____ _____.

4 _____ see what our lives _____ _____ _____ in the _____ future.

5 Sangho in the _____ _____

6 Shopping is _____ _____.

7 There are _____ _____ and _____ _____.

8 Sangho enters a shop _____ his smartphone which has a _____ _____ _____.

9 In the shop, he _____ _____ _____ he wants.

10 The items _____ _____ _____ _____ a _____ card on his smartphone.

11 If Sangho _____ an item _____, it _____ _____ _____ _____ his _____ _____ _____.

12 When he finishes _____, Sangho _____ _____ _____ _____ wait _____ _____ to pay.

13 His virtual card _____ _____ all the _____ and will _____ him _____.

14 _____ that _____?

---

1 변화하는 사회

2 과학과 기술의 발전은 지금까지 우리의 삶에 많은 변화를 초래해 왔다.

3 미래에 과학 기술은 더 많은 변화를 만들 것이다.

4 가까운 미래에 우리의 삶이 어떻게 될지 살펴보자.

5 쇼핑 센터에 있는 상호

6 쇼핑이 훨씬 쉽다.

7 줄도 없고 계산대도 없다.

8 상호는 특별한 쇼핑 앱이 있는 스마트폰을 가지고 가게로 들어간다.

9 가게에서 그는 그가 원하는 물건들을 집는다.

10 그 물건들은 자동으로 그의 스마트폰에 있는 가상 카드에 더해진다.

11 만약 상호가 물건을 되돌려 놓으면 그것은 자동으로 그의 구매 목록에서 제거된다.

12 쇼핑을 끝냈을 때 상호는 돈을 지불하기 위해 줄을 설 필요가 없다.

13 그의 가상 카드가 모든 가격을 더해서 나중에 그에게 청구할 것이다.

14 정말 멋지지 않은가?

15 Sumin's _____ _____ House and _____

16 Sumin _____ in a _____ _____ house.

17 _____ a 3D printed house is _____ _____ _____ than building a house _____ _____ _____.

18 Sumin's house _____ _____ because of its unique design.

19 A 3D printer can produce _____ _____ that people cannot make with _____ _____ _____ _____.

20 Sumin also likes to make _____ _____ at home _____ _____ a 3D printer.

21 She can choose colors and materials and can design clothes _____ _____ her body and _____ her _____.

22 Sumin is now a _____ _____!

23 Dongmin _____ _____ _____

24 Dongmin _____ _____ his grandfather in the hospital.

25 _____ _____ nurse _____ the room.

26 It _____ _____ the room and _____ the patients' _____.

27 When the AI nurse finds that Dongmin's grandfather has a _____ _____, it gives him some medicine _____ _____ _____ _____.

28 _____ _____ _____ _____ about these changes?

29 Some changes have already started to _____ _____ while _____ may start _____ _____ _____.

30 Can you _____ _____ _____?

31 _____ _____ _____ _____ _____ about them.

15 수민이의 3D 프린터로 만든 집과 옷

16 수민이는 3D 프린터로 만든 집에 산다.

17 3D 프린터로 집을 짓는 것은 전통적인 방법으로 집을 짓는 것보다 더 빠르고 저렴하다.

18 수민이의 집은 독특한 디자인 때문에 멋져 보인다.

19 3D 프린터는 사람들이 전통 건축 방법과 재료들로 만들 수 없는 집 모양을 만들어 낼 수 있다.

20 수민이는 또한 집에서 3D 프린터를 사용해 옷을 만드는 것을 좋아한다.

21 그녀는 색깔과 재료를 고를 수 있고 자신의 몸과 취향에 맞는 옷을 디자인할 수 있다.

22 수민이는 이제 패션 디자이너이다!

23 병원에 있는 동민

24 동민이는 병원에 계시는 그의 할아버지를 방문하고 있다.

25 AI 간호사가 병실로 들어온다.

26 그것은 병실을 돌아다니고, 환자들의 상태를 확인한다.

27 AI 간호사가 동민이 할아버지가 열이 높다는 것을 알았을 때 그것은 그의 체온을 낮추기 위해 그에게 약을 준다.

28 여러분은 이러한 변화에 대해 생각해 본 적 있는가?

29 어떤 변화는 이미 일어나기 시작했고 반면 다른 것들은 가까운 미래에 일어날지도 모른다.

30 여러분은 다른 변화들을 상상할 수 있는가?

31 그것들에 대해 잠깐 생각해 보자.

※ 다음 문장을 우리말로 쓰시오.

1 ▶ Changing Society

➡ _____

2 ▶ Advances in science and technology have caused many changes in our lives so far.

➡ _____

3 ▶ In the future, science and technology will make more changes.

➡ _____

4 ▶ Let's see what our lives may be like in the near future.

➡ _____

5 ▶ Sangho in the Shopping Center

➡ _____

6 ▶ Shopping is much easier.

➡ _____

7 ▶ There are no lines and no counters.

➡ _____

8 ▶ Sangho enters a shop with his smartphone which has a special shopping app.

➡ _____

9 ▶ In the shop, he takes the items he wants.

➡ _____

10 ▶ The items are automatically added to a virtual card on his smartphone.

➡ _____

11 ▶ If Sangho puts an item back, it is automatically removed from his list of purchases.

➡ _____

12 ▶ When he finishes shopping, Sangho does not need to wait in line to pay.

➡ _____

13 ▶ His virtual card adds up all the prices and will charge him later.

➡ _____

14 ▶ Isn't that fancy?

➡ _____

15 ▶ Sumin's 3D Printed House and Clothes

➡ _____

16 ▶ Sumin lives in a 3D printed house.

➡ _____

17 ▶ Building a 3D printed house is faster and cheaper than building a house with traditional methods.

➡ _____

18 Sumin's house looks fantastic because of its unique design.

➡ _____

19 A 3D printer can produce house shapes that people cannot make with traditional building methods and materials.

➡ _____

20 Sumin also likes to make her clothes at home by using a 3D printer.

➡ _____

21 She can choose colors and materials and can design clothes that fit her body and suit her tastes.

➡ _____

22 Sumin is now a fashion designer!

➡ _____

23 Dongmin in the Hospital

➡ _____

24 Dongmin is visiting his grandfather in the hospital.

➡ _____

25 An AI nurse enters the room.

➡ _____

26 It moves around the room and checks the patients' conditions.

➡ _____

27 When the AI nurse finds that Dongmin's grandfather has a high temperature, it gives him some medicine to lower his temperature.

➡ _____

28 Have you ever thought about these changes?

➡ _____

29 Some changes have already started to take place while others may start in the near future.

➡ _____

30 Can you imagine other changes?

➡ _____

31 Take some time to think about them.

➡ _____

※ 다음 괄호 안의 단어들을 우리말에 맞도록 바르게 배열하시오.

1 (Society / Changing)
➡ _____

2 (in / advances / science / and / have / technology / caused / changes / many / our / in / lives / far. / so)
➡ _____

3 (the / in / future, / technology / and / science / make / will / changes. / more)
➡ _____

4 (see / let's / our / what / lives / be / may / like / the / in / future. / near)
➡ _____

5 (in / Sangho / the / Center / Shopping)
➡ _____

6 (is / shopping / easier. / much)
➡ _____

7 (are / there / lines / no / and / countries. / no)
➡ _____

8 (enters / Sangho / shop / a / with / smartphone / his / has / which / special / a / app. / shopping)
➡ _____

9 (the / in / shop, / takes / he / items / the / wants. / he)
➡ _____

10 (items / the / automatically / are / to / added / a / card / virtual / on / smartphone. / his)
➡ _____

11 (Sangho / if / an / puts / back, / item / is / it / removed / automatically / from / list / his / purchases. / of)
➡ _____

12 (he / when / shopping, / finishes / does / Sangho / need / not / wait / to / line / in / pay. / to)
➡ _____

13 (virtual / his / adds / card / all / up / the / and / prices / charge / will / later. / him)
➡ _____

14 (that / isn't / fancy?)
➡ _____

15 (3D / Sumin's / House / Printed / Clothes / and)
➡ _____

16 (lives / Sumin / a / in / 3D / house. / printed)
➡ _____

17 (a / building / printed / 3D / house / faster / is / and / than / cheaper / building / house / a / traditional / with / methods.)
➡ _____

---

1 변화하는 사회

2 과학과 기술의 발전은 지금까지 우리의 삶에 많은 변화를 초래해 왔다.

3 미래에 과학 기술은 더 많은 변화를 만들 것이다.

4 가까운 미래에 우리의 삶이 어떻게 될지 살펴보자.

5 쇼핑 센터에 있는 상호

6 쇼핑이 훨씬 쉽다.

7 줄도 없고 계산대도 없다.

8 상호는 특별한 쇼핑 앱이 있는 스마트폰을 가지고 가게로 들어간다.

9 가게에서 그는 그가 원하는 물건들을 집는다.

10 그 물건들은 자동으로 그의 스마트폰에 있는 가상 카드에 추가해진다.

11 만약 상호가 물건을 되돌려 놓으면 그것은 자동으로 그의 구매 목록에서 제거된다.

12 쇼핑을 끝냈을 때 상호는 돈을 지불하기 위해 줄을 설 필요가 없다.

13 그의 가상 카드가 모든 가격을 더해서 나중에 그에게 청구할 것이다.

14 정말 멋지지 않은가?

15 수민이의 3D 프린터로 만든 집과 옷

16 수민이는 3D 프린터로 만든 집에 산다.

17 3D 프린터로 집을 짓는 것은 전통적인 방법으로 집을 짓는 것보다 더 빠르고 저렴하다.

18 (house / Sumin's / fantastic / looks / of / because / its / design. / unique)
➡ _____

19 (3D / a / can / printer / produce / shapes / house / that / cannot / people / with / make / building / traditional / materials. / and / methods)
➡ _____

20 (also / Sumin / to / likes / her / make / at / clothes / home / using / by / 3D / printer. / a)
➡ _____

21 (she / choose / can / materials / and / colors / and / design / can / that / clothes / her / fit / body / and / her / suit / tastes.)
➡ _____

22 (is / Sumin / a / now / designer! / fashion)
➡ _____

23 (in / Dongmin / Hospital / the)
➡ _____

24 (is / Dongmin / his / visiting / grandfather / the / hospital. / in)
➡ _____

25 (AI / an / and / enters / nurse / room. / the)
➡ _____

26 (moves / it / the / around / room / checks / and / patients' / the / conditions.)
➡ _____

27 (the / when / nurse / AI / that / finds / grandfather / Dongmin's / has / a / temperature, / high / gives / it / some / him / to / medicine / lower / temperature. / his)
➡ _____

28 (you / have / thought / ever / these / about / changes?)
➡ _____

29 (changes / some / already / have / to / started / place / take / while / may / others / start / the / in / future. / near)
➡ _____

30 (you / can / other / imagine / changes?)
➡ _____

31 (some / take / to / time / them. / about / think)
➡ _____

18 수민이의 집은 독특한 디자인 때문에 멋져 보인다.

19 3D 프린터는 사람들이 전통 건축 방법과 재료들로 만들 수 없는 집 모양을 만들어 낼 수 있다.

20 수민이는 또한 집에서 3D 프린터를 사용해 옷을 만드는 것을 좋아한다.

21 그녀는 색깔과 재료를 고를 수 있고 자신의 몸과 취향에 맞는 옷을 디자인할 수 있다.

22 수민이는 이제 패션 디자이너이다!

23 병원에 있는 동민

24 동민이는 병원에 계시는 그의 할아버지를 방문하고 있다.

25 AI 간호사가 병실로 들어온다.

26 그것은 병실을 돌아다니고, 환자들의 상태를 확인한다.

27 AI 간호사가 동민이 할아버지가 열이 높다는 것을 알았을 때 그것은 그의 체온을 낮추기 위해 그에게 약을 준다.

28 여러분은 이러한 변화에 대해 생각해 본 적 있는가?

29 어떤 변화는 이미 일어나기 시작했고 반면 다른 것들은 가까운 미래에 일어날지도 모른다.

30 여러분은 다른 변화들을 상상할 수 있는가?

31 그것들에 대해 잠깐 생각해 보자.

※ 다음 우리말을 영어로 쓰시오.

1 변화하는 사회

➡ _____

2 과학과 기술의 발전은 지금까지 우리의 삶에 많은 변화를 초래해 왔다.

➡ _____

3 미래에 과학 기술은 더 많은 변화를 만들 것이다.

➡ _____

4 가까운 미래에 우리의 삶이 어떻게 될지 살펴보자.

➡ _____

5 쇼핑 센터에 있는 상호

➡ _____

6 쇼핑이 훨씬 쉽다.

➡ _____

7 줄도 없고 계산대도 없다.

➡ _____

8 상호는 특별한 쇼핑 앱이 있는 스마트폰을 가지고 가게로 들어간다.

➡ _____

9 가게에서 그는 그가 원하는 물건들을 집는다.

➡ _____

10 그 물건들은 자동으로 그의 스마트폰에 있는 가상 카드에 더해진다.

➡ _____

11 만약 상호가 물건을 되돌려 놓으면 그것은 자동으로 그의 구매 목록에서 제거된다.

➡ _____

12 쇼핑을 끝냈을 때 상호는 돈을 지불하기 위해 줄을 설 필요가 없다.

➡ _____

13 그의 가상 카드가 모든 가격을 더해서 나중에 그에게 청구할 것이다.

➡ _____

14 정말 멋지지 않은가?

➡ _____

15 수민이의 3D 프린터로 만든 집과 옷

➡ _____

16 수민이는 3D 프린터로 만든 집에 산다.

➡ _____

17 3D 프린터로 집을 짓는 것은 전통적인 방법으로 집을 짓는 것보다 더 빠르고 저렴하다.

➡ _____

18 수민이의 집은 독특한 디자인 때문에 멋져 보인다.

➡ _____

19 3D 프린터는 사람들이 전통 건축 방법과 재료들로 만들 수 없는 집 모양을 만들어 낼 수 있다.

➡ _____

20 수민이는 또한 집에서 3D 프린터를 사용해 옷을 만드는 것을 좋아한다.

➡ _____

21 그녀는 색깔과 재료를 고를 수 있고 자신의 몸과 취향에 맞는 옷을 디자인할 수 있다.

➡ _____

22 수민이는 이제 패션 디자이너이다!

➡ _____

23 병원에 있는 동민

➡ _____

24 동민이는 병원에 계시는 그의 할아버지를 방문하고 있다.

➡ _____

25 AI 간호사가 병실로 들어온다.

➡ _____

26 그것은 병실을 돌아다니고, 환자들의 상태를 확인한다.

➡ _____

27 AI 간호사가 동민이 할아버지가 열이 높다는 것을 알았을 때 그것은 그의 체온을 낮추기 위해 그에게 약을 준다.

➡ _____

28 여러분은 이러한 변화에 대해 생각해 본 적 있는가?

➡ _____

29 어떤 변화는 이미 일어나기 시작했고 반면 다른 것들은 가까운 미래에 일어날지도 모른다.

➡ _____

30 여러분은 다른 변화들을 상상할 수 있는가?

➡ _____

31 그것들에 대해 잠깐 생각해 보자.

➡ _____

※ 다음 우리말과 일치하도록 빈칸에 알맞은 말을 쓰시오.

Enjoy Writing B

1. Schools _____ 20 _____
2. _____ you ever _____ of _____ _____ _____ over the next 20 years?
3. Students _____ _____ drone design.
4. _____ drones _____ _____ students at school.
5. _____ _____ _____ an AI teachers' room _____ _____ _____.
6. Students _____ _____ to school only _____ _____ _____ _____ a week.

1. 20년 후 학교의 모습
2. 다음 20년에 걸쳐 학교의 모습이 어떻게 변할지 생각해 본 적이 있나요?
3. 학생들은 드론 디자인을 배울지도 모릅니다.
4. 청소 드론이 학교에서 학생들을 도울지도 모릅니다.
5. 모든 학교에 AI 선생님들이 교무실이 있을지도 모릅니다.
6. 학생들은 일주일에 오직 두세 번만 학교에 갈지도 모릅니다.

Project

1. _____ you ever _____ life _____ _____ _____?
2. People _____ use personal drones _____ _____ _____ _____.
3. So there _____ _____ _____ _____ for drones in the sky.
4. _____ _____ _____ AI helpers _____ _____ _____ soon and they may help humans _____ _____ _____ _____.

1. 미래의 삶을 상상해 본 적이 있나요?
2. 사람들은 매일의 삶에서 개인 드론을 사용할지도 모릅니다.
3. 그래서 하늘에는 드론들을 위한 교통 신호등이 있을지도 모릅니다.
4. 많은 AI 도우미들이 곧 만들어져서 많은 방식으로 인간을 도울지 모릅니다.

Wrap Up 1

1. G: _____ you _____ _____ your trip to London?
2. B: Yes, but I'm _____ _____ _____ _____. I'm not _____ _____ _____ places.
3. G: _____ worry. _____ _____ many good smartphone _____ _____ _____ _____.
4. B: Can you _____ _____ _____?
5. G: Sure. Use this one. It _____ _____ _____ _____ of the city and _____ _____ _____.
6. B: Oh, _____.

1. G: 너의 런던 여행은 준비됐니?
2. B: 응, 하지만 나는 길을 잃는 것에 대해 걱정하고 있어. 나는 장소 찾는 것을 잘 못해.
3. G: 걱정 마. 네가 사용할 수 있는 좋은 스마트폰 앱이 많이 있어.
4. B: 나에게 하나 보여줄 수 있니?
5. G: 물론이지. 이것을 사용해 봐. 그것은 도시의 지도와 길의 사진을 보여줘.
6. B: 오, 고마워.

※ 다음 우리말을 영어로 쓰시오.

Enjoy Writing B

1. 20년 후 학교의 모습
➡ _____

2. 다음 20년에 걸쳐 학교의 모습이 어떻게 변할지 생각해 본 적이 있나요?
➡ _____

3. 학생들은 드론 디자인을 배울지도 모릅니다.
➡ _____

4. 청소 드론이 학교에서 학생들을 도울지도 모릅니다.
➡ _____

5. 모든 학교에 AI 선생님들 교무실이 있을지도 모릅니다.
➡ _____

6. 학생들은 일주일에 오직 두세 번만 학교에 갈지도 모릅니다.
➡ _____

Project

1. 미래의 삶을 상상해 본 적이 있나요?
➡ _____

2. 사람들은 매일의 삶에서 개인 드론을 사용할지도 모릅니다.
➡ _____

3. 그래서 하늘에는 드론들을 위한 교통 신호등이 있을지도 모릅니다.
➡ _____

4. 많은 AI 도우미들이 곧 만들어져서 많은 방식으로 인간을 도울지 모릅니다.
➡ _____

Wrap Up 1

1. G: 너의 런던 여행은 준비됐니?
➡ _____

2. B: 응, 하지만 나는 길을 잃는 것에 대해 걱정하고 있어. 나는 장소 찾는 것을 잘 못해.
➡ _____

3. G: 걱정 마. 네가 사용할 수 있는 좋은 스마트폰 앱이 많이 있어.
➡ _____

4. B: 나에게 하나 보여줄 수 있니?
➡ _____

5. G: 물론이지. 이것을 사용해 봐. 그것은 도시의 지도와 길의 사진을 보여줘.
➡ _____

6. B: 오, 고마워.
➡ _____

※ 다음 영어를 우리말로 쓰시오.

01	single		17	meal
02	break		18	customer
03	tap		19	novel
04	chair		20	bedroom
05	producer		21	player
06	owner		22	counter
07	turn		23	treat
08	yet		24	bowl
09	count		25	have to 동사원형
10	order		26	be about to
11	elderly		27	treat A(사람) to B(사물)
12	grandson		28	can't wait to 동사원형
13	chew		29	pick up
14	if		30	say to oneself
15	even		31	help+목적어+동사원형
16	raise		32	think up

※ 다음 우리말을 영어로 쓰시오.

01 침실

02 계산대

03 생산자, 제작자

04 (음식을) 씹다

05 (가볍게) 톡톡 두드리다

06 (무엇을 할) 차례, 순번

07 아직

08 (음식을) 주문하다

09 참가자, 선수

10 의자

11 대접하다, 다루다

12 연세가 드신

13 수를 세다, 계산하다

14 (우묵한) 그릇, 통

15 (자금 등을) 모으다

16 주인, 소유주

17 휴식, (학교의) 쉬는 시간

18 손자

19 만일 ~라면

20 식사

21 손님, 고객

22 소설

23 ~도, ~조차

24 단 하나의, 단일의

25 ~을 생각해 내다

26 ~해야 한다

27 들어올리다, 집다

28 A에게 B를 대접하다

29 (목적어)가 ~하는 것을 돕다

30 빨리 ~하고 싶다

31 막 ~하려는 참이다

32 혼잣말을 하다

※ 다음 영영풀이에 알맞은 단어를 <보기>에서 골라 쓴 후, 우리말 뜻을 쓰시오.

1 _____ : someone who owns something: _____

2 _____ : comprising only one part: _____

3 _____ : a son of one's son or daughter: _____

4 _____ : a room that you sleep in: _____

5 _____ : a book telling a long story in prose: _____

6 _____ : a person who buys goods from a shop, etc.: _____

7 _____ : to buy or give someone something special: _____

8 _____ : to break food etc. with the teeth before swallowing: _____

9 _____ : an occasion when you eat food such as breakfast, lunch, and dinner: _____

10 _____ : the place where customers are served or pay in a restaurant or shop: _____

11 _____ : to invent or to imagine something, especially an excuse: _____

12 _____ : a piece of furniture for one person to sit on, with a back, legs, and sometimes two arms: _____

보기			
chair	counter	think up	grandson
novel	treat	bedroom	chew
single	owner	meal	customer

※ 다음 우리말과 일치하도록 빈칸에 알맞은 것을 골라 쓰시오.

1 The _____
   A. Customer   B. 100th

2 One day, an _____ woman _____ _____ a restaurant.
   A. into   B. elderly   C. walked

3 She was _____ _____ _____.
   A. her   B. with   C. grandson

4 _____, the woman _____ Mr. Kang, the _____ of the restaurant.
   A. asked   B. owner   C. quietly

5 "_____ _____ is a _____ of Gukbap?"
   A. bowl   B. much   C. how

6 "It's 4,000 won, ma'am," Mr. Kang _____ _____ a _____.
   A. with   B. smile   C. answered

7 She was too _____ to _____ for two _____.
   A. bowls   B. pay   C. poor

8 She _____ a _____ bowl for her _____.
   A. single   B. ordered   C. grandson

9 "Are you _____ you are not _____, Grandma?" the boy asked, _____ he _____ the hot soup.
   A. as   B. sure   C. hungry   D. ate

10 "_____, I'm not _____."
   A. hungry   B. no

11 _____ _____ about me."
   A. worry   B. don't

12 She _____ _____ some Gimchi and _____ _____ it happily.
   A. up   B. on   C. chewed   D. picked

13 Mr. Kang watched them _____, and a warm _____ came _____ him.
   A. over   B. eat   C. feeling

14 He _____ _____ a plan to give the boy a _____ _____.
   A. free   B. up   C. meal   D. thought

15 When the woman was _____ to _____, Mr. Kang _____ his hands and said, "No _____, ma'am.
   A. about   B. need   C. pay   D. waved

16 In my restaurant, you don't _____ you're the _____ _____ of the day."
   A. if   B. pay   C. customer   D. 100th

17 The _____ and her grandson _____ Mr. Kang and _____.
   A. left   B. thanked   C. woman

1 백 번째 손님

2 어느 날 한 할머니가 식당으로 걸어 들어왔다.

3 그녀는 손자와 함께 있었다.

4 그녀는 조용히 식당 주인인 강 씨에게 물었다.

5 "국밥 한 그릇이 얼마인가요?"

6 "4,000원입니다. 할머니." 강 씨는 미소 지으며 답했다.

7 그녀는 너무 가난해서 두 그릇 값을 지불할 수 없었다.

8 그녀는 손자를 위해 한 그릇을 주문했다.

9 "정말 배고프지 않으세요, 할머니?" 남자아이는 따뜻한 국물을 먹으며 물었다.

10 "응. 난 배고프지 않단다.

11 내 걱정하지 마라."

12 그녀는 행복하게 김치를 집어서 먹었다.

13 강 씨는 그들이 먹는 것을 지켜보았고, 따뜻한 감정이 밀려왔다.

14 그는 남자아이에게 무료로 식사를 주기 위해 계획을 생각해 냈다.

15 할머니가 돈을 내려고 할 때, 강 씨는 손을 흔들며 말했다. "필요 없습니다, 할머니.

16 저희 식당에서는 그 날의 백 번째 손님이 되면 돈을 내지 않아도 됩니다."

17 할머니와 손자는 강 씨에게 감사해 하며 떠났다.

18 A _____ _____, Mr. Kang _____ the boy in the street _____ the restaurant.

    A. outside   B. later   C. saw   D. month

19 The boy _____ _____ _____.

    A. gathering   B. stones   C. was

20 "_____ are you _____?" _____ Mr. Kang.

    A. doing   B. what   C. asked

21 "I'm _____ the _____ of customers _____ _____ your restaurant.

    A. number   B. enter   C. counting   D. who

22 _____ _____ my _____ birthday."

    A. grandma's   B. is   C. today

23 'He wants to be the 100th customer and _____ his grandmother _____ a _____ of Gukbap!' Mr. Kang said to _____.

    A. himself   B. treat   C. bowl   D. to

24 Mr. Kang _____ _____.

    A. down   B. looked

25 He could see that the _____ of stones _____ not yet _____ fifty.

    A. even   B. number   C. was

26 He _____ to do something _____ _____ the boy _____ 100 stones.

    A. gather   B. had   C. help   D. to

27 Mr. Kang _____ _____ _____ the restaurant and _____ his friends.

    A. back   B. went   C. called   D. into

28 "Come to my restaurant now and _____ _____ who _____ you.

    A. bring   B. with   C. everyone   D. works

29 _____ is a boy who _____ your _____."

    A. help   B. there   C. needs

30 People began _____ _____ _____ the restaurant.

    A. arrive   B. to   C. at

31 When the 99th customer _____, Mr. Kang _____ the boy say, "It's our _____, Grandma."

    A. heard   B. turn   C. arrived

32 Mr. Kang _____ them and _____ the woman a _____ _____ of Gukbap.

    A. served   B. free   C. welcomed   D. bowl

33 "Are you _____ you're not _____?" the woman _____ the boy.

    A. asked   B. sure   C. hungry

34 The boy _____ _____ _____ on some Gimchi and said _____ a _____, "No, I'm not hungry, Grandma.

    A. loudly   B. with   C. chewed   D. smile

35 _____ _____ about _____. Happy birthday!"

    A. me   B. worry   C. don't

18 한 달 후, 강 씨는 식당 밖 거리에서 그 남자아이를 보았다.

19 그 남자아이는 돌멩이를 모으고 있었다.

20 너 뭐 하고 있니?" 강 씨가 물었다.

21 "저는 아저씨 식당에 들어가는 손님들의 수를 세고 있어요.

22 오늘이 우리 할머니 생신이거든요"

23 '저 아이는 백 번째 손님이 되어서 할머니께 공짜 국밥 한 그릇을 대접하고 싶어 하는구나.' 강 씨는 혼잣말을 했다.

24 강 씨는 아래를 내려다보았다.

25 그는 돌멩이의 개수가 아직 오십 개도 안 되는 것을 볼 수 있었다.

26 그는 남자아이가 돌멩이 백 개를 모으는 것을 돕기 위해 무언가를 해야 했다.

27 강 씨는 식당으로 되돌아가 그의 친구들에게 전화했다.

28 "지금 내 식당으로 오고, 자네와 함께 일하는 모든 사람들을 데려와 주게.

29 자네 도움이 필요한 남자아이가 있어."

30 사람들이 식당에 도착하기 시작했다.

31 아흔아홉 번째 손님이 도착했을 때 강 씨는 남자아이가 "우리 차례예요. 할머니."라고 말하는 것을 들었다.

32 강 씨는 그들을 반기며 할머니께 공짜 국밥 한 그릇을 제공했다.

33 "너 정말 배고프지 않니?" 할머니가 남자아이에게 물었다.

34 남자아이는 큰 소리로 김치를 씹고 미소 지으며 말했다. "네, 전 배고프지 않아요, 할머니.

35 제 걱정 마세요, 생신 축하드려요!"

※ 다음 우리말과 일치하도록 빈칸에 알맞은 말을 쓰시오.

1 The _____ _____

2 One day, an _____ woman _____ _____ a restaurant.

3 She was _____ _____ _____ .

4 _____ , the woman _____ Mr. Kang, _____ _____ of the restaurant.

5 "_____ _____ is _____ _____ Gukbap?"

6 "It's 4,000 won, ma'am," Mr. Kang answered _____ _____ _____ .

7 She was _____ _____ _____ _____ for two bowls.

8 She ordered a _____ bowl _____ _____ _____ .

9 "_____ _____ _____ you are not hungry, Grandma?" the boy asked, as he _____ the hot soup.

10 "_____ , I'm _____ _____ .

11 _____ _____ _____ me."

12 She picked up some Gimchi and _____ _____ it _____ .

13 Mr. Kang _____ them _____ , and a warm feeling _____ _____ him.

14 He _____ _____ a plan _____ _____ _____ _____ _____ _____ _____ .

15 When the woman _____ _____ _____ _____ _____ , Mr. Kang _____ his hands and said, "No need, ma'am.

16 In my restaurant, you don't _____ if you're _____ _____ of the day."

17 The woman and her grandson _____ _____ _____ and left.

2 어느 날 한 할머니가 식당으로 걸어 들어왔다.

3 그녀는 손자와 함께 있었다.

4 그녀는 조용히 식당 주인인 강 씨에게 물었다.

5 "국밥 한 그릇이 얼마인가요?"

6 "4,000원입니다, 할머니." 강 씨는 미소 지으며 답했다.

7 그녀는 너무 가난해서 두 그릇 값을 지불할 수 없었다.

8 그녀는 손자를 위해 한 그릇을 주문했다.

9 "정말 배고프지 않으세요, 할머니?" 남자아이는 따뜻한 국물을 먹으며 물었다.

10 "응, 난 배고프지 않단다.

11 내 걱정하지 마라."

12 그녀는 행복하게 김치를 집어서 먹었다.

13 강 씨는 그들이 먹는 것을 지켜 보았고, 따뜻한 감정이 밀려왔다.

14 그는 남자아이에게 무료로 식사를 주기 위해 계획을 생각해 냈다.

15 할머니가 돈을 내려고 할 때, 강 씨는 손을 흔들며 말했다. "필요 없습니다. 할머니.

16 저희 식당에서는 그 날의 백 번 째 손님이 되면 돈을 내지 않아 도 됩니다."

17 할머니와 손자는 강 씨에게 감 사해 하며 떠났다.

18 _____ _____ _____, Mr. Kang _____ the boy in the street _____ the restaurant.

19 The boy _____ _____ _____.

20 "_____ are you _____?" asked Mr. Kang.

21 "I'm _____ the number of customers _____ enter your restaurant.

22 _____ _____ my grandma's birthday."

23 'He wants to be the 100th customer and _____ his grandmother to a bowl of Gukbap!' Mr. Kang _____ _____ _____.

24 Mr. Kang _____ _____.

25 He could see that _____ _____ of stones _____ not yet _____.

26 He had to do something _____ _____ the boy gather 100 stones.

27 Mr. Kang _____ _____ _____ the restaurant and _____ his friends.

28 "Come to my restaurant now and _____ _____ _____ _____ _____ you.

29 There is a boy _____ _____ _____ _____."

30 People _____ _____ _____ _____ the restaurant.

31 When the 99th customer arrived, Mr. Kang heard the boy say, "_____ _____ _____, Grandma."

32 Mr. Kang _____ _____ and _____ the woman _____ _____ _____ _____ _____.

33 "_____ _____ _____ you're not hungry?" the woman asked the boy.

34 The boy _____ _____ on some Gimchi and said _____ _____ _____, "No, I'm not hungry, Grandma.

35 _____ _____ about me. Happy birthday!"

---

18 한 달 후, 강 씨는 식당 밖 거리에서 그 남자아이를 보았다.

19 그 남자아이는 돌멩이를 모으고 있었다.

20 너 뭐 하고 있니?" 강 씨가 물었다.

21 "저는 아저씨 식당에 들어가는 손님들의 수를 세고 있어요.

22 오늘이 우리 할머니 생신이거든요."

23 '저 아이는 백 번째 손님이 되어서 할머니께 공짜 국밥 한 그릇을 대접하고 싶어 하는구나.' 강 씨는 혼잣말을 했다.

24 강 씨는 아래를 내려다보았다.

25 그는 돌멩이의 개수가 아직 오십 개도 안 되는 것을 볼 수 있었다.

26 그는 남자아이가 돌멩이 백 개를 모으는 것을 돕기 위해 무언가를 해야 했다.

27 강 씨는 식당으로 되돌아가 그의 친구들에게 전화했다.

28 "지금 내 식당으로 오고, 자네와 함께 일하는 모든 사람들을 데려와 주게.

29 자네 도움이 필요한 남자아이가 있어."

30 사람들이 식당에 도착하기 시작했다.

31 아흔아홉 번째 손님이 도착했을 때 강 씨는 남자아이가 "우리 차례예요, 할머니."라고 말하는 것을 들었다.

32 강 씨는 그들을 반기며 할머니께 공짜 국밥 한 그릇을 제공했다.

33 "너 정말 배고프지 않니?" 할머니가 남자아이에게 물었다.

34 남자아이는 큰 소리로 김치를 씹고 미소 지으며 말했다. "네, 전 배고프지 않아요, 할머니.

35 제 걱정 마세요, 생신 축하드려요!"

※ 다음 문장을 우리말로 쓰시오.

1 The 100th Customer

➡ _____

2 One day, an elderly woman walked into a restaurant.

➡ _____

3 She was with her grandson.

➡ _____

4 Quietly, the woman asked Mr. Kang, the owner of the restaurant.

➡ _____

5 "How much is a bowl of Gukbap?"

➡ _____

6 "It's 4,000 won, ma'am," Mr. Kang answered with a smile.

➡ _____

7 She was too poor to pay for two bowls.

➡ _____

8 She ordered a single bowl for her grandson.

➡ _____

9 "Are you sure you are not hungry, Grandma?" the boy asked, as he ate the hot soup.

➡ _____

10 "No, I'm not hungry.

➡ _____

11 Don't worry about me."

➡ _____

12 She picked up some Gimchi and chewed on it happily.

➡ _____

13 Mr. Kang watched them eat, and a warm feeling came over him.

➡ _____

14 He thought up a plan to give the boy a free meal.

➡ _____

15 When the woman was about to pay, Mr. Kang waved his hands and said, "No need, ma'am.

➡ _____

16 In my restaurant, you don't pay if you're the 100th customer of the day."

➡ _____

17 The woman and her grandson thanked Mr. Kang and left.

➡ _____

18 A month later, Mr. Kang saw the boy in the street outside the restaurant

➡ _____

19 The boy was gathering stones.

➡ _____

20 "What are you doing?" asked Mr. Kang.

➡ _____

21 "I'm counting the number of customers who enter your restaurant.

➡ _____

22 Today is my grandma's birthday."

➡ _____

23 'He wants to be the 100th customer and treat his grandmother to a bowl of Gukbap!' Mr. Kang said to himself.

➡ _____

24 Mr. Kang looked down.

➡ _____

25 He could see that the number of stones was not yet even fifty.

➡ _____

26 He had to do something to help the boy gather 100 stones.

➡ _____

27 Mr. Kang went back into the restaurant and called his friends.

➡ _____

28 "Come to my restaurant now and bring everyone who works with you.

➡ _____

29 There is a boy who needs your help."

➡ _____

30 People began to arrive at the restaurant.

➡ _____

31 When the 99th customer arrived, Mr. Kang heard the boy say, "It's our turn, Grandma."

➡ _____

32 Mr. Kang welcomed them and served the woman a free bowl of Gukbap.

➡ _____

33 "Are you sure you're not hungry?" the woman asked the boy.

➡ _____

34 The boy chewed loudly on some Gimchi and said with a smile, "No, I'm not hungry, Grandma.

➡ _____

35 Don't worry about me. Happy birthday!"

➡ _____

※ 다음 괄호 안의 단어들을 우리말에 맞도록 바르게 배열하시오.

1 (100th / The / Customer)
➡ _____

2 (day, / one / elderly / an / walked / woman / into / restaurant. / a)
➡ _____

3 (was / she / her / with / grandson.)
➡ _____

4 (the / quietly, / asked / woman / Kang, / Mr. / owner / the / of / restaurant. / the)
➡ _____

5 (much / "how / a / is / bowl / Gukbap?" / of)
➡ _____

6 (4,000 / "it's / ma'am," / won, / Kang / Mr. / with / answered / smile. / a)
➡ _____

7 (was / she / poor / too / pay / to / two / bowls. / for)
➡ _____

8 (ordered / she / single / a / for / bowl / grandson. / her)
➡ _____

9 ("are / sure / you / are / you / not / Grandma?" / hungry, / boy / the / asked, / he / as / ate / hot / the / soup.)
➡ _____
_____

10 ("no, / not / I'm / hungry.)
➡ _____

11 (worry / don't / me." / about)
➡ _____

12 (picked / she / up / Gimchi / some / and / on / chewed / happily. / it)
➡ _____

13 (Kang / Mr. / them / watched / eat, / a / and / warm / came / feeling / him. / over)
➡ _____

14 (thought / he / a / up / plan / give / to / boy / the / free / a / meal.)
➡ _____

15 (the / when / woman / was / to / about / pay, / Kang / Mr. / his / waved / hands / said, / and / "no / ma'am. / need,)
➡ _____

16 (my / in / restaurant, / don't / you / pay / you're / if / 100th / the / of / customer / day." / the)
➡ _____

17 (woman / the / and / grandson / her / Mr. / thanked / Kang / left. / and)
➡ _____

1 백 번째 손님

2 어느 날 한 할머니가 식당으로 걸어 들어왔다.

3 그녀는 손자와 함께 있었다.

4 그녀는 조용히 식당 주인인 강 씨에게 물었다.

5 "국밥 한 그릇이 얼마인가요?"

6 "4,000원입니다. 할머니." 강 씨는 미소 지으며 답했다.

7 그녀는 너무 가난해서 두 그릇 값을 지불할 수 없었다.

8 그녀는 손자를 위해 한 그릇을 주문했다.

9 "정말 배고프지 않으세요, 할머니?" 남자아이는 따뜻한 국물을 먹으며 물었다.

10 "응. 난 배고프지 않단다.

11 내 걱정하지 마라."

12 그녀는 행복하게 김치를 집어서 먹었다.

13 강 씨는 그들이 먹는 것을 지켜보았고, 따뜻한 감정이 밀려왔다.

14 그는 남자아이에게 무료로 식사를 주기 위해 계획을 생각해 냈다.

15 할머니가 돈을 내려고 할 때, 강 씨는 손을 흔들며 말했다. "필요 없습니다. 할머니.

16 저희 식당에서는 그 날의 백 번째 손님이 되면 돈을 내지 않아도 됩니다."

17 할머니와 손자는 강 씨에게 감사해 하며 떠났다.

18 (month / a / later, / Kang / Mr. / the / saw / boy / the / in / street / the / outside / restaurant.)
➡ _____

19 (boy / the / was / stones. / gathering)
➡ _____

20 (are / "what / doing?" / you / Mr. / asked / Kang.)
➡ _____

21 ("I'm / the / counting / number / customers / of / enter / who / restaurant. / your)
➡ _____

22 (is / today / grandma's / my / birthday.")
➡ _____

23 (wants / 'he / be / to / 100th / the / customer / and / his / treat / grandmother / a / to / bowl / Gukbap!' / of / Kang / Mr. / to / said / himself.)
➡ _____

24 (Kang / Mr. / down. / looked)
➡ _____

25 (could / he / see / the / that / of / number / stones / not / was / yet / fifty. / even)
➡ _____

26 (had / he / do / to / to /something / help / boy / the / gather / stones. / 100)
➡ _____

27 (Kang / Mr. / back / went / the / into / restaurant / called / and / friends. / his)
➡ _____

28 (to / "come / restaurant / my / now / and / everyone / bring / who / with / works / you.)
➡ _____

29 (is / there / boy / a / who / your / needs / help.")
➡ _____

30 (began / people / arrive / to / the / at / restaurant.)
➡ _____

31 (when / 99th / the / arrived, / customer / Kang / Mr. / the / heard / boy / say, / "it's / our / Grandma." / turn,)
➡ _____

32 (Kang / Mr. / them / welcomed / and / the / served / woman / a / bowl / free / Gukbap. / of)
➡ _____

33 (you / "are / sure / not / you're / hungry?"/ woman / the / the / asked / boy.)
➡ _____

34 (boy / the / loudly / chewed / some / on / Gimchi / said / and / a / with / smile, / "no, / not / I'm / Grandma. / hungry)
➡ _____

35 (worry / don't / me. / about // birthday!" / happy)
➡ _____

18 한 달 후, 강 씨는 식당 밖 거리에서 그 남자아이를 보았다.

19 그 남자아이는 돌멩이를 모으고 있었다.

20 너 뭐 하고 있니?" 강 씨가 물었다.

21 "저는 아저씨 식당에 들어가는 손님들의 수를 세고 있어요.

22 오늘이 우리 할머니 생신이거든요.

23 '저 아이는 백 번째 손님이 되어서 할머니께 공짜 국밥 한 그릇을 대접하고 싶어 하는구나.' 강 씨는 혼잣말을 했다.

24 강 씨는 아래를 내려다보았다.

25 그는 돌멩이의 개수가 아직 오십 개도 안 되는 것을 볼 수 있었다.

26 그는 남자아이가 돌멩이 백 개를 모으는 것을 돕기 위해 무언가를 해야 했다.

27 강 씨는 식당으로 되돌아가 그의 친구들에게 전화했다.

28 "지금 내 식당으로 오고, 자네와 함께 일하는 모든 사람들을 데려와 주게.

29 자네 도움이 필요한 남자아이가 있어."

30 사람들이 식당에 도착하기 시작했다.

31 아흔아홉 번째 손님이 도착했을 때 강 씨는 남자아이가 "우리 차례예요, 할머니."라고 말하는 것을 들었다.

32 강 씨는 그들을 반기며 할머니께 공짜 국밥 한 그릇을 제공했다.

33 "너 정말 배고프지 않니?" 할머니가 남자아이에게 물었다.

34 남자아이는 큰 소리로 김치를 씹고 미소 지으며 말했다. "너전 배고프지 않아요, 할머니.

35 제 걱정 마세요. 생신 축하드려요!

※ 다음 우리말을 영어로 쓰시오.

1 백 번째 손님

➡ _____

2 어느 날 한 할머니가 식당으로 걸어 들어왔다.

➡ _____

3 그녀는 손자와 함께 있었다.

➡ _____

4 그녀는 조용히 식당 주인인 강 씨에게 물었다.

➡ _____

5 "국밥 한 그릇이 얼마인가요?"

➡ _____

6 "4,000원입니다, 할머니." 강 씨는 미소 지으며 답했다.

➡ _____

7 그녀는 너무 가난해서 두 그릇 값을 지불할 수 없었다.

➡ _____

8 그녀는 손자를 위해 한 그릇을 주문했다.

➡ _____

9 "정말 배고프지 않으세요, 할머니?" 남자아이는 따뜻한 국물을 먹으며 물었다.

➡ _____

10 "응, 난 배고프지 않단다.

➡ _____

11 내 걱정하지 마라."

➡ _____

12 그녀는 행복하게 김치를 집어서 먹었다.

➡ _____

13 강 씨는 그들이 먹는 것을 지켜보았고, 따뜻한 감정이 밀려왔다.

➡ _____

14 그는 남자아이에게 무료로 식사를 주기 위해 계획을 생각해 냈다.

➡ _____

15 할머니가 돈을 내려고 할 때, 강 씨는 손을 흔들며 말했다. "필요 없습니다, 할머니.

➡ _____

16 저희 식당에서는 그 날의 백 번째 손님이 되면 돈을 내지 않아도 됩니다."

➡ _____

17 할머니와 손자는 강 씨에게 감사해 하며 떠났다.

➡ _____

18 한 달 후, 강 씨는 식당 밖 거리에서 그 남자아이를 보았다.
➡ _____

19 그 남자아이는 돌멩이를 모으고 있었다.
➡ _____

20 "너 뭐 하고 있니?" 강 씨가 물었다.
➡ _____

21 "저는 아저씨 식당에 들어가는 손님들의 수를 세고 있어요.
➡ _____

22 오늘이 우리 할머니 생신이거든요."
➡ _____

23 '저 아이는 백 번째 손님이 되어서 할머니께 공짜 국밥 한 그릇을 대접하고 싶어 하는구나.' 강 씨는 혼잣말을 했다.
➡ _____

_____

24 강 씨는 아래를 내려다보았다.
➡ _____

25 그는 돌멩이의 개수가 아직 오십 개도 안 되는 것을 볼 수 있었다.
➡ _____

26 그는 남자아이가 돌멩이 백 개를 모으는 것을 돕기 위해 무언가를 해야 했다.
➡ _____

27 강 씨는 식당으로 되돌아가 그의 친구들에게 전화했다.
➡ _____

28 "지금 내 식당으로 오고, 자네와 함께 일하는 모든 사람들을 데려와 주게.
➡ _____

29 자네 도움이 필요한 남자아이가 있어."
➡ _____

30 사람들이 식당에 도착하기 시작했다.
➡ _____

31 아흔아홉 번째 손님이 도착했을 때 강 씨는 남자아이가 "우리 차례예요, 할머니."라고 말하는 것을 들었다.
➡ _____

32 강 씨는 그들을 반기며 할머니께 공짜 국밥 한 그릇을 제공했다.
➡ _____

33 "너 정말 배고프지 않니?" 할머니가 남자아이에게 물었다.
➡ _____

34 남자아이는 큰 소리로 김치를 씹고 미소 지으며 말했다. "네, 전 배고프지 않아요, 할머니.
➡ _____

35 제 걱정 마세요. 생신 축하드려요!"
➡ _____

MEMO

MEMO

영어 기출 문제집

적중100

2학기

정답 및 해설

시사 | 박준언

중 2

2학기

정답 및 해설

시사 | 박준언

중 2

Work on Your Dreams

시험대비 실력평가 p.08

01 ⑤ 02 ① 03 ③ 04 ②
05 ② 06 ① 07 ②

01 overcome: 극복하다 / 그는 인생에서 많은 어려움을 극복할 것입니다.

02 earn: 얻다, 획득하다 / 그녀는 많은 돈을 벌지는 못하지만 일을 즐긴다.

03 turn down: ~을 거절하다, 거부하다, 소리를 줄이다 / • 그녀는 그의 제안을 거절하기를 위해서, 그에게 'no'라고 말했다. • 소리 좀 줄여주시겠어요? 내가 공부에 집중할 수 없어요.

04 keep calm: 평온을 유지하다 / • 그는 심호흡을 하며 평온을 유지하려고 노력했다. keep 동명사: ~하는 것을 계속하다 / • 휘발유 값이 계속 올라간다면, 어떻게 해야 할지 모르겠어요.

05 although: 비록 ~일지라도 in spite of: ~에도 불구하고 / 재정상의 문제들에도 불구하고, 그는 새 차를 구입했다.

06 calm: 침착한 / 흥분, 화, 충격 또는 공포 같은 강한 감정에 의해 영향을 받지 않은

07 honor: 예우하다, ~을 공경하다 / 특히 상이나 타이틀을 주거나, 공적으로 칭찬함으로써 어떤 사람에게 존경이나 칭찬을 보여주다

서술형 시험대비 p.09

01 (a)fraid
02 at
03 (1) They became faster with practice.
    (2) I failed to follow the summer vacation plan.
    (3) I couldn't believe my eyes when I first saw that.
04 (1) talented (2) major (3) excellent (4) positive
05 (1) color line (2) baseman (3) (A)lthough
    (4) effort (5) ever

01 그 꼬마 사내아이는 너무 무서워서 많은 실수를 했다. / scared: 무서운

02 at bat: 타석에서 / 지금 타석에 있는 선수는 누구인가? be poor at: ~을 못하다 become good at: ~을 잘하게 되다 / 나는 수학을 정말 못해서 수학을 잘하고 싶어.

03 (1) with: ~함에 따라 (2) fail: 실패하다, ~하지 못하다 (3) cannot believe one's eyes: ~ 눈을 의심하다

04 (1) talented: 재능이 있는 / 그는 또한 재능 있는 예술가를 찾는 데 많은 시간을 보내고 있습니다. (2) major: 주요한 / 이것은 주요한 우려의 원인이다. (3) excellent: 뛰어난 / 그곳은 휴식을 취하기에 최적의 장소입니다. (4) positive: 긍정적인 / 당신은 긍정적인 사람인가요 아니면 부정적인 사람인가요?

05 (1) color line: 인종 차별 (2) baseman: (1·2·3) 루수 (3) although: 비록 ~일지라도 (4) effort: 노력 (5) ever: 언젠가, 한 번이라도

교과서 Conversation

핵심 Check p.10~11

1 It's important to be
2 (C) → (B) → (A)
3 It is important to practice a lot.
4 (B) → (C) → (A)
5 Could you explain about that?

교과서 대화문 익히기

Check(√) True or False p.12

1 T   2 T   3 F   4 T

교과서 확인학습 p.14~15

Listen & Speak 1 A

1. find, problem / too hard, I'm not good at math / It's important that, solve
2. looks / finish / draw, How, good / takes, important, as often as / keep practicing

Listen & Speak 1 B

1. hard to be, What / important, never / not forget
2. hard to / It's important that / will not

Listen & Talk 2 A

1. hard to do / how to / What do you mean by / mean
2. have, want to win / crossed / What do you mean by / means, luck

Listen & Talk 2 B

1. are , than / What, mean by / mean, together, than, alone
2. Practice / mean / mean, by doing, over

Conversation A

To achieve, failed, However, up / took, Finally, achieved, never give

Conversation B

look / achieve / What do you mean by that / fail auditions, give up / famous / more than / trying, practice / you never give up

시험대비 기본평가   p.16

01 ③   02 ①   03 ④

01 It's important that 주어 동사 ~: ~하는 것이 중요해 use: 사용하다 rule: 규칙 solve: 풀다, 해결하다

02 'I mean ~.(그것은 ~ 뜻이야.)'은 설명을 요청할 때의 대답이므로 설명을 요청하는 질문이 어울린다. What do you mean by that?: 그게 무슨 뜻이니?

03 노래 경연 대회에서 1등을 하고 싶다는 말에 (C) "keep my fingers crossed"한다고 말하니까 (B) "keep my fingers crossed"가 무슨 뜻인지 물어보고 (A) 행운을 빈다는 뜻이라고 대답한다. (D) 행운을 빌어줘 고맙다고 대답한다.

시험대비 실력평가   p.17~18

01 ②   02 ①   03 ④   04 ②
05 ②   06 ④   07 ⑤   08 ④
09 ③   10 ②
11 It is important that you never give up.

01 yours는 your poster를 의미한다. 너의 포스터를 다 끝냈는지 물어보는 질문에 'Not yet.(아직 못 끝냈어.)'이 어울리므로 ②가 적절하다

02 (A) 그림을 잘 그리기 위해서 자주 그림을 그리는 것이 중요하다고 했으므로 시간이 걸린다는 말이 적절하다. (B) keep 동명사: ~하는 것을 계속하다

03 여자아이는 그림을 잘 그리지 못하고, 그림을 잘 그리기를 원한다. 남자아이의 포스터는 멋져 보였고, 그림을 잘 그리기 위한 조언을 해 주는 것을 보아 남자아이는 잘 그리는 것으로 유추할 수 있다.

04 지호는 배우가 되고 싶지만, 항상 오디션에 떨어져서 포기를 하고 싶다는 말을 하고 있다.

05 ⓑ always fail

06 지호가 아닌 유명한 영화배우가 백 번 이상 오디션에서 떨어졌다.

07 Two heads are better than one: 두 개의 머리가 머리 하나보다 낫다(= 백지장도 맞들면 낫다)

08 'What do you mean by ~?(~이 무슨 뜻이니?)'는 Yes나 No로 대답할 수 없다.

09 계속 공부하는 것이 중요하다는 말에 음악을 끌 것이라고 대답하는 것은 어색하다.

10 What should I do?: 내가 무엇을 해야 할까? 훌륭한 댄서가 되기 위해 무엇을 해야 할지 묻자, 절대 포기하지 않는 것이 중요하다고 대답한다.

11 It's important that 주어 동사 ~: ~하는 것이 중요해. give up: 포기하다

서술형 시험대비   p.19

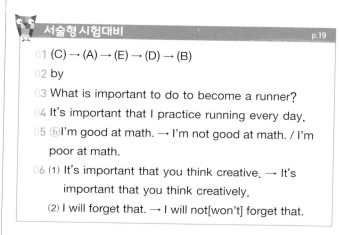

01 (C) → (A) → (E) → (D) → (B)
02 by
03 What is important to do to become a runner?
04 It's important that I practice running every day.
05 ⓑI'm good at math. → I'm not good at math. / I'm poor at math.
06 (1) It's important that you think creative. → It's important that you think creatively.
   (2) I will forget that. → I will not[won't] forget that.

01 포스터가 멋져 보인다는 말에 (C) 고맙다고 대답하며, 상대방도 포스터를 끝냈는지 물어본다. (A) 아직 안 끝냈다고 대답하고, 그림을 잘 그리지 못 한다며 어떻게 해야 그림을 잘 그릴 수 있는지 질문한다. (E) 가능한 한 자주 그리는 것이 중요하다는 말을 하자, (D) 계속 그리는 연습을 해야 한다는 의미인지 질문하고 (B) 맞다고 대답한다.

02 What do you mean by ~?: ~이 무슨 뜻이니?

03 important: 중요한 become: ~이 되다 'to become a runner'는 to부정사의 부사적 용법(목적, ~하기 위해)으로 사용하였다.

04 'It은 가주어 that절이 진주어로 사용되었다. practice는 동명사를 목적어로 받는다.

05 남자아이는 수학 문제의 정답을 찾지 못했고, 너무 어렵다고 말하고 있으므로, 수학을 잘하지 못한다는 말과 어울린다. be good at: ~을 잘하다

06 (1) 동사를 수식할 수 있는 것은 부사이므로 creative가 아니라 creatively를 사용해야 한다. (2) 영화를 만드는 것이 어렵다는 상대방에게 창의적으로 생각하는 것이 중요하다는 말을 했는데, 이에 'I will forget that.(그것을 잊을게.)'은 어색하다.

p.20~21

핵심 Check

1 (1) to live (2) to be (3) to think
2 (1) who (2) which

시험대비 기본평가

p.22

01 (1) bring → to bring (2) borrow → to borrow

  (3) which → who, whom 또는 that

  (4) who → which 또는 that

02 ⑤   03 ①

04 (1) to believe (2) to help (3) who(m)[that]

  (4) which[that]

01 (1), (2) 목적어와 목적격보어가 능동 관계일 때 tell과 ask의 목적격보어로 to부정사가 적절하다. (3) 선행사가 사람일 때 목적격 관계대명사로 which가 아니라 who, whom이나 that을 쓴다. (4) 선행사가 사물일 때 목적격 관계대명사로 who가 아니라 which나 that을 쓴다.

02 목적어와 목적격보어가 능동 관계일 때 advise의 목적격보어는 to부정사이다.

03 선행사가 사물일 때 목적격 관계대명사로 which나 that을 쓴다.

04 (1) 목적어와 목적격보어가 능동 관계일 때 expect의 목적격보어로 to부정사가 적절하다. (2) 목적어와 목적격보어가 능동 관계일 때 encourage의 목적격보어로 to부정사가 적절하다. (3) 선행사가 사람일 때 목적격 관계대명사로 who, whom이나 that을 쓴다. (4) 선행사가 사물일 때 목적격 관계대명사로 which나 that을 쓴다.

시험대비 실력평가

p.23~25

01 ⑤   02 ②   03 ③   04 ④

05 ③

06 (1) that (2) which (3) which (4) play (5) warned

07 ④   08 ①   09 ④   10 ①

11 (1) to spend (2) to keep (3) (to) carry (4) finish

  (5) to assemble   12 ③

13 (1) Sophie asked her dad to help her to finish her homework.

  (2) Mom wanted Lily to come home by 8.

  (3) She invited me to go to New York with her.

  (4) The blue watch is the gift which[that] I bought there for my brother.

(5) The man who[whom/that] my mother is talking to is my art teacher.

(6) The girl and her cat that I met this morning were playing in the park.

14 ⑤   15 (1) who (2) that (3) which is

16 ①   17 ⑤

01 목적어와 목적격보어가 능동 관계일 때 tell은 목적격보어로 to부정사가 나온다.

02 <보기>와 나머지는 목적격 관계대명사이지만, ②번은 주격 관계대명사이다.

03 모두 주격이나 목적격으로 사용된 관계대명사 that이 들어갈 수 있지만 ③번은 소유격 관계대명사 whose가 들어가야 한다.

04 enable은 목적격보어로 to부정사가 나온다.

05 want는 목적격보어로 동사원형이 아니라 to부정사가 나온다. to lend가 되어야 한다.

06 (1) 선행사가 사람이므로 that, (2) 선행사가 사물이므로 which, (3) 전치사 about이 있으므로 that은 쓸 수 없다. (4) 'help'는 목적격보어로 원형부정사와 to부정사 둘 다 취할 수 있다. (5) to부정사를 목적격보어로 쓸 수 있는 것은 warn이다. hope는 5형식으로 쓰이지 않는다.

07 관계대명사의 선행사가 사람이면 who, whom이나 that을 쓰고 사물이면 which나 that을 쓴다. ② This is the house in which she lives. 또는 This is the house which[that] she lives in.

08 빈칸에는 to부정사를 목적격보어로 취할 수 있는 동사가 들어가야 한다. watch는 목적격보어로 동사원형이나 현재분사가 나와야 한다.

09 She allowed me to eat ice cream for dessert.

10 ①번은 접속사이지만 나머지는 모두 관계대명사이다.

11 (1), (2), (5) ask, encourage, request는 to부정사를 목적격보어로 취하는 동사이다. (3) help는 to부정사나 동사원형을 쓸 수 있다. (4) have는 사역동사로 목적격보어로 원형부정사를 쓴다.

12 warn은 목적격보어로 to부정사를 쓴다.

13 (1), (2), (3) ask, want, invite는 모두 목적격보어로 to부정사가 나와야 한다. (4) 선행사가 사물일 때 목적격 관계대명사로 who가 아니라 which나 that을 쓴다. (5) 선행사가 사람일 때 목적격 관계대명사로 which가 아니라 who, whom이나 that을 쓴다. (6) 선행사가 '사람+동물'일 경우 목적격 관계대명사로 that을 쓴다.

14 feel은 지각동사로 동사원형이나 현재분사를 목적격보어로 취한다. 나머지는 모두 to부정사를 목적격보어로 취하는 동사들로 부정사의 형태가 들어가야 한다.

15 목적격 관계대명사와 '주격 관계대명사+be동사'는 생략할 수 있다.

16 cause, force, warn, want, ask는 모두 목적격보어로 to부정사를 취하는 동사이다. The heavy rain caused the river to

overflow.

17 관계대명사 that은 전치사 다음에는 쓰지 않는다. 또한 목적격 관계대명사는 생략될 수 있다.

01 (1) I want you to be happy.
  (2) Jack asked his mother to wake him up at 8 o'clock.
  (3) Tina told me to find a quiet place to study.
  (4) Jessy got her dad to drop her off at the bus stop.
  (5) His teacher advised him not to spend all his time on one subject.

02 (1) The man who[whom/that] you met on Sunday is my brother.
  (2) That is the computer which[that] I bought last week.
  (3) This is the cake which[that] was made by Ann.
  (4) I visited the church which[that] I took some pictures of. 또는 I visited the church of which I took some pictures.
  (5) It is an experience which[that] I look forward to. 또는 It is an experience to which I look forward.
  (6) Does Eddie have any friends who[whom/that] he can depend on? 또는 Does Eddie have any friends on whom he can depend?

03 (1) to bring (2) take (3) burning

04 (1) This is the bridge which[that] my father built.
  (2) They are the people who[whom/that] I met in the plane.
  (3) I like the new computer that I bought last week.
  (4) Can you tell me about the church of which you took the picture last weekend? 또는 Can you tell me about the church (which/that) you took the picture of last weekend?

05 (1) to come (2) to be (3) not to give up

06 (1) I bought a book.
  (2) I invited her to the party.
  (3) I need to do them[three things] to achieve my dream.
  (4) Is the novel fun?

07 (1) She asked you to clean her room.
  (2) Mom[My mom] expects me to take care of the puppy.
  (3) The people who(m)[that] we met were very

nice.
  (4) The bag (which/that) I bought yesterday is blue.

01 (1) want는 that절을 목적어로 하는 3형식으로 쓰이지 않으며 목적어와 목적격보어가 능동 관계일 때 목적격보어로 to부정사가 나와야 한다. (2) ask, (3) tell, (4) get (5) advise 등의 동사도 목적어와 목적격보어가 능동 관계일 때 목적격보어로 to부정사가 나와야 한다. 또한 to부정사의 부정형은 'not to 동사원형'으로 쓴다.

02 목적격 관계대명사는 수식하는 선행사가 사람이면 who나 whom, that을, 사람이나 동물이면 which나 that을 쓴다. 일반적으로 목적격 관계대명사는 생략될 수 있다. 목적격 관계대명사가 전치사의 목적어인 경우 전치사는 관계대명사절의 끝에 오거나 관계대명사 앞에 올 수 있다. 전치사가 관계대명사절의 끝에 올 경우에는 관계대명사를 생략할 수 있다. 전치사가 관계대명사 앞에 올 경우에는 관계대명사 that을 쓸 수 없으며, 관계대명사를 생략하지 않는다.

03 목적어와 목적격보어가 능동 관계일 때 (1) would like는 목적격보어로 to부정사를 쓴다. (2) make는 사역동사로 목적격보어로 원형부정사를 쓴다. (3) smell은 목적격보어로 현재분사를 쓴다.

04 (1) 선행사가 사물이므로 which나 that, (2) 선행사가 사람이므로 who, whom이나 that, (3) 관계대명사가 접속사와 대명사의 역할을 하므로 목적어로 쓰인 it을 삭제해야 한다. (4) 전치사가 관계대명사 앞에 올 경우에는 관계대명사 that을 쓸 수 없으며, 관계대명사를 생략하지 않는다.

05 (1) tell (2) order (3) encourage 모두 목적격보어로 to부정사를 쓴다.

06 목적격 관계대명사는 선행사가 사람이면 who나 whom, that, 사물이나 동물이면 which나 that을 쓰고 관계대명사절에서 목적어 역할을 한다.

07 (1), (2) ask와 expect의 목적격보어로 to부정사를 쓴다. (3), (4) 선행사가 사람이면 who, whom이나 that, 사물이나 동물이면 which나 that을 쓴다.

교과서
Reading

확인문제   p.28

1 T 2 F 3 T 4 F 5 T 6 F

1 T   2 F   3 T   4 F   5 T   6 F

교과서 확인학습 A   p.30~31

01 Breaks the Color Line

02 on April 15, 1947

03 as, for   04 couldn't believe

05 the first African American player

06 the color line was broken

07 faced many difficulties

08 Although, to play with him

09 turned the team down

10 was at bat   11 thought to himself

12 who people like

13 there will be more

14 put, into

15 With practice, batting, base running

16 moved

17 one of his teammates, tapped him on the

18 Do not listen to   19 fine

20 to play   21 earned the respect

22 Thanks to   23 recognized, presented, with

24 asked, to join

25 uniform number

26 no longer, to honor him

27 however, wore   28 is called

교과서 확인학습 B   p.32~33

1 Jackie Robinson Breaks the Color Line

2 It was New York City on April 15, 1947.

3 Jackie Robinson, an African American, went on the field as second baseman for the Brooklyn Dodgers.

4 People couldn't believe their eyes.

5 He was the first African American player to play on a Major League team.

6 That day, the color line was broken.

7 Robinson faced many difficulties.

8 Although Robinson was a talented player and a gentle person, his teammates did not want to play with him.

9 Every hotel turned the team down because Robinson was on the team.

10 When he was at bat, people in the stands rudely

shouted at him.

11 Robinson thought to himself, 'I need to keep calm and focus on baseball.

12 I will try and become a player who people like.

13 Then, next season, there will be more African American players in the league.'

14 Robinson put all his time and energy into baseball.

15 With practice, he became great at batting and base running.

16 Robinson's effort moved his teammates.

17 When people shouted at Robinson, one of his teammates walked up to Robinson and tapped him on the shoulder.

18 "Do not listen to them.

19 You're doing fine," he said.

20 His support helped Robinson to play harder.

21 Finally, Robinson earned the respect of other players and fans.

22 Thanks to Robinson, the Dodgers won the National League Championship in 1947.

23 The league recognized Robinson's excellence and presented him with the Rookie of the Year Award in the same year.

24 After that season, other teams asked African American players to join them.

25 Robinson's uniform number was 42.

26 Baseball players in Major League teams no longer wear the number 42 to honor him.

27 Every year, however, on April 15, every player wears the number that Robinson wore.

28 The day is called "Jackie Robinson Day."

시험대비 실력평가   p.34~37

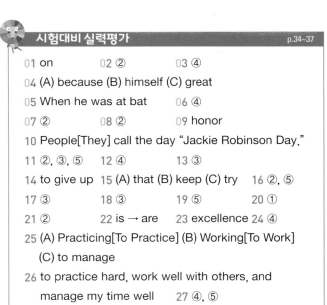

01 on   02 ②   03 ④

04 (A) because (B) himself (C) great

05 When he was at bat   06 ④

07 ②   08 ②   09 honor

10 People[They] call the day "Jackie Robinson Day."

11 ②, ③, ⑤   12 ④   13 ③

14 to give up   15 (A) that (B) keep (C) try   16 ②, ⑤

17 ③   18 ③   19 ⑤   20 ①

21 ②   22 is → are   23 excellence 24 ④

25 (A) Practicing[To Practice] (B) Working[To Work] (C) to manage

26 to practice hard, work well with others, and manage my time well   27 ④, ⑤

01 (A) 날짜 앞에 on을 쓰는 것이 적절하다. (B) '소속'을 나타내는 on을 쓰는 것이 적절하다.

02 ⓐ와 ②번: (전치사) '~로(서)'라는 뜻으로 자격을 나타낸다. ① (접속사) [상태] …인 대로, …인 채로, ③ (접속사) [비례] …함에 따라, …할수록, ④ (접속사) [이유] …이므로, …이기 때문에, ⑤ (접속사) 때

03 ④ 가족 관계는 알 수 없다. ① 아프리카계, ② 미국, ③ 2루수, ⑤ 브루클린 다저스

04 (A) 뒤에 절(주어+동사)이 나오므로 because가 적절하다. because of+구, (B) Robinson은 '마음속으로 생각했다'고 해야 하므로 himself가 적절하다. think to oneself: 조용히 생각하다, 마음속으로 생각하다, (C) become의 보어로 형용사를 써야 하므로 great가 적절하다.

05 at bat: 타석에 서서

06 ④ Robinson의 노력 덕분에 몇 명의 아프리카계 미국인들이 메이저리그 팀에서 경기할 수 있었는지는 대답할 수 없다. ① Yes, he did. ② Because Robinson was on the team. ③ No, they didn't. ⑤ With practice, he became great at batting and base running.

07 ② 앞에 나오는 내용과 상반되는 내용이 뒤에 이어지므로 however가 가장 적절하다. ① 그러므로, ④ 사실은, ⑤ 게다가

08 ⓐ와 ①, ⑤: 부사적 용법 ② 명사적 용법 ③, ④ 형용사적 용법

09 메이저리그 팀의 야구 선수들은 Robinson에 대한 '존경을 보여 주기 위해' 더 이상 42번을 달지 않는다.

10 People[They]을 주어로 해서 고치는 것이 적절하다.

11 선행사가 사람이고 목적어 자리이므로, 목적격 관계대명사 who, whom, that을 쓰는 것이 적절하다.

12 ④ 연습이 완벽하게 만들어 준다. ① 늦어도 안 하는 것보다 낫다. ② 제때의 바늘 한 뜸이 아홉 번의 수고를 던다. (때를 놓치지 않고 신속하게 행동해야 생길 수 있는 문제를 예방할 수 있다.) ③ 남에게 받고 싶은 대로 남에게 해 주어라. ⑤ 뛰기 전에 살펴봐라. (신중하게 행동하라.)

13 Robinson은 '자신이 노력해서 사람들이 좋아하는 선수가 되면, 다음 시즌에는 아프리카계 미국인 선수가 리그에 더 많이 생길 것'이라고 마음속으로 생각했다.

14 꿈을 성취하기 위해 필요한 세 가지인 to be healthy, to be creative, and never to give up 중에서 세 번째인 never to give up을 쓰는 것이 적절하다. tell + 목적어 + to부정사

15 (A) 선행사가 있기 때문에 that이 적절하다. (B) 'help+목적어+to부정사 또는 원형부정사'이므로 keep이 적절하다. (C) 'make+목적어+원형부정사'이므로 try가 적절하다.

16 ② '남들과 잘 일하기'와 ⑤ '남들은 도우기'는 디자이너의 꿈을 성취하기 위해 필요한 요소에 속하지 않는다.

17 so as to 동사원형 = in order to 동사원형 = in order that 주어 can = so that 주어 can: ~하기 위하여

18 ⓐ와 ③번: 감동시켰다, ① (몸을) 움직였다, ② 바꿨다, ④ 이사했다, ⑤ 옳겼다

19 ⑤는 Robinson의 팀 동료 중 한 명을 가리키고, 나머지는 다 Robinson을 가리킨다.

20 ① 마지막으로, 끝으로(무엇을 열거하면서 마지막 요소 앞에 붙이는 말), ⓐ와 나머지: 마침내

21 ⓐ와 ②번: 의지(명사), ①, ④: …일[할] 것이다(조동사), ③ 무엇을 해 달라는 부탁을 할 때 씀. ⑤ 유언장(명사)

22 주어가 being, working, and being이므로 are로 고치는 것이 적절하다.

23 소유격 다음이므로 명사를 쓰는 것이 적절하다. excellence: 우수, 탁월, 뛰어남

24 주어진 문장의 His support에 주목한다. ④번 앞 문장의 내용을 받고 있으므로 ④번이 적절하다.

25 꿈을 성취하기 위해 필요한 세 가지인 to practice hard, to work well with others, and to manage my time well을 알맞은 형태로 쓰는 것이 적절하다. (A)와 (B)는 주어, (C)는 tell+목적어+to부정사

26 꿈을 성취하기 위해 필요한 세 가지인 to practice hard, to work well with others, and to manage my time well을 가리킨다.

27 ⓑ와 ④, ⑤번: 가목적어, ①, ②, ③: 가주어

서술형 시험대비 p.38~39

01 color line

02 April fifteen(th), nineteen forty-seven

03 African American player

04 to join

05 to

06 other teams

07 He won it in 1947.

08 talented

09 Every hotel turned the team down 또는 Every hotel turned down the team

10 (A) gentle (B) difficulties

11 Robinson's teammates were moved by his effort. 또는 His teammates were moved by Robinson's effort.

12 people

13 (A) teammates (B) shouted at

14 Robinson earned the respect of other players and fans.

15 (A) batting (B) base running

16 thought to himself

17 I will try and become a player people like.

01 a color line: 인종 차별, (정치적·사회적) 흑인과 백인의 차별, 흑인들이 백인과 함께 다양한 활동에 참여하는 것을 막는 장벽

02 날짜는 서수로 읽는 것이 원칙이지만 기수로도 읽는다. 그리고

7

April the fifteenth도 가능하다(보통 April 15th, 1947로 표기된 경우).

03 come out into the field: 출전하다, 그 이전에 메이저리그 팀에서 경기한 '아프리카계 미국인 선수'가 없었기 때문이다. (그는 메이저리그 팀에서 경기한 최초의 아프리카계 미국인 선수였다.)

04 ask+목적어+to부정사

05 present A with B = present B to A: A에게 B를 수여하다

06 '다른 팀들'을 가리킨다.

07 그는 1947년에 신인상을 수여했다.

08 talented = gifted: 재능이 있는

09 이어동사 turned down의 목적어인 'the team'을 turned down 사이에 써도 되고 뒤에 써도 된다.

10 그의 재능과 '온화한' 성격에도 불구하고, Robinson은 많은 '어려움'을 경험했다. 예를 들면, 그의 팀원들은 그와 함께 경기하기를 원하지 않았다. in spite of: ~에도 불구하고, personality: 성격

11 Robinson's teammates[his teammates]를 주어로 해서 고치는 것이 적절하다.

12 '사람들'을 가리킨다.

13 Robinson의 '팀 동료' 중 한 명이 Robinson에게 다가가 어깨를 두드리고, "너는 잘하고 있어."라고 덧붙이면서 그에게 소리치고 있는 사람들 말을 듣지 말라고 말했다.

14 earn the respect: 존경을 얻다

15 전치사 'at'의 목적어로 동명사 'batting'과 'base running'을 쓰는 것이 적절하다.

16 think to oneself: 조용히 생각하다, 마음속으로 생각하다

17 목적격 관계대명사 'whom' 대신에 쓰인 'who'를 생략할 수 있다.

영역별 핵심문제
p.41~45

01 ③	02 ④	03 (F)inally	04 ④
05 ⑤	06 ④	07 ①	08 by
09 ③	10 ②	11 ②	12 ②

13 (1) The computer (which/that) my parents bought for me is broken.
  (2) The man and his dog that I took a picture of won the first prize.
  (3) The man (who/whom/that) you met on Sunday is my brother.
  (4) His family wanted him to take part in the swimming competition.
  (5) She invited me to go to Paris with her.
  (6) I told him not to make a noise.

| 14 ⑤ | 15 ④ | 16 ③ | 17 ⑤ |

18 (1) He asked me to take him to the hospital.
  (2) Did you hear her go[going] out?
  (3) I can't forget the woman who[whom/that] I met in Rome.

19 ①, ④, ⑤
20 (A) Jackie Robinson (B) color line
21 ② 22 ② 23 ④
24 ①
25 other teams asked African American players to join them
26 ② 27 ⓐ wears ⓑ wore
28 want to wear → no longer wear

01 give up: 포기하다 / 그들은 1점도 득점하지 못하고 경기를 포기했어요. thanks to: ~ 덕분에 / 당신 덕분에, 나는 많은 좋은 사람들을 만났다.

02 present A with B: A에게 B를 수여하다 / 그들은 그에게 훌륭한 시민상을 수여할 것이다.

03 finally: 마침내 / 결국, 우리 모두는 부활절 콘서트를 조직하기로 결정했다.

04 earn the respect: 존경을 얻다 / 존경을 얻기 위한 방법들 중 하나는 사회를 위한 책임감을 보여주는 것이다.

05 'keep my fingers crossed'는 행운을 빈다는 뜻이다.

06 ① 여자아이는 "keep my fingers crossed"의 뜻을 알고 있는가? ② 남자아이는 경연 대회에서 무엇을 원하는가? ③ 남자 아이는 어떤 종류의 대회에 나갈 것인가? ④ 어디서 노래 경연 대회가 열리는가? ⑤ 언제 노래 경연 대회가 있는가?

07 반복해서 무언가를 하면 배우게 된다는 뜻을 가진 말은 'Practice makes perfect.(연습이 완벽함을 만든다.)'이다.

08 What do you mean by ~?: ~가 무슨 뜻이니? by 동사-ing: ~함으로써

09 주어진 문장은 어떻게 하면 그림을 잘 그릴 수 있는지 묻는 질문이다. 이 질문에 대한 대답으로 그림을 잘 그릴 수 있도록 하는 조언이 어울린다. 여기서는 시간이 많이 걸리고 자주 그림을 그리라고 조언했다.

10 뒤에 나오는 You mean I should keep practicing?과 어울리는 것은 가능한 한 자주 그림을 그리라는 것이다.

11 ② 이외의 보기들은 설명을 요청할 때 사용하는 표현들이다.

12 take: (얼마의 시간이) 걸리다 achieve: 이루다, 달성하다 Rome was not built in a day.: 로마는 하루아침에 이루어지지 않았다.(= 무언가를 이루는 데는 시간이 걸린다.)

13 (1) 선행사가 사물일 때 목적격 관계대명사로 which나 that을 쓰며, 생략할 수 있다. (2) 선행사가 '사람+동물'일 때 목적격 관계대명사로 that을 쓰며, 생략할 수 있다. (3) 선행사가 사람일 때 목적격 관계대명사로 who, whom이나 that을 쓴다. (4), (5), (6) want, tell, invite는 목적격보어로 to부정사가 나온다. to부정사의 부정형은 'not to 동사원형'으로 쓴다.

14 ⑤ The bag (which/that) I bought yesterday was sent

to Wendy.

15 ① I didn't expect him to talk to you. ② They asked John to do something for them. ③ Mom wanted Sam to finish his homework. ⑤ His doctor ordered Simon to take some rest.

16 ③번은 주격 관계대명사이고 나머지는 모두 목적격 관계대명사 이다.

17 ⓐ to not → not to ⓑ live → to live ⓒ to go → go ⓕ which → who ⓖ it → 삭제

18 (1) ask의 목적격 보어로 to부정사가 나와야 한다. (2) 지각동사 hear의 목적격 보어로 동사원형이나 현재분사가 나와야 한다. (3) 선행사가 사람이므로 목적격 관계대명사로 who나 whom 또는 that을 쓴다.

19 ⓐ와 ②, ③: 형용사적 용법, ①, ⑤: 부사적 용법, ④ 명사적 용법, a major leaguer: 메이저 리그 선수

20 1947년 4월 15일, 'Jackie Robinson'이 브루클린 다저스의 2 루수로 경기장에 나갔을 때, '인종 차별'이 깨졌다.

21 'Robinson은 재능 있는 선수이고 온화한 사람이었지만 그의 팀원들은 그와 함께 경기하길 원하지 않았다.'고 해야 하므로 'Although'를 쓰는 것이 적절하다.

22 ②번 다음 문장의 Then에 주목한다. 주어진 문장의 내용을 받 고 있으므로 ②번이 적절하다.

23 ④ diligent: 근면한, 성실한, Robinson은 자신의 모든 시간과 에너지를 야구에 집중했고, 연습을 함으로써 타격과 주루를 잘 하게 되었다고 했으므로 성격이 '성실하다'고 하는 것이 적절하 다. ① 호기심 많은, ② 외향적인, ③ 사교적인, ⑤ 창의적인

24 ⓐ 정관사가 다른 사람의 신체의 일부를 나타내는 명사 앞에서 소유격 대명사를 대신한 구문이고, tap이나 pat과 같이 '두드 리다'는 뜻일 때는 전치사 'on'을 사용하는 것이 적절하다. ⓑ present A with B = present B to A: A에게 B를 수여[제공] 하다

25 'to'를 보충하면 된다. ask+목적어+to부정사

26 이 글은 Robinson이 자신의 노력을 통해 사람들의 인정을 얻 었다는 내용의 글이다.

27 ⓐ every는 단수로 취급하므로 wears, ⓑ Robinson이 예전 에 42번을 달았던 것이므로 wore

28 메이저리그 팀의 야구 선수들은 그에 대한 존경을 보여 주기 위해 '더 이상' 42번을 '달지 않는다.'

🐾 단원별 예상문제   p.46~49

01 ④   02 ⑤   03 ③   4 ①
05 ③   6 ②, ⑤
07 it's important that you choose the right books to read.
08 ①   09 ③   10 achieved
11 It's important that you never give up.
12 (C) → (A) → (B)   13 ②   14 ③

15 ④   16 ③   17 African American
18 April 15, 1947   19 ②   20 ④
21 refused(rejected)   22 ②
23 touched
24 ④   25 ①, ③, ⑤   26 ①, ③, ④

01 ④번은 동사와 명사의 관계이고 나머지 보기는 형용사와 명 사의 관계이다. ① different: 다른 difference: 다름, 차이 ② important: 중요한 importance: 중요성 ③ silent: 조용 한 silence: 침묵 ④ allow: 허락하다 allowance: 허용 ⑤ excellent: 우수한 excellence: 우수, 장점

02 face: 직면하다, 직시하다 / 나는 그들이 많은 문제들에 직면해 있다는 것을 압니다.

03 think to oneself: 마음속으로 생각하다

04 win first place: 1등을 하다, 우승하다 / 그녀는 수영대회에서 1등을 했다. award: 상 win an award: 상을 타다 / 그녀는 최 고의 여배우 상을 받았다.

05 이것을 하기 어렵다는 말에 (C) 무슨 일인지 물어보자 (A) 쿠 키를 만드는 방법을 가르쳐 줄 수 있는지 물었다. (B) 물론이라 고 대답하며, 그것이 'a walk in the park'라고 말한다. (D) 'a walk in the park'가 무슨 뜻인지 물어보자 그것은 하기 쉽다 는 뜻이라고 대답한다.

06 ⓑ never stop ⓔ how

07 It's important that 주어 동사 ~: ~하는 것이 중요하다 choose: 고르다

08 ⓐ to win ⓑ keep ⓒ crossed ⓓ mean ⓔ It means

09 빈칸 (A)의 앞, 뒤의 말이 역접의 관계이므로('많은 오디션에 갔 지만 자주 떨어졌다'와 '나는 절대 포기하지 않았다.') 그러므로 However(하지만)가 어울린다.

10 achieve: 이루다, 달성하다 achieve a goal: 목표를 달성하다

11 It's important that 주어 동사 ~: ~하는 것이 중요하다 give up: 포기하다

12 (C) 훌륭한 댄서가 되는 것이 어렵다고 말하면서 무엇을 해야 하는지 상대방에게 질문했다. (A) 절대로 포기하지 않는 것이 중요하다고 말하자, (B) 알았다고 잊지 않겠다고 대답한다.

13 ① Her parents were worried and asked her to stop surfing. ③ Mr. Johnson told us to shake hands after the game. ④ His parents encouraged him to have an interest in art. ⑤ I didn't expect you to understand me at all.

14 ③번은 목적격 관계대명사가 생략된 것이므로 it이 없어야 한다.

15 선행사가 사물일 때 목적격 관계대명사로 which나 that을 쓴다.

16 ③ 인종 차별이 '깨졌다'고 해야 하므로, break를 과거 수동태로 쓰 는 것이 적절하다.

17 African American: 아프리카계 미국인

18 '1947년 4월 15일'을 가리킨다.

9

ⓐ face: 직면하다, ② encounter: 만나다, 마주치다, ① express: 표현하다, ③ accept: 수락하다, 받아들이다, ④ look into: ~을 조사하다, ⑤ solve: 해결하다

20 ④ 부사적 용법, ⓑ와 나머지: 명사적 용법

21 turn down = refuse = reject: 거절하다

22 이 글은 'Robinson이 자신의 노력을 통해 사람들의 인정을 얻었다'는 내용의 글이므로, 제목으로는 'Robinson의 노력이 결실을 맺었다'가 적절하다. bear fruit: 결실을 맺다

23 move = touch: 감동시키다

24 ④ Thanks to Robinson, the Dodgers won the National League Championship in 1947.

25 no longer = no more = not ~ any longer = not ~ any more: 더 이상 ~ 않다

26 ⓑ와 ①, ③, ④번: 관계대명사, ②, ⑤: 접속사

서술형 실전문제　　　　　　　p.50~51

01 I mean[It means] working together is better than working alone.

02 ⓑIt's too easy for me. → It's too hard[difficult]] for me.

03 It's important that you use this math rule to solve the problem.

04 I mean you learn something by doing it over and over.

05 (1) The Korean dishes which[that] we had last night tasted yummy.
　　(2) I have a dog with which I take a walk every night. 또는 I have a dog which[that] I take a walk with every night.

06 (1) not to go out alone at night
　　(2) to win first prize at the singing contest

07 (1) 그의 팀원들은 그와 함께 경기하기를 원하지 않았다.
　　(2) Robinson이 팀에 있었기 때문에 모든 호텔에서 그 팀을 거절했다.
　　(3) 그가 타석에 있을 때, 관중석에 있는 사람들이 그에게 무례 하게 소리치기도 했다.

08 (A) down (B) rudely (C) calm

09 I try and become a player who people like

10 playing → (to) play

11 (1) Robinson 덕분에 다저스는 1947년에 내셔널리그 챔피언십에서 우승하게 되었다.
　　(2) 리그에서는 Robinson의 탁월함을 인정했고, 같은 해에 그에게 신인상을 수여했다.

12 to win

---

01 설명을 할 때는 '~을 의미하다'의 뜻을 가진 'mean'을 사용해 'It means ~.'나 'I mean ~.'으로 대답할 수 있다. better than: ~보다 나은

02 ⓑ의 수학 문제가 너무 쉽다는 말과 ⓒ의 수학을 못한다는 말은 반대의 말이므로 어색하다. 여자아이가 수학 문제에 대한 조언을 해 주고 있으므로, 수학이 어렵다는 말이 어울린다.

03 It's important that 주어 동사 ~: ~하는 것이 중요하다 use: 사용하다 solve: 풀다, 해결하다

04 by 동사ing: ~함으로써 over and over: 반복해서

05 목적격 관계대명사는 수식하는 선행사가 사람이면 who나 whom, that을, 사람이 아니면 which나 that을 쓴다. 일반적으로 목적격 관계대명사는 생략될 수 있다. 목적격 관계대명사가 전치사의 목적어인 경우 전치사는 관계대명사절의 끝에 오거나 관계대명사 앞에 올 수 있다. 전치사가 관계대명사절의 끝에 올 경우에는 관계대명사를 생략할 수 있다. 전치사가 관계대명사 앞에 올 경우에는 관계대명사 that을 쓸 수 없으며, 관계대명사를 생략하지 않는다.

06 order와 expect는 목적어와 목적격보어가 능동 관계일 때 목적격보어로 to부정사를 쓴다.

07 뒤에 이어지는 내용을 쓰는 것이 적절하다.

08 (A) 'Robinson이 팀에 있었기 때문에 모든 호텔에서 그 팀을 거절했다.'고 해야 하므로 down이 적절하다. turn down: ~을 거절하다, 거부하다, turn up: 나타나다, (B) 동사 shouted를 수식하므로 부사 rudely가 적절하다. (C) keep의 보어이므로 형용사 calm이 적절하다.

09 때나 조건을 나타내는 부사절에서는 현재시제가 미래를 대신한다.

10 help+목적어+to부정사 또는 원형부정사

11 두 번째 단락의 내용을 쓰면 된다.

12 Robinson의 노력이 다저스가 1947년에 내셔널리그 챔피언십에서 우승하도록 해주었다.

창의사고력 서술형 문제　　　　　　　p.52

|모범답안|

01 I think music helps me to study better. /
It's important to focus when you study. /
I'll turn down the music.

02 (1) I expect Mina to get good grades.
　　(2) I expect Luke to do exercise regularly.
　　(3) I expect my mom to be healthy. / I expect my dad to stop smoking.

03 (A) to practice hard (B) cook well and easily
　　(C) to work at a restaurant
　　(D) make food in time to serve

---

01 help+목적어+(to)동사원형: (목적어)가 ~하는 것을 돕다 It's important that 주어 동사 ~: ~하는 것이 중요해 focus: 집중하다 turn down: 소리를 줄이다

01 ①   02 ①

03 (1) difficulties (2) excellence

04 support   05 ②

06 I mean[It means] you can achieve your dream with a strong will.

07 (C) → (A) → (D) → (B)   08 ④   09 ③

10 ③   11 He failed more than 100 auditions.

12 give up

13 (1) She is the girl who[whom/that] I love.

   (2) Have you ever fallen in love with a lady to whom you haven't even talked? 또는 Have you ever fallen in love with a lady who[whom/that] you haven't even talked to?

14 (1) to do (2) to go (3) to insist (4) not to be

15 ⑤   16 ②

17 (1) drank → to drink (2) trying → to try

   (3) stay → to stay (4) who → which[that]

18 but   19 ⑤번 → at   20 ③

21 take part in 또는 participate in   22 ①

23 ⑤   24 ③, ⑤   25 42

---

01 shout at: ~을 향해 외치다 / 너는 왜 항상 나에게 소리를 지르니?

02 earn the respect: 존경을 얻다 / 그녀는 의사로서 환자들의 존경을 얻었다. give up: 포기하다 pursue: 추구하다 / 당신이 꿈을 갖고 있다면, 절대 포기하지 말고 당신의 열정을 추구하세요.

03 (1) difficult: 어려운 difficulty: 어려움, 곤경, 장애 (2) excellent: 뛰어난 excellence: 우수, 탁월, 뛰어남

04 support: 지지 / 어려움을 겪고 있는 사람에게 주는 도움과 친절 / 나는 그의 도움과 지지가 필요하다.

05 대화의 will은 '의지'의 뜻이다. ② ~할 것이다 / 그는 보고서를 즉시 끝낼 것이다. ① 그 결정은 그녀의 자유 의지로 되었다. ③ 의지가 강할수록 더 많이 배울 것이다. ④ 사람은 의지의 자유가 있다. ⑤ 의지가 있는 곳에 길이 있습니다.

06 achieve: 이루다, 달성하다 will: 의지

07 A가 자신을 "The Wizard of Goyang"으로 불러달라고 하자 B가 그것이 무슨 뜻인지 물어본다. (C) "The Wizard of Goyang"의 뜻이 자신이 발명가가 되고 싶다는 의미라고 설명한다. (A) 상대방에게 발명가가 되기 위해서는 무엇이 중요한지 질문하자 (D) 창의적으로 생각하는 것이 중요하다고 말하고 (B) 상대방이 성공할 것을 확신한다고 대답한다.

08 주어진 문장은 '하지만, 읽을 알맞은 책을 고르는 것이 중요하다.'란 의미이다. ④번 다음 문장에서 책을 고르는 법을 언급하고 있으므로 ④번이 적절하다. It's important that 주어 동사 ~: ~하는 것이 중요하다 right: 올바른, 알맞은

09 하나가 지호에게 무슨 일인지 묻는 질문에 꿈을 이룰 수 없을 것

10 What do you mean by ~?: ~가 무슨 뜻이니?

11 fail: 실패하다, ~하지 못하다 more than: ~보다 많이

12 give up: 포기하다

13 목적격 관계대명사는 수식하는 선행사가 사람이면 who나 whom, that을, 사람이 아니면 which나 that을 쓴다. 일반적으로 목적격 관계대명사는 생략될 수 있다. 목적격 관계대명사가 전치사의 목적어인 경우 전치사는 관계대명사절의 끝에 오거나 관계대명사 앞에 올 수 있다. 전치사가 관계대명사절의 끝에 올 경우에는 관계대명사를 생략할 수 있다. 전치사가 관계대명사 앞에 올 경우에는 관계대명사 that을 쓸 수 없으며, 관계대명사를 생략하지 않는다.

14 ask, allow, cause, warn의 목적격보어로 to부정사가 적절하다. to부정사의 부정형은 'not to 동사원형'으로 쓴다.

15 I love the jacket which[that] Hana is wearing.

16 ① tell의 목적격보어로 to부정사가 적절하다. ③, ④ 선행사가 사물일 때 목적격 관계대명사로 which나 that을 쓴다. ⑤ 목적어로 쓰인 them을 삭제해야 한다.

18 Although 대신 문장 중간에 but을 쓰는 것이 적절하다.

19 연습을 함으로써 그는 타격과 주루를 '잘하게 되었다'라고 해야 하므로, at으로 고치는 것이 적절하다. become great for: ~에 좋게 되다, become great at: ~에 잘하게 되다

20 전치사의 목적어로 동명사 'batting'과 'base running'이 쓰였다. ⓑ와 ②, ③, ④: 동명사, ①, ⑤: 현재분사

21 join = take part in = participate in: ~에 참가하다

22 ① 지성이면 감천이다. ② 서두르면 일을 그르친다. ③ 엎질러진 우유를 놓고 울어봐야 소용없다.(되돌릴 수 없는 잘못을 하고 후회해 봐야 아무 소용이 없다.) ④ 모두의 일은 어느 누구의 일도 아니다.(누군가에게 직접 책임이 지워지지 않은 일은 서로 미루다가 결국은 아무도 하지 않게 된다.) ⑤ 요리사가 너무 많으면 국을 망친다.(사공이 많으면 배가 산으로 올라간다.)

23 ⑤ 그 시즌 이후, 몇 명의 아프리카계 미국인 선수들이 다른 팀에 합류했는지는 대답할 수 없다. ① One of his teammates. ② Yes. ③ In 1947. ④ The Rookie of the Year Award.

24 목적격 관계대명사 that이나 which가 적절하다.

25 Robinson의 등 번호 '42번'을 가리킨다.

Science Is Making Big Changes

01 (1) put on   (2) take place   02 ④   03 ②
04 ②   05 ①   06 ①   07 ③

01 <보기>의 단어들은 유의어 관계이다. huge: 거대한 large: 큰
(1) wear: 입다 put on: 입다, 쓰다, 신다 (2) happen: 발생하
다 take place: 일어나다

02 in trouble: 곤경에 빠져서, 난처하여 / 그는 항상 어려움에 처
한 사람들을 보호하려고 노력했습니다.

03 heavily: 심하게, 아주 많이 / 간밤에 비가 심하게 왔다, 그래서
오늘은 좀 춥다.

04 work: 작동하다 / 이것이 그 제품이 작동하는 방법입니다.

05 be ready for: ~할 준비가 되다 / • 아무래도 내일 시험은 잘 못
볼 것 같아! look for: ~을 찾다 / • 나는 3시간 동안 나의 가방
을 찾았고, 마침내 그것을 발견했다.

06 take care of: ~을 돌보다 / • 방과 후에 나의 딸을 보살펴 줄 사람
이 필요하다. take place: 일어나다, 개최되다 / • 많은 문화 축제
들이 가을 동안 개최된다.

07 <보기>의 문장의 may의 뜻은 '~일지도 모른다'로 사용되었다.
그는 오늘 결석이다. 아플지도 모른다. ③ 이외의 may는 '~해
도 좋다'로 허락의 의미를 지닌다. ① 전화 끝나셨으면 제가 좀
써도 될까요? ② 제가 내일 두 시간 늦게 출근해도 될까요? ③
늦을 지도 몰라, 그러니 기다리지 마. ④ 이 방을 사용해도 좋다.
⑤ 이 컴퓨터 잠시 좀 써도 될까요?

01 don't have to
02 (s)imilarity
03 (1) (c)harge   (2) (m)aterial   (3) (r)ecommended
     (4) (s)uits   (5) (m)ethod
04 (1) on   (2) of   (3) by   (4) in
05 (1) The Earth moves around the Sun.
     (2) I got lost on my way to the flower shop.
     (3) People are not worried about air pollution.
     (4) Be sure to put on safety helmets and life jackets.

01 don't have to 동사원형: ~할 필요가 없다(= need not) / 우리
는 만나는 장소를 바꿀 필요가 없다.

02 반의어 관계이다. ever: 어느 때고, 언제든, 한번이라도 never:
지금까지[어느 때건] 한 번도 ~ 않다 difference: 차이점
similarity: 유사점

03 (1) charge: (지불, 대금 등을) 청구하다 (2) material: 물질, 물
체 (3) recommend: ~을 추천하다 (4) suit: (입맛, 취향 등에)
맞다 (5) method: 방법, 방식

04 (1) turn on: (전기·가스·수도 등을) 켜다 / 여름에 우리는 선풍
기를 틀어 시원하게 한다. (2) take care of: ~을 돌보다 / 당신
이 없는 동안 아이들은 누가 돌보나요? (3) by 동명사: ~함으로
써 / 그들은 그들의 숙제를 함으로써 책임감을 배울 수 있다. (4)
wait in line: 줄을 서서 기다리다 / 나는 표를 사기 위해 줄을
서서 기다렸다.

05 (1) move around: ~의 주위를 돌다 (2) get lost: 길을 잃다
(3) be worried about: ~에 대해 걱정하다 (4) put on: 입다,
쓰다, 신다

1 I'm surprised th at
2 (D) → (B) → (A) → (C)
3 I'm surprised that you think so.
4 you help me / teach me now / I'm afraid I can't.
5 Could I ask you to open the door

1 T   2 F   3 T   4 F

Listen & Speak 1 A
1. to turn off / to return / turn, off / surprised that, off
2. to / put / I'm surprised

Listen & Speak 1 B
1. there, surprises / surprised, walk
2. there anything, that surprises / I'm surprised that,
itself

Listen & Talk 2 A
1. help / looking for / for / search for, by
2. don't have / tell, how / on

Listen & Talk 2 B
1. play / play
2. messy / clean
3. out / walk

Conversation A
work like / travel / simple, by talking to / I'm surprised that, living

Conversation B
are, books / Where can, gravity / librarian / looking for, gravity, recommend / that you can recommend books / amazing / on

---

시험대비 기본평가 p.68

01 ④　　　02 ②　　　03 ②

01 I'm surprised that 주어 동사 ~: ~하는 것이 놀라워 / 놀람을 표현할 때는 'I'm surprised that ~.' 또는 'I'm amazed that ~.'이라고 표현한다.

02 스마트 워치를 찾고 있는 남자아이가 스마트 워치 하나를 보여 줄 수 있는지 여직원에게 묻는 말이 적절하다. Can you 동사 ~?: ~해 줄 수 있니? show: 보여주다

03 런던 여행 준비가 다 되었는지 묻는 질문에 (B) 준비는 다 되었지만, 길을 잃을 것을 걱정하고 있다고 말한다. (C) 상대방은 걱정 말라고 말하며, 좋은 스마트폰 앱을 추천한다. (A) 스마트폰 앱 하나를 보여 달라는 요청에 (D) 물론이라고 대답하면서, 도시의 지도와 길의 사진을 보여주는 앱을 사용해 보라고 권한다.

시험대비 실력평가 p.69~70

01 ③　　02 ⑤　　03 ③, ④　　04 ④
05 ③　　06 ⑤　　07 ④　　08 ②
09 ④　　10 ⑤

01 put on: 입다, 쓰다, 신다 남자아이는 VR(Virtual Reality: 가상현실)로 나이아가라 폭포를 보기 위해서 어떤 것을 쓰고 체험하고 있다.

02 I'm surprised that 주어 동사 ~: ~하는 것이 놀라워 feel: ~을 느끼다

03 ③ VR(가상현실)을 이용해 나이아가라 폭포를 보고 있다. ④ VR(가상현실)을 통해 본 나이가라 폭포는 거대했다.

04 가게에 가 달라고 요청하는 말에 'Sure.(물론이지.)'라고 긍정의

대답을 하고 'I'm busy now.(난 지금 바빠.)'라고 말하는 것은 어울리지 않는다.

05 (A)는 anything을 수식하는 주격 관계대명사 that이 어울린다. I'm surprised that 주어 동사 ~: ~하는 것이 놀라워

06 (C) 스마트 워치를 찾고 있고, 하나를 보여 달라고 요청했다. (D) 하나를 보여주면서, 음악의 연주 기능에 대해 언급한다. (B) 멋지다고 대답하고 (A) 점원이 스마트 워치가 말로 검색하는 또 다른 기능을 가지고 있다고 말한다. 남자아이는 그것을 산다고 말하며 대화가 끝난다.

07 스마트 전등을 켜고 끄기 위해 손을 사용할 필요가 없다는 말에 대한 응답으로 그것을 켜고 끄는 방법을 묻는 것이 어울린다.

08 새로운 스마트 전등을 켜기 위해서 "불 켜!"라고 말해도 되므로 손을 꼭 사용할 필요는 없다. should: ~해야 한다

09 히터 끄는 것을 잊어버렸다는 여자아이의 말에 남자아이가 집으로 돌아가야 하는지 물었고 'No'라고 대답했으므로, 이어서 집에 안 가고 끌 수 있는 방법인 스마트폰으로 히터를 끌 수 있다는 말을 하는 것이 어울린다.

10 ① 여자아이는 지금 그녀의 집에 있다. ② 여자아이는 히터를 끄기 위해 집에 갈 것이다. ③ 남자아이는 이미 스마트폰으로 히터를 끌 수 있다는 것을 알고 있었다. ④ 남자아이는 히터 끄는 것을 잊어버렸다. ⑤ 남자아이는 여자아이가 스마트폰으로 히터를 끌 수 있다는 것에 놀랐다.

서술형 시험대비 p.71

01 (A) off　(B) No　(C) surprised
02 I'm surprised that this drone can deliver things.
03 ⓑ have to → don't have to
04 (1) Can I ask you to recommend one
　(2) Do[Would] you mind recommending one
　(3) Will you recommend one
05 I'm surprised that you can recommend books.

01 (A) turn off: (전기·가스·수도 등을) 끄다 (B) 남자아이가 히터를 끄기 위해 집에 가야 하는지 묻자, 여자 아이가 스마트폰을 이용해 끌 수 있다고 말하므로 'No'가 어울린다. (C) I'm surprised that 주어 동사 ~: ~하는 것이 놀라워

02 I'm surprised that 주어 동사 ~: ~하는 것이 놀라워 drone: (원격 조종의) 드론 deliver: 배달하다

03 don't have to 동사원형: ~할 필요가 없다

04 요청하는 표현에는 'Can[Will] you 동사 ~?(~해 줄 수 있니?)', 'Could[Can] I ask you to 동사 ~?(~을 부탁해도 될까?)', 'Do[Would] you mind 동명사 ~?(~해 줄 수 있니?)' 등이 있다.

05 I'm surprised that 주어 동사 ~: ~하는 것이 놀라워 can+동사원형: ~할 수 있다 recommend: ~을 추천하다

13

Grammar

핵심 Check   p.72~73

1 (1) has, spent   (2) have, heard   (3) Have, thought
2 (1) may   (2) use   (3) be

시험대비 기본평가   p.74

01 May   02 ⑤   03 ①   04 ④
05 ③

01 may의 '허가' 용법을 이용한다. Can을 May 대신 쓸 수도 있다.

02 현재완료의 결과적 용법(…해서 (그 결과) 지금 ~하다)을 이용하여 과거에 미국으로 간 것이 아직도 거기에 있다는 현재의 결과를 나타내도록 한다.

03 '그들이 정원에 있을 가능성이 있다.'는 말은 '그들이 어쩌면 정원에 있을지도 모른다.'고 말할 수 있다. may의 '추측' 용법을 이용한다.

04 부정문이므로 yet이 적절하다.

05 may의 '추측' 용법을 이용한다. 조동사 다음에는 동사원형이 나온다.

시험대비 실력평가   p.75~77

01 ④   02 ⑤   03 ③
04 (1) has   (2) haven't   (3) gone   (4) happened
    (5) happen   (6) may not
05 ②   06 ①
07 (1) start → started
    (2) have you done → did you do
    (3) do you have been → have you been
    (4) for → since   (5) since → for
08 ⑤   09 ④   10 ③   11 ②
12 ①   13 ②
14 (1) mays → may   (2) rains → rain
    (3) does not may → may not   (4) is → be
15 ⓐ visited   ⓑ been
16 (1) Bill has known Alice since 2017.
    (2) Olivia has lived in Seoul for three years.
17 ④
18 (1) Cleaning drones may not help students at school.
    (2) May I see your passport?
19 ④

01 언제 주차했는지 묻는 문장으로 특정한 과거의 한 시점을 묻는 것이므로 현재완료가 아니라 과거시제가 되어야 한다. 보통 when은 현재완료와 쓰이지 않는다. **When did you park your car at the garage?**

02 조동사는 인칭에 따른 변화가 없고 조동사 다음에는 항상 동사원형이 나와야 하며 'may' 다음에 'not'을 써서 부정문을 만든다.

03 현재완료의 의문문은 'Have[Has]+주어+과거분사~?'이다. 조동사 'may'가 나와 있으므로 그 다음에는 동사원형이 나와야 한다. 그러므로 ③번이 적절하다.

04 (1) 주어가 3인칭 단수이므로 has가 적절하다. (2) 현재완료의 부정문은 'have[has]+not[never]+과거분사'로 나타낸다. (3) have[has] gone to'는 '~에 가고 없다'는 결과를 나타낸다. (4) 현재완료는 과거를 나타내는 어구(in 2010)와 함께 쓸 수 없다. (5) 조동사 다음에는 동사원형이 나와야 한다. (6) 'may' 다음에 'not'을 써서 부정문을 만든다.

05 현재완료 시제의 의문문에 대한 답은 have를 이용하여 답한다.

06 '허가(~해도 좋다)'를 나타내는 may를 이용한다.

07 (1) 현재완료는 'have[has]+과거분사'의 형태이다. (2) 현재완료는 과거를 나타내는 어구와 함께 쓸 수 없다. (3) 현재완료의 의문문은 have 동사를 주어 앞으로 보낸다. (4), (5) 현재완료에서 'since+시간 명사', 'for+기간 명사'를 쓴다.

08 ⑤번은 '추측'의 의미로 쓰였다. 나머지는 '허가'의 의미이다.

09 현재완료에서 'since+시간 명사', 'for+기간 명사'로 쓰는 것이 적절하다.

10 'have[has] been to'는 '~에 가 본 적이 있다'는 경험을 나타내고, 'have[has] gone to'는 '~에 가고 없다'는 결과를 나타내며 현재완료는 'have[has]+과거분사'의 형태이다.

11 '~일지도 모른다, 아마 ~일 것이다'라는 '추측'의 의미로 쓰일 수 있는 것은 may이다.

12 현재완료에서 'since+시간 명사', 'for+기간 명사'로 쓰는 것이 적절하다.

13 <보기>와 ②는 계속 용법이다. ①, ⑤ 결과 용법 ③ 경험 용법 ④ 완료 용법

14 (1) 조동사는 인칭이나 시제에 따른 어형 변화가 없다. (2), (4) 조동사 뒤에 나오는 be동사나 일반동사는 동사원형으로 쓴다. (3) 'may' 다음에 'not'을 써서 부정문을 만든다.

15 ⓐ yesterday라는 과거를 나타내는 말이 있으므로 과거형으로 써야 한다. ⓑ 'have gone to'는 결과를 나타내는 말로 1인칭을 주어로 쓸 수 없다. 여기서 there는 to the Technology Fair를 의미한다.

16 (1) 2017년에 Alice를 처음 알고 지금도 알고 있으므로 현재완료의 '계속' 용법으로 나타낸다. (2) 3년 전에 살기 시작해서 아직도 살고 있으므로 현재완료의 '계속' 용법으로 나타낸다. 현재완료에서 'since+시간 명사', 'for+기간 명사'를 쓴다는 것에 유의한다.

17 '허가'를 나타내어 '~해도 좋다'의 뜻을 나타내는 may 대신에 can을 사용할 수도 있다.

18 (1) 'may' 다음에 'not'을 써서 부정문을 만든다. (2) 'may'의 의문문은 'may'를 문두로 옮겨 'May+주어+동사 ~?'의 어순으로 쓴다.

19 ④번은 현재완료의 '경험' 용법이고, 나머지는 모두 '계속' 용법이다.

01 (1) He has lived in Busan since he was 15 years old.

  (2) Have you ever seen giraffes?

  (3) I haven't finished my homework yet.

  (4) I have lost my diary.

  (5) Paul may not be in the classroom.

  (6) May[Can] I turn on the air conditioner?

02 (1) It has rained since last Thursday.

  (2) Has William gone to buy sandwiches?

03 (1) I have never used a drone before.

  (2) I have been to the tomato festival once. 등
  어법에 맞게 쓰면 정답

04 (1) '~할지도 모른다' (추측)

  (2) '~해도 좋다' (허가)

05 (1) may come   (2) may not park   (3) may sell

06 (1) When did you start working at the company?

  (2) She has worked as a drone designer since 2035.

  (3) Have you ever been to Vietnam before?

  (4) So there may be traffic lights for drones in the sky.

  (5) Schools may be open only three days a week, so students may not go to school every day.

07 **부정문:** You have never[haven't] thought of how schools may change over the next 20 years.

  의문문: Have you ever thought of how schools may change over the next 20 years?

08 (1) I have studied English for 6 years.

  (2) I have not sent the letter yet.

  (3) Have you ever swum in the sea?

  (4) Some changes have already started to take place while others may start in the near future.

09 (1) have visited, four times

  (2) may have

01 (1)~(4) 현재완료를 이용하여 영작한다. 각각 '계속', '경험', '완

료', '결과' 용법이다. (5)~(6) may를 이용한다. (5)번은 '추측'을, (6)번은 '허가'를 의미한다. '허가'의 경우에는 may 대신 can을 쓸 수 있다.

02 (1) 지난 목요일에 비가오기 시작해서 지금도 오고 있는 것이므로 현재완료의 '계속'을 이용한다. (2) 샌드위치를 사러 가서 지금 여기 없는 것이므로 현재완료의 '결과'를 이용한다.

03 현재완료의 '경험' 용법을 이용하여 쓴다.

04 조동사 'may'는 '추측'과 '허가'의 의미로 쓰인다.

05 (1) '올 것 같다'는 것을 '올지도 모른다'라고 may를 써서 나타낸다. (2) '허가'를 나타내는 can과 may를 이용한다. (3) maybe는 '아마도'라는 뜻으로 may를 이용하여 나타낼 수 있다.

06 (1) 현재완료는 과거의 특정 시점을 나타내는 의문사 when과 함께 쓸 수 없다. (2) 현재완료에서 'since+시간 명사', 'for+기간 명사' (3) have[has] been to는 '~에 가 본적이 있다'는 경험을 나타내고, have[has] gone to는 '~에 가고 없다'는 결과를 나타내므로 3인칭만 주어가 될 수 있다. 주어가 you이므로 have been to로 고쳐야 한다. (4) maybe는 부사로 '어쩌면, 아마'라는 뜻이다. 동사가 없으므로 'maybe'를 'may be'로 고쳐 쓴다. (5) 조동사 다음에는 동사원형이 나와야 하고 'may' 다음에 'not'을 써서 부정문을 만든다.

07 현재완료의 부정문은 'have[has]+not[never]+과거분사'로, 의문문은 'Have[Has]+주어+과거분사 ~?'로 나타낸다.

08 (1) 현재완료의 '계속' 용법, (2) 현재완료의 '완료' 용법, (3) 현재완료의 '경험' 용법을 이용한다. (4) 현재완료의 '완료' 용법과 '추측'의 may를 이용한다.

09 (1) 현재완료의 '경험' 용법을 이용한다. (2) '추측'의 may를 이용한다. be likely to: ~할 것 같다

확인문제   p.80

1 T   2 F   3 T   4 F

확인문제   p.81

1 F   2 F   3 T   4 F   5 T

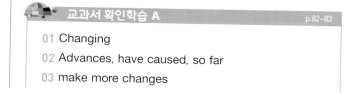

01 Changing

02 Advances, have caused, so far

03 make more changes

04 may be like   05 Shopping Center

06 much easier   07 no lines, no counters

08 special shopping app

09 takes the items

10 are automatically added to

11 puts, back, is automatically removed from

12 shopping, in line

13 adds up, charge

14 fancy   15 3D Printed

16 3D printed

17 Building, faster and cheaper, with traditional methods

18 looks fantastic

19 house shapes, traditional building methods and materials

20 by using   21 that fit, suit

22 fashion designer   23 in the Hospital

24 is visiting   25 An AI

26 checks, conditions

27 high temperature, to lower

28 Have you ever thought

29 take place, in the near future

30 imagine

31 Take some time

p.84~85

교과서 확인학습 B

1 Changing Society

2 Advances in science and technology have caused many changes in our lives so far.

3 In the future, science and technology will make more changes.

4 Let's see what our lives may be like in the near future.

5 Sangho in the Shopping Center

6 Shopping is much easier.

7 There are no lines and no counters.

8 Sangho enters a shop with his smartphone which has a special shopping app.

9 In the shop, he takes the items he wants.

10 The items are automatically added to a virtual card on his smartphone.

11 If Sangho puts an item back, it is automatically removed from his list of purchases.

12 When he finishes shopping, Sangho does not need to wait in line to pay.

13 His virtual card adds up all the prices and will

charge him later.

14 Isn't that fancy?

15 Sumin's 3D Printed House and Clothes

16 Sumin lives in a 3D printed house.

17 Building a 3D printed house is faster and cheaper than building a house with traditional methods.

18 Sumin's house looks fantastic because of its unique design.

19 A 3D printer can produce house shapes that people cannot make with traditional building methods and materials.

20 Sumin also likes to make her clothes at home by using a 3D printer.

21 She can choose colors and materials and can design clothes that fit her body and suit her tastes.

22 Sumin is now a fashion designer!

23 Dongmin in the Hospital

24 Dongmin is visiting his grandfather in the hospital.

25 An AI nurse enters the room.

26 It moves around the room and checks the patients' conditions.

27 When the AI nurse finds that Dongmin's grandfather has a high temperature, it gives him some medicine to lower his temperature.

28 Have you ever thought about these changes?

29 Some changes have already started to take place while others may start in the near future.

30 Can you imagine other changes?

31 Take some time to think about them.

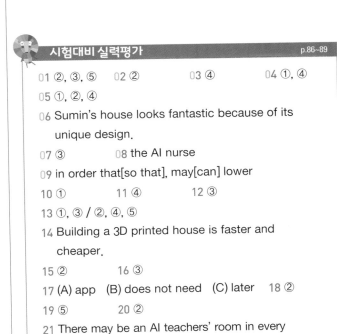

p.86~89

시험대비 실력평가

01 ②, ③, ⑤   02 ②   03 ④   04 ①, ④

05 ①, ②, ④

06 Sumin's house looks fantastic because of its unique design.

07 ③   08 the AI nurse

09 in order that[so that], may[can] lower

10 ①   11 ④   12 ③

13 ①, ③ / ②, ④, ⑤

14 Building a 3D printed house is faster and cheaper.

15 ②   16 ③

17 (A) app   (B) does not need   (C) later   18 ②

19 ⑤   20 ②

21 There may be an AI teachers' room in every

school.

22 it gives some medicine to him　23 ⑤

24 (A) lower　(B) high

01 ⓐ와 ①, ④번: 계속 용법, ② 경험 용법, ③ 완료 용법, ⑤ 결과 용법

02 이 글은 '과학과 기술의 발전으로 인한 변화'에 관한 글이다.

03 본문 끝에서 '가까운 미래에 우리의 삶이 어떻게 될지 살펴보자'라고 했으므로, ④번이 적절하다.

04 (A)에는 목적격 관계대명사를, (B)에는 주격 관계대명사를 써야 하고, 선행사가 사물이므로 that이나 which가 적절하다.

05 ⓐ와 ③, ⑤번: 동명사, ①, ②, ④: 현재분사

06 look+형용사: ~하게 보이다, because of+명사구

07 '어떤' 변화는 이미 일어나기 시작했고 반면 '다른 것들'은 가까운 미래에 일어날지도 모른다고 해야 하므로, some과 others가 적절하다.

08 'AI 간호사'를 가리킨다.

09 목적을 나타내는 to부정사는 'in order that 주어 may[can]'나 'so that 주어 may[can]'로 고치는 것이 적절하다.

10 (A) add A to B: A를 B에 더하다, (B) remove A from B: B로부터 A를 제거하다

11 very는 원급을 강조하고, ⓐ와 나머지는 비교급을 강조한다.

12 물건을 되돌려 놓으면 그것은 자동으로 구매 목록에서 제거된다.

13 ⓐ와 ①, ③: 목적격 관계대명사, ⓑ와 ②, ④, ⑤: 주격 관계대명사

14 '3D 프린터로 집을 짓는 것'이 전통적인 방법으로 집을 짓는 것보다 더 빠르고 저렴하다.

15 ② 3D 프린터로 집을 짓는 것이 얼마나 걸리는지는 대답할 수 없다. ① In a 3D printed house. ③ Because of its unique design. ④ By using a 3D printer. ⑤ Sumin does.

16 주어진 문장의 The items에 주목한다. ③번 앞 문장의 the items를 받고 있으므로 ③번이 적절하다.

17 (A) 특별한 쇼핑 '앱'이 있는 스마트폰을 가지고 가게로 들어간다고 해야 하므로 app이 적절하다. list: 목록, (B) 가상 카드가 모든 가격을 더해서 나중에 그에게 청구한다고 했으므로, 돈을 지불하기 위해 줄을 설 '필요가 없다'고 하는 것이 적절하다. (C) 가상 카드가 모든 가격을 더해서 '나중에' 그에게 청구할 것이라고 해야 하므로 later가 적절하다. later: 나중에, latter: 후자의

18 ⓐ와 ②번: (요금, 값을) 청구하다, ① 돌격[공격]하다, ③ 책임(명사), ④ 청구 금액, 대가(명사), free of charge: 무료로, ⑤ <축전지에> 충전하다

19 이 글은 '훨씬 쉬워진 미래의 쇼핑'에 관한 글이다.

20 ⓐ와 ②, ⑤번: 경험 용법, ① 완료 용법, ③ 계속 용법, ④ 결과 용법

21 There may be: ~이 있을지도 모른다

22 give는 'to'를 사용하여 3형식으로 고친다.

23 ⓐ와 ⑤번: [주절 뒤에서 반대·비교·대조를 나타내어] 그런데, 한편(으로는), ①, ②, ③, ④: …하는 동안, …하는 사이, …와 동시에

24 AI 간호사는 동민이 할아버지가 열이 '높다'는 것을 알았을 때 그것은 그의 체온을 '낮추기' 위해 그에게 약을 준다.

🦉 서술형 시험대비
p.90~91

01 have caused

02 (A) advances　(B) changes

03 (1) seeing　(2) Why don't we

04 (1) 특별한 쇼핑 앱이 있는 스마트폰을 가지고 가게로 들어간다.

(2) 가게에서 그가 원하는 물건들을 집는다.

(3) 그 물건들은 자동으로 그의 스마트폰에 있는 가상 카드에 더해지고, 만약 그가 물건을 되돌려 놓으면 그것은 자동으로 그의 구매 목록에서 제거된다.

(4) 쇼핑을 끝내면 돈을 지불하기 위해 줄을 설 필요가 없고, 그의 가상 카드가 모든 가격을 더해서 나중에 그에게 청구할 것이다.

05 In the shop, he takes the items that[which] he wants.

06 he does not need to wait in line to pay

07 unique design

08 fits → fit, suits → suit

09 (1) 색깔과 재료를 고른다.

(2) 자신의 몸과 취향에 맞는 옷을 디자인한다.

(3) 3D 프린터를 사용해 집에서 옷을 만든다.

10 application

11 item

12 to shop → shopping

13 may

14 how schools may change over the next 20 years

15 no more[longer]

01 뒤에 'so far'가 있으므로 현재완료 시제로 쓰는 것이 적절하다.

02 과학과 기술의 '발전' 때문에 지금까지 우리의 삶에 많은 '변화들'이 있어 왔다.

03 Let's see ~. = How[What] about seeing ~? = Why don't we see ~?: ~을 보는 게 어때?

04 본문에서 소개하고 있는 쇼핑 방법을 쓰는 것이 적절하다.

05 생략된 목적격 관계대명사 that[which]을 넣어 문장을 다시 쓰는 것이 적절하다.

06 wait in line: 줄을 서서 기다리다

07 수민이의 집의 '독특한 디자인'이 집을 멋져 보이게 만든다.

08 선행사가 clothes이므로 fit과 suit으로 고치는 것이 적절하다.

09 수민이는 색깔과 재료를 고를 수 있고 자신의 몸과 취향에 맞는 옷을 디자인하여 집에서 3D 프린터를 사용해 옷을 만들 수 있다고 했다.

10 app: 스마트폰 앱, 어플리케이션(application)

11 상호가 되돌려 놓는 '물건'을 가리킨다.

12 finish는 목적어로 동명사를 취한다.

13 추측을 표현하는 'may'를 쓰는 것이 적절하다.

14 'next'를 보충하면 된다.

15 not ~ anymore = no more[longer]: 더 이상 ~ 아닌

영역별 핵심문제
p.93~97

01 ③ 02 ① 03 ② 04 ⑤
05 ② 06 (C) → (A) → (B)
07 (A) → (D) → (B) → (C) 08 ⑤
09 ④ 10 rescue
11 If there is a person in trouble, it flies over and drops a tube.
12 Can I ask you to show me how it works?
13 (A) for (B) about (C) at
14 ⑤ 15 ① 16 ⑤ 17 ⑤
18 (1) I bought it only a couple of hours ago.
   (2) She has studied science and technology for 10 years.
   (3) Have you ever been to Paris?
   (4) There may be an AI teachers' room in every school.
19 (1) He has never bought a lottery ticket.
   (2) I have lost my passport at the airport.
   (3) We have known each other since 1999.
   (4) He has just finished his science project.
   (5) They may come back tomorrow.
   (6) May[Can] I use your smartphone?
20 Advances in science and technology have caused many changes in our lives so far.
21 ③, ⑤ 22 (A) added (B) virtual (C) charge
23 automatically removes → is automatically removed
24 he needs to pay at the counter → he does not need to wait in line to pay
25 ①, ④ 26 make them → make
27 ③ 28 lower
29 ⓐ Dongmin's grandfather ⓑ other changes

01 ③은 유의어 관계이며, 나머지 보기들은 반의어 관계이다. ① difference: 차이, 차이점 similarity: 유사점 ② ever: 어느 때고, 언제든, 한번이라도 never: 지금까지[어느 때건] 한 번도 ~ 않다 ③ law: 법칙, 법 principle: 원칙, 법칙 ④ lower: 낮

추다 heighten: 강화하다, 높이다 ⑤ true: 참된 false: 거짓의

02 ① have, don't have to 동사원형: ~할 필요가 없다 / 너는 도시락을 가져올 필요는 없다. ② waiting, wait in line: 줄을 서서 기다리다 / 그들은 음식을 주문하기 위해 줄서서 기다리고 있다. ③ Add, add up: 합산하다 / 다음의 숫자를 합산하세요. ④ get, get lost: 길을 잃다 / 만약 길을 잃으시면 제 휴대폰 010-744-2996으로 전화주세요. ⑤ move, move around: 돌아다니다 / 우리는 모든 과목마다 교실을 옮겨다닌다.

03 cover: 덮다 / 바다는 지구 표면의 70% 정도를 덮고 있습니다.

04 suit: (입맛, 취향 등에) 맞다 / 그는 자기 적성에 맞는 그 일을 좋아했다.

05 ⓑ I'm good at finding places. → I'm not good at finding places. 길을 잃을 것에 대해 걱정하는 말을 했으므로, 장소를 잘 찾는다는 말이 나오는 것은 어색하다.

06 (C) 상대의 물건에 대해 설명을 요청하는 말에 (A) 미래의 신발이라고 말하며, 이 신발을 신은 사람은 100미터를 5초 안에 달릴 것이라고 설명한다. (B) 그 정도로 빨리 달릴 수 있는 것에 대해 놀람을 표현한다.

07 (A) 집에 나오기 전에 히터 끄는 것을 잊어버렸고 말한다. (D) 그러면 히터를 끄기 위해 집으로 돌아가야 하는지 질문하자, (B) 스마트폰으로 히터를 끌 수 있다고 말한다. (C) 상대방이 스마트폰으로 히터를 끌 수 있다는 사실에 대해 놀라워한다.

08 ⓐ to visit, would like to 동사원형: ~하고 싶다 ⓑ put this on, 이어동사는 '동사+부사(on, off, up, over 등)'로 이루어져 있다. '동사+부사+목적어'의 어순이나 '동사+목적어+부사'의 어순 둘 다 가능하지만 목적어 자리에 대명사(it, them, this 등)가 올 때는 '동사+목적어+부사'의 어순으로 쓴다. ⓒ real, look+형용사: ~하게 보이다 ⓓ isn't it ⓔ I'm surprised that 주어 동사 ~: ~하는 것이 놀라워

09 save: 구하다

10 rescue: 구조하다 / 위험이나 손상으로부터 누군가나 어떤 것을 구하다

11 if: ~라면 there is+단수 명사: ~가 있다 in trouble: 곤경에 빠져서, 난처하여 drop: 떨어뜨리다 tube: 튜브

12 Can[Could/Will/Would] you 동사 ~?(~해 줄 수 있니?)', 'Could[Can] I ask you to 동사 ~?(~을 부탁해도 될까?)'는 상대방에게 어떤 행동을 요청할 때 사용하는 표현들이다.

13 be ready for: ~의 준비가 되다 be worried about: ~에 대해 걱정하다 be good at: ~을 잘하다

14 ① 남자아이는 무엇을 걱정하는가?(길을 잃는 것) ② 남자 아이는 어디를 여행할 것인가?(런던) ③ 남자아이는 무엇을 잘 못하는가?(장소 찾는 것) ④ 여자아이가 남자아이에게 추천해 준 앱은 무엇을 보여주는가?(도시의 지도와 길의 사진) ⑤ 남자아이는 얼마나 많은 스마트폰 앱을 사용할 수 있는가?

15 since(~ 이래로)는 보통 현재완료와 함께 많이 쓰인다. 이때 since절에는 과거 시제가 쓰인다.

16 ⓐ mays → may ⓑ are → be ⓒ gone → been ⓕ for →

since ⓗ has met → met

17 ⑤번은 '허가'의 의미로 쓰였지만 나머지는 모두 '추측'의 의미로 쓰였다.

18 (1) 현재완료는 과거를 나타내는 ~ ago와는 함께 쓰이지 않는다. (2) 현재완료의 '계속' 용법이다. 'since+시간 명사', 'for+ 기간 명사'임에 유의한다. (3) have[has] been to는 '~에 가 본 적이 있다'는 경험을 나타내고, have[has] gone to는 '~에 가고 없다'는 결과를 나타내므로 have been to로 고쳐야 한다. (4) 조동사 may 다음에는 동사원형이 나와야 한다.

19 (1) 현재완료의 '경험' 용법을 이용한다. (2) 현재완료의 '결과' 용법을 이용한다. (3) 현재완료의 '계속' 용법을 이용한다. (4) 현재완료의 '완료' 용법을 이용한다. (5) '추측'의 may를 이용한다. (6) '허가'의 may를 이용한다. '허가'의 경우에는 may 대신 can을 쓸 수 있다.

20 'have'를 보충하면 된다.

21 ⓑ와 ③, ⑤번: (추측) ~일지도 모른다, ① (허락) …해도 되다[좋다], ② [목적을 나타내는 부사절에서] …하기 위하여, …할 수 있도록, ④ (바람, 소망) …이기를 (빌다)

22 (A) 그의 스마트폰에 있는 가상 카드에 '더해진다'라고 수동태로 써야 하므로 added가 적절하다. (B) 그의 '가상' 카드라고 해야 하므로 virtual이 적절하다. actual: 실제의, virtual: (컴퓨터를 이용한) 가상의, (C) 나중에 그에게 '청구할 것'이라고 해야 하므로 charge가 적절하다.

23 자동으로 그의 구매 목록에서 '제거된다'고 해야 하므로, 수동태로 고치는 것이 적절하다.

24 쇼핑을 끝냈을 때 상호는 '돈을 지불하기 위해 줄을 설 필요가 없다.'

25 ① 주어 자리에 동명사와 to부정사를 쓸 수 있다. ④ 전통적인 방법으로 집을 짓는 것은 3D 프린터로 집을 짓는 것만큼 빠르고 저렴하지 않다.

26 목적격 관계대명사 that이 있으므로, them을 삭제하는 것이 적절하다.

27 3D 프린터는 사람들이 전통적인 건축 방법과 재료들로 만들 수 '없는' 집 모양을 만들어 낼 수 '있다'.

28 체온을 '낮추기' 위해 그에게 약을 준다고 하는 것이 적절하다. lower: …을 내리다[낮추다]

29 ⓐ는 '동민이 할아버지'를, ⓑ는 '다른 변화들'을 가리킨다.

단원별 예상문제

p.98~101

01 (1) (l)ibrarian (2) (o)ffer   02 ④

03 (1) interested in drones (2) technology
   (3) materials (4) (f)ancy

04 (1) Advances in technology have brought us many good things.
   (2) This watch can run many applications like smartphones.

05 (A) before (B) turn it off

06 I'm surprised that you can turn off the heater with your smartphone.

07 ③   08 recommend

09 (A) surprised (B) amazing   10 ⑤

11 ③   12 ⑤   13 ②

14 Advances 15 ③   16 ①, ④   17 ②

18 ②

19 The items are automatically added to a virtual card on his smartphone. 또는 The items are added to a virtual card on his smartphone automatically.

20 ④   21 ③, ⑤   22 ②

23 AI 간호사는 병실을 돌아다니면서 환자들의 상태를 확인하고, 환자의 열이 높다는 것을 알면 체온을 낮추기 위해 환자에게 약을 준다.

24 ②

01 (1) 장소와 직업의 관계이다. farm: 농장 farmer: 농부 library: 도서관 librarian: 사서 (2) 동의어 관계이다 material: 재료 matter: 물질, 물체 provide: 공급하다 offer: 제공하다

02 since: ~ 이후로 / 대학교를 떠난 이후로 럭비를 하지 않았다.

03 (1) be interested in: ~에 관심이 있다 drone: (원격 조종의) 드론 (2) technology: 과학 기술, 생산 기술 (3) different: 다른 material: 재료 (4) fancy: 화려한, 공들인, 고급의

04 (1) advance: 발전 technology: 과학 기술, 생산 기술 (2) app: 스마트폰 앱, 어플리케이션(application)

05 (A) 집에서 나오기 전에 히터를 끄는 것을 잊어버린 것을 말하고, 이어 상대방이 히터를 끄기 위해 집에 다시 가야 하는지 물어 보는 것이 어울리므로 before가 적절하다. (B) turn off는 이어동사로 '동사+부사'로 이루어져 있다. 목적어 자리에 대명사가 올 때는 '동사+목적어+부사'의 어순으로 쓴다.

06 I'm surprised that 주어 동사 ~: ~하는 것이 놀라워 with: ~을 써서, 이용하여

07 주어진 문장은 '추천해 줄 수 있니?'라는 의미의 문장이다. 여기서 one은 a book about gravity이며, 이 질문에 대한 대답으로 책을 추천해야 하므로, 'The Law of Gravity'를 추천하는 말 앞에 나와야 어울린다.

08 recommend: ~을 추천하다 / 어떤 것을 지지하여 말하다

09 I'm surprised that 주어 동사 ~: ~하는 것이 놀라워 amazing: 놀라운 감정을 나타내는 동사의 경우 현재분사는 '~하게 하는'의 뜻으로 감정을 유발하는 대상에 쓰이고, 과거분사는 '~하게 된'의 뜻으로 감정을 느끼는 대상에 쓰인다.

10 AI가 책을 추천해서 놀라움을 표현한 것은 하나와 Amy이다.

11 현재완료에서 'since+시간 명사', 'for+기간 명사'

12 ① Koreans have played *jegichagi*, a traditional Korean

game, for a long time. ② The children have already had dinner. ③ He left for New York last night. ④ Has he done his homework?

13 ② The math problem is difficult. Chris may not know the answer.

14 더 나은 쪽으로의 변화; 발달에 있어서의 진전 / advance: 발달, 진보

15 ③ so far = until now: 지금까지, ①과 ⑤: 최근에, ② 그 때까지, ④ 우선은, 현재로는, 당분간은

16 ⓒ와 ①, ④번: (외관·내용 등이) …을 닮아, …와 유사하여(전치사), ②, ③, ⑤: ~을 좋아하다(동사)

17 쇼핑이 훨씬 쉬워진 것이므로, '정말 멋지지 않은가?'라고 하는 것이 적절하다. ① 지루한, ③ 소박한, ④ 끔찍한, ⑤ 복잡한

18 ② 계산대는 없다.

19 'automatically'를 보충하면 된다.

20 ④번 다음 문장부터 3D 프린터를 사용해 옷을 만드는 내용이 나오므로 ④번이 적절하다.

21 ⓐ와 ③, ⑤번: 관계대명사, ①, ②, ④: 접속사

22 이 글은 '수민이가 3D 프린터를 사용하여 집을 짓고 옷을 만든다'는 내용의 글이다.

23 첫 단락의 내용을 쓰는 것이 적절하다.

24 ⓐ와 ①, ③번: 완료 용법, ② 결과 용법, ④ 경험 용법, ⑤ 계속 용법

서술형 실전문제 p.102~103

01 I'm surprised that this car can drive itself automatically.

02 ⓔ That's very difficult. → That's very simple[easy].

03 Then do you mind telling me how to do it? / Then can I ask you to tell me how to do it?

04 (1) for (2) since (3) before

05 (1) You may not leave this room now.
   (2) My friend may be sad because of the news.
   (3) My parents have raised the dog since I was born.
   (4) She has gone to see the movie.
   (5) She has swum in the river once.
   (6) The children have not had dinner yet.

06 (1) may (2) Maybe

07 more difficult → easier

08 virtual

09 그의 가상 카드가 모든 가격을 더해서 나중에 그에게 청구할 것이기 때문이다.

10 using

11 looks like → looks

12 (1) 3D 프린터로 집을 짓는 것은 전통적인 방법으로 집을 짓는 것보다 더 빠르고 저렴하다.
   (2) 독특한 디자인 때문에 멋져 보인다.
   (3) 3D 프린터는 사람들이 전통적인 건축 방법과 재료들로 만들 수 없는 집 모양을 만들어 낼 수 있다.

01 I'm surprised that 주어 동사 ~: ~하는 것이 놀라워 automatically: 자동적으로 itself: 그 자신, 스스로

02 전등을 켜고 끄기 위해서 단지 "불 켜!" 또는 "불 꺼!"라고 말하는 것은 간단한[쉬운] 일이다.

03 요청하는 표현에는 'Could[Can] I ask you to 동사 ~?(~을 부탁해도 될까?)', 'Do[Would] you mind 동명사 ~?(~해 줄 수 있니?)' 등이 있다.

04 (1), (2) 현재완료에서 'since+시간 명사', 'for+ 기간 명사' (3) ago는 현재완료와 함께 사용할 수 없으나 before는 사용할 수 있다.

05 (1) '허가'의 may를 이용한다. (2) '추측'의 may를 이용한다. (3) 현재완료의 '계속' 용법을 이용한다. (4) 현재완료의 '결과' 용법을 이용한다. have[has] been to는 '~에 가 본 적이 있다'는 경험을 나타내고, have[has] gone to는 '~에 가고 없다'는 결과를 나타낸다. (5) 현재완료의 '경험' 용법을 이용한다. (6) 현재완료의 '완료' 용법을 이용한다. 부정문이므로 yet을 쓰는 것에 주의한다.

06 (1) '추측'의 may를 쓰는 것이 적절하다. (2) maybe를 이용한다. maybe는 부사로 '어쩌면, 아마'라는 뜻이다.

07 줄도 없고 계산대도 없다고 했기 때문에 쇼핑이 '훨씬 쉽다'고 하는 것이 적절하다.

08 어떤 장소에 가거나 직접 사람들을 만나지 않고 컴퓨터나 인터넷을 사용하여 행해지거나 보여지는, virtual: (컴퓨터를 이용한) 가상의

09 뒷문장의 내용을 쓰는 것이 적절하다.

10 전치사 다음에 동명사를 쓰는 것이 적절하다.

11 look+형용사: ~하게 보이다

12 본문의 앞부분의 내용을 쓰는 것이 적절하다.

창의사고력 서술형 문제 p.104

|모범답안|

01 I'm surprised that it looks like a leaf but it's moving.

02 (1) Advances in science and technology have caused many changes.
   (2) Have you ever imagined life in the future? / I have never been to Austria.
   (3) I have finished my homework. / I have visited Jejudo twice.

03 (A) 3D printing (B) AI teachers
   (C) a drone station (D) paper textbooks

01 ②

02 (1) (l)aw, gravity   (2) patient   (3) (m)ethod   (4) take

03 Virtual

04 (1) They are waiting in line to get coffee.

    (2) When I was in trouble, she tried to support me a lot.

    (3) The woman is trying to exchange her purchase.

    (4) Take this medicine after meals.

05 I'm surprised that we're already living in the future.

06 ⑤   07 law   08 ①   09 drone

10 ③

11 Can you tell me how shoes will change our lives in the future?

12 (C) → (D) → (B) → (A)

13 ②   14 ③

15 Cindy may live in a 3D printed house in the future.

16 해석: (1) 나는 스마트폰을 잃어버렸다.

     해석: (2) 나는 스마트폰을 잃어버렸다.

     차이: (1)번은 '스마트폰을 잃어버렸다'는 사실만을 나타내지만, (2)번은 '스마트폰을 잃어버려서 현재 스마트폰이 없다'는 현재의 상황까지 나타낸다.

17 ③   18 (A) takes   (B) puts back

19 ③   20 ④   21 ③   22 ①

---

01 fit: (치수·모양 등이) 꼭 맞다 / 이 재킷은 나에게 꽤 잘 맞는다. charge: (지불·대금 등을) 청구하다 / 우리 웹사이트에 들어온 주문품을 배달하는 비용을 얼마나 청구하지요?

02 (1) law: 법칙, 법 gravity: 중력 (2) patient: 환자 condition: 상태, 조건 (3) method: 방법, 방식 (4) take place: 일어나다, 개최되다

03 virtual: 가상의 / 컴퓨터에 의해 만들어진 또는 컴퓨터나 인터넷에 나타나는 / 가상 현실 기술은 아주 우수한 컴퓨터를 필요로 한다.

04 (1) wait in line: 줄을 서서 기다리다 (2) in trouble: 곤경에 빠져서, 난처하여 (3) purchase: 구입(품) (4) medicine: 약

05 I'm surprised that 주어 동사 ~: ~하는 것이 놀라워 in the future: 미래에

06 주어진 문장은 책이 어디에 있는지 위치를 묻는 질문이므로, 'It's on the third floor.(그건 3층에 있어.)'의 대답과 잘 어울린다.

07 law: 법칙, 법 / 특정한 조건에서 항상 발생하는 것에 관련된 사실의 진술; 과학적 원리

08 중력에 관한 책이 57권이 있다고 말했지만, 도서관에 책이 몇 권 있는지는 언급되지 않았다. ① 도서관에 책이 몇 권 있니? ② Amy와 하나는 어디에 있는가? ③ 어떤 책이 Terry에 의해

추천되었는가? ④ 대화 후에 그들은 어디에 갈 것인가? ⑤ The Law of Gravity는 몇 층에 있는가?

09 drone: (원격 조종의) 드론 / 원격조종이나 내장 컴퓨터로 조종되는 무인의 항공기나 배

10 ⓐ to save people's lives, to부정사의 부사적 용법 (~ 하기 위해서) ⓒ drops a tube, flies와 병렬 관계 ⓓ I'm surprised that, I'm surprised that 주어 동사 ~: ~하는 것이 놀라워

11 Can you 동사 ~?: ~해 줄 수 있니? tell의 직접목적어 자리에 간접의문문(의문사+주어+동사)이 들어갔다. in the future: 미래에

12 (C) 새로운 전등을 보여 주면서, 전등을 켜고 끄기 위해 손을 사용할 필요가 없다고 말한다. (D) 전등을 켜고 끄는 방법을 말해 줄 수 있는지 물어보자 (B) "불 꺼" 또는 "불 켜"라고 말하면 된다고 답한다. (A) 말로 전등을 켜고 끄는 것이 간단하다고 말한다.

13 then은 과거의 특정 시점을 나타내는 부사이므로 현재완료와 함께 쓸 수 없다.

14 주어진 문장과 ③번은 '허가'의 의미로 쓰이고 있다. 나머지는 모두 '추측'을 나타낸다.

15 '추측'의 may를 이용한다.

16 (1) 과거 시제는 과거에 있었던 사실만을 나타낸다. (2) 현재완료는 과거의 어느 한 시점에 일어난 일이 현재까지 영향을 미칠 때 사용한다.

17 ⓐ와 ①, ④: 부사적 용법, ② 형용사적 용법 ③, ⑤: 명사적 용법

18 가게에서 상호가 '집는' 물건들은 자동으로 그의 스마트폰에 있는 가상 카드에 더해지고, 상호가 '되돌려 놓는' 물건들은 자동으로 그의 구매 목록에서 제거된다.

19 물건들을 자동으로 상호의 스마트폰에 있는 가상 카드에 더하기 위해 앱이 무슨 작동방식을 사용하는지는 대답할 수 없다. ① No. ② Yes. ④ Yes. ⑤ He doesn't need to wait in line to pay. His virtual card adds up all the prices and will charge him later.

20 자신의 몸과 취향에 맞는 옷을 디자인할 수 있다고 했기 때문에, '패션 디자이너'라고 하는 것이 적절하다. ① 건축가, ③ (기계·도로·교량 등을) 설계·건축하는) 기사, 엔지니어 ⑤ 화가

21 ③ ~에도 불구하고

22 ⓑ와 ①번: 취향, ② <음식이> (~한) 맛이 나다, ③ 맛이 ~하다, ~한 맛이 나다, ④ 맛, ⑤ 맛을 보다, 시식[시음]하다

The 100th Customer

교과서
Reading

확인문제	p.112

1 T 2 F 3 T 4 F

확인문제	p.113

1 T 2 F 3 T 4 F

교과서 확인학습 A   p.114~115

01 100th	02 elderly
03 with her grandson	04 Quietly, the owner
05 How much	06 with a smile
07 too poor to pay	08 for her grandson
09 Are you sure	10 No
11 Don't worry	12 chewed on
13 eat, came over	
14 to give the boy a free meal	
15 was about to pay	16 the 100th customer
17 thanked Mr. Kang	
18 A month later, outside	19 was gathering
20 What	21 counting, who
22 Today is	23 treat, said to himself
24 looked down	25 the number, was
26 to help	27 went back into
28 bring everyone who	29 who needs
30 to arrive at	31 It's our turn
32 welcomed them, a free bowl of Gukbap	
33 Are you sure	34 with a smile
35 Don't worry	

교과서 확인학습 B   p.116~117

1 The 100th Customer

2 One day, an elderly woman walked into a restaurant.

3 She was with her grandson.

4 Quietly, the woman asked Mr. Kang, the owner of the restaurant.

5 "How much is a bowl of Gukbap?"

6 "It's 4,000 won, ma'am," Mr. Kang answered with a smile.

7 She was too poor to pay for two bowls.

8 She ordered a single bowl for her grandson.

9 "Are you sure you are not hungry, Grandma?" the boy asked, as he ate the hot soup.

10 "No, I'm not hungry.

11 Don't worry about me."

12 She picked up some Gimchi and chewed on it happily.

13 Mr. Kang watched them eat, and a warm feeling came over him.

14 He thought up a plan to give the boy a free meal.

15 When the woman was about to pay, Mr. Kang waved his hands and said, "No need, ma'am.

16 In my restaurant, you don't pay if you're the 100th customer of the day."

17 The woman and her grandson thanked Mr. Kang and left.

18 A month later, Mr. Kang saw the boy in the street outside the restaurant.

19 The boy was gathering stones.

20 "What are you doing?" asked Mr. Kang.

21 "I'm counting the number of customers who enter your restaurant.

22 Today is my grandma's birthday."

23 'He wants to be the 100th customer and treat his grandmother to a bowl of Gukbap!' Mr. Kang said to himself.

24 Mr. Kang looked down.

25 He could see that the number of stones was not yet even fifty.

26 He had to do something to help the boy gather 100 stones.

27 Mr. Kang went back into the restaurant and called his friends.

28 "Come to my restaurant now and bring everyone who works with you.

29 There is a boy who needs your help."

30 People began to arrive at the restaurant.

31 When the 99th customer arrived, Mr. Kang heard the boy say, "It's our turn, Grandma."

32 Mr. Kang welcomed them and served the woman a free bowl of Gukbap.

33 "Are you sure you're not hungry?" the woman

asked the boy.

34 The boy chewed loudly on some Gimchi and said with a smile, "No. I'm not hungry, Grandma.

35 Don't worry about me. Happy birthday!"

서술형 실전문제
p.118~120

01 (1) (s)ingle　(2) (t)reating　(3) (e)lderly
02 (1) up　(2) to
03 (1) raise　(2) chew　(3) Order　(4) count
04 can't, to take
05 (1) even　(2) meals　(3) turn　(4) yet
06 (c)hair / (c)hew
07 (1) I saw you enter(또는 entering) the museum.
　(2) I heard my friend laugh(또는 laughing) loudly in English class.
　(3) The kid is too short to reach that book.
　(4) I am so tired that I can't get up early.
08 (A) burning　(B) to carry
09 (1) The shirt is too large to wear.
　(2) I heard Tom talk[talking] about me.
　(3) He is honest enough to tell the truth.
10 with
11 price
12 so, that, couldn't
13 (A) No (B) to pay (C) customer
14 to eat → eat 또는 eating
15 "자신의 식당에서는 그 날의 백 번째 손님이 되면 돈을 내지 않아도 된다."고 말하면서 돈을 받지 않는 것
16 that
17 그의 친구들에게 전화해서 함께 일하는 모든 사람들을 데리고 지금 자신의 식당으로 오라고 말하는 것
18 the 100th customer
19 say 또는 saying
20 get to 또는 reach
21 served a free bowl of Gukbap to the woman

01 (1) only: 유일한 single: 단 하나의, 단일의 / 이것은 이 지역의 유일한 은행이다. (2) deal with: (문제 등을) 다루다 treat: 다루다 / 비조직 범죄를 다룰 수 있는 새로운 방법들이 있다. (3) old: 나이든 elderly: 연세가 드신 / Sarah는 그녀의 나이 든 부모님을 돌본다.

02 (1) think up: ~을 생각해 내다 / 누가 새로운 상품의 이름을 생각해 냈니? pick up: 들어올리다, 집다 / 승객들이 가방을 집어 들고 있다. (2) treat A(사람) to B(사물): A에게 B를 대접하다 / 나는 그들에게 오늘 밤 저녁을 대접할 것이다. say to oneself: 혼잣말을 하다 / Johnson은 항상 혼잣말을 한다.

03 (1) raise: (자금 등을) 모으다 / 그들은 땅을 사기 위해 백만 달러를 모으기를 희망했다. (2) chew: (음식을) 씹다 / 나는 치통 때문에 음식을 잘 씹을 수가 없다. (3) order: (음식, 음료 등을) 주문하다 / 비용을 생각하지 말고 원하는 것을 무엇이든 주문하여라. regardless of: ~에 상관없이 (4) count: 수를 세다, 계산하다 / John은 동물들의 수를 세어야 했다.

04 can't wait to 동사원형: 빨리 ~하고 싶다, ~하는 것이 기다려지다 look forward to 동명사: ~하는 것을 기대하다

05 (1) even: (예상 밖의 놀라운 일을 나타내어) ~도, ~조차 (2) meal: 식사 (3) turn: (무엇을 할) 차례, 순번 (4) yet: (부정문, 의문문에서) 아직(안 했거나 못 했다는 뜻을 나타낼 때)

06 chair: 의자 / 한 사람이 앉기 위한, 등받이와 다리, 때때로 팔걸이가 있는 가구
chew: (음식을) 씹다 / 음식을 삼키기 전에 이로 음식을 부수다

07 (1), (2) 지각동사의 목적어가 목적격보어의 행위의 주체가 될 경우 목적격보어로 원형부정사나 현재분사를 쓰는 것이 적절하다. (3), (4) 'too+형용사/부사+to 동사원형' 구문으로 '너무 ~해서 …할 수 없다, ~하기에는 너무 …하다'는 뜻을 나타내며, 'so+형용사/부사+that+주어+can't[couldn't]+동사원형'의 구문으로 바꾸어 쓸 수 있다.

08 (A) smell은 목적격보어로 현재분사가 적절하다. (B) '너무 ~해서 …할 수 없다, ~하기에는 너무 …하다'는 뜻을 나타내는 'too+형용사/부사+to 동사원형' 구문이다.

09 (1) 'too+형용사/부사+to 동사원형' 구문을 이용한다. (2) 지각동사의 목적격보어로 원형부정사나 현재분사를 쓴다. (3) '형용사/부사+enough+to부정사' 구문은 '~할 만큼 …하다, 충분히 ~해서 …할 수 있다'는 뜻이다.

10 ⓐ with her grandson: 손자와 함께, ⓒ with a smile: 미소 지으며

11 How much is ~? = What's the price of ~?

12 too ~ to = so ~ that 주어 can't

13 (A) '배고프지 않다'고 했으므로 No가 적절하다. (B) 돈을 '내려고 할 때'라고 해야 하므로 to pay가 적절하다. be about to: 막 ~하려는 참이다, (C) (상점의) 고객을 말하는 것이므로 customer가 적절하다. guest: 손님, 하객

14 지각동사는 목적격보어로 동사원형이나 현재분사가 온다.

15 다음에 이어지는 문장의 내용을 쓰면 된다.

16 ⓐ와 ⓓ에는 관계대명사 who나 that, ⓑ에는 접속사 that이 적절하다.

17 그의 친구들에게 전화해서 말한 내용을 쓰는 것이 적절하다.

18 그 소년을 그 날의 '백 번째 손님'이 되게 하고 싶었기 때문이다.

19 hear의 목적격보어로 동사원형이나 현재분사를 쓴다.

20 arrive at = get to = reach: ~에 도착하다

21 serve는 'to'를 사용하여 3형식으로 고친다.

01 ②　　02 (1) (p)ick up　(2) (R)aise, (r)aise

03 (1) She treated him to lunch.

(2) When he called me, I was about to leave.

(3) The girl helped her sister make a cake.

(4) I can't wait to watch it.

04 ③　　05 ⑤　　06 ③　　07 ⑤

08 ③

09 (1) I felt something biting my leg.

(2) We enjoyed listening to the bird sing.

(3) Did you see the children playing soccer on the ground?

10 (1) Kate felt someone touch[touching] her bag.

(2) I didn't hear you call[calling] me.

(3) I watched the boy building a sandcastle at the beach.

(4) I was so young that I couldn't watch the movie.

(5) She got up early enough to catch the first train.

(6) The tea is too hot to drink.

11 (1) She is so shy that she can't ask for help.

(2) The stars in the sky are so many that we can't count them.

(3) The problem is so easy that he can solve it.

12 ②, ⑤　　13 ③

14 to give a free meal to the boy

15 할머니 : 자신은 배고프지 않다고 말하며, 손자에게만 국밥을 사준 것.

Mr. Kang : 할머니와 손자에게 '그 날의 백 번째 손님이 되면 돈을 내지 않아도 된다'고 말하며, 국밥 값을 받지 않은 것.

16 to　　17 ⑤　　18 ②　　19 ③

20 served the woman a free bowl of Gukbap

21 ①　　22 ⑤　　23 ④

24 if you're the 100th customer of the day

25 ⑤

26 (A) himself (B) was (C) gather

27 ④　　28 ②

29 the boy and his grandmother

30 free　　31 ④　　32 ③

33 touched　　34 a free bowl of Gukbap

01 ② 접미사 -er을 붙여 '~하는 것'이라는 뜻의 명사가 되는 동사이다. dry: 건조하다 dryer: 건조기, 드라이어. 이외의 보기들은 접미사 -er을 붙여 '~하는 사람'이라는 뜻의 명사가 되는 동사들이다. ① own: 소유하다 owner: 주인, 소유주 ③ write: 쓰다, (작품·문서 등을) 저술하다 writer: 작가 ④ teach: 가르치다 teacher: 교사 ⑤ produce: 생산하다, 만들다 producer: 생산자, 제작자

02 (1) pick up: 들어올리다, 집다, ~을 (차에) 태우러 가다 / 나는 공항에 내 여동생을 태우러 갈 것이다. • 우리는 길거리의 쓰레기를 주워야 한다. (2) raise: (자금 등을) 모으다, 올리다 / • 정답을 안다면, 손을 올리세요. • 그들은 홍수 이재민을 돕기 위해서 자금을 모았다.

03 (1) treat A(사람) to B(사물): A에게 B를 대접하다 (2) be about to: 막 ~하려는 참이다 (3) help+목적어+동사원형: (목적어)가 ~하는 것을 돕다 (4) can't wait to 동사원형: 빨리 ~하고 싶다, ~하는 것이 기다려지다

04 ③ think up: ~을 생각해 내다 / 나는 더 나은 변명을 생각해 내야 했다.

05 be about to: 막 ~ 하려고 하다 What about ~ing?: ~하는 것이 어때?

06 raise: (자금 등을) 모으다 / 그는 자선기금 모금을 위한 연주회를 열었다.

07 ① It is too hot to go out today. ② He was so poor that he couldn't buy a car. ③ The problem is so easy that he can solve it. ④ Mike felt someone tap[tapping] him on the shoulder.

08 지각동사의 목적격보어로 원형부정사나 현재분사를 써야 한다. I felt the ground shake[shaking] once.

09 지각동사의 목적격보어로 원형부정사나 현재분사를 써야 한다. (1), (3)에는 진행형이 사용되고 있으므로 원형부정사보다는 현재분사가 적절하다.

10 (1)~(3) 지각동사의 목적격보어로 원형부정사나 현재분사를 쓴다. (4)~(6) too+형용사/부사+to+동사원형 = so+형용사/부사+that+주어+can't[couldn't]+동사원형, 형용사/부사+enough+to부정사 = so+형용사/부사+that+주어+can[could]+동사원형

11 too+형용사/부사+to+동사원형 = so+형용사/부사+that+주어+can't[couldn't]+동사원형, 형용사/부사+enough+to부정사 = so+형용사/부사+that+주어+can[could]+동사원형 (2), (3)번의 경우 to부정사의 목적어가 문장의 주어이므로 문제에서는 to부정사의 목적어를 쓰지 않았지만 that절로 바꿀 때는 써 주어야 함에 주의한다.

12 지각동사는 목적격보어로 동사원형이나 현재분사가 온다.

13 ⓐ와 ③번 [때] ~하고 있을 때, ~하면서(접속사), ① ~한 대로(접속사), ② ~로서(전치사), ④ ~라고(전치사), ⑤ [보통 as ... as ~로 형용사·부사 앞에서] ~와 같은 정도로, (앞의 as는 지시부사, 뒤의 as는 접속사)

14 give는 'to'를 사용하여 3형식으로 고친다.

15 할머니는 손자에게, Mr. Kang은 할머니와 손자에게 각각 배려하는 마음을 보였다.

16 ⓐ treat A(사람) to B(사물): A에게 B를 대접하다, ⓑ say to oneself: 혼잣말을 하다

17 주어진 문장의 **do something**에 주목한다. ⑤번 뒤 문장의 내용을 가리키므로 ⑤번이 적절하다.

18 ② 사려 깊은, (남을) 배려하는, ① 끈기 있는, ③ 재미있는, ④ 호기심 많은, ⑤ 외향적인

19 ⓐ와 ③번: 차례, ① 돌다(동사), ② (어떤 나이, 시기가) 되다 (동사), ④ 돌리다(동사), ⑤ (방향) 전환

20 'free'를 보충하면 된다.

21 위 글은 배려와 사랑이 담긴 이야기이므로, 글의 분위기는 '감동적'이라고 하는 것이 적절하다. ① 가슴[마음]을 뭉클하게 하는, 감동적인, ② 우울하게 만드는, 우울한, ③ (특이해서) 웃기는 [재미있는], ④ 비참한, ⑤ 지루한

22 ⑤ 감동한, ① 부끄러운, ② 흥분한, ③ 실망한, ④ 지루한

23 ⓑ와 ④번: 무료의, ① 자유로운, ② 다른 계획[약속]이 없는, ③ (갇히거나 걸린 데서) 풀어 주다[빼내다](동사), ⑤ (새장 등에) 갇혀 있지 않은

24 the 100th: 백 번째의

25 ⑤는 **Mr. Kang**을 가리키고, 나머지는 다 소년을 가리킨다.

26 (A) 주어와 목적어가 같으므로 재귀대명사 himself가 적절하다. (B) the number of는 단수 취급하므로 was가 적절하다. (C) 'help'는 동사원형과 to부정사를 목적격보어로 취하므로 gather가 적절하다.

27 ④ 강 씨가 아래를 내려다보았을 때 돌멩이의 개수가 아직 오십 개도 안 되는 것을 볼 수 있었다고 했기 때문에, 식당의 손님은 아직 오십 명을 넘지 않았다.

28 ⓐ와 ②, ⑤: 명사적 용법, ① 형용사적 용법, ③, ④: 부사적 용법

29 소년과 그의 할머니를 가리킨다.

30 free: 무료의, 비용이 들지 않는

31 위 글은 '일기'이다. ② (신문·잡지의) 글, 기사, ③ 수필, ⑤ (책·연극·영화 등에 대한) 논평[비평], 감상문

32 ③ 오늘 소년은 할머니께 공짜 국밥 한 그릇을 대접하고 싶어 했다.

33 moved = touched: 감동받은

34 free: 무료의, 비용이 들지 않는

교과서 파헤치기

Lesson 7

p.02

단어 TEST Step 1

01 팀 동료
02 완벽한
03 침착한
04 이루다, 달성하다
05 어려움, 곤경, 장애
06 직면하다, 직시하다
07 상
08 무서운
09 실패하다, ~하지 못하다
10 마침내
11 긍정적인
12 점잖은
13 야구의 루
14 인정하다, 알아보다
15 문장
16 비록 ~일지라도
17 재활용하다
18 극복하다
19 얻다, 획득하다
20 우수, 탁월, 뛰어남
21 아픔, 고통
22 주다, 수여하다, 증정하다
23 노력
24 예우하다, ~을 공경하다
25 빌려주다
26 주요한
27 뛰어난
28 존경
29 풀다, 해결하다
30 무례하게
31 지지
32 재능이 있는
33 구, 구절
34 인종 차별
35 마음속으로 생각하다
36 더 이상 ~ 아닌
37 1등을 하다, 우승하다
38 ~을 거절하다, 거부하다, 소리를 줄이다
39 포기하다
40 반복해서
41 A에게 B를 수여하다, 증정하다
42 타석에서
43 눈을 의심하다(놀람)

단어 TEST Step 2

01 achieve
02 calm
03 recognize
04 difficulty
05 perfect
06 earn
07 although
08 excellence
09 pain
10 award
11 excellent
12 positive
13 face
14 recycle
15 respect
16 honor
17 fail
18 solve
19 talented
20 support
21 finally
22 gentle
23 present
24 rudely
25 teammate
26 sentence
27 bat
28 effort
29 lend
30 major
31 overcome
32 terrible
33 stadium
34 base
35 give up
36 think to oneself
37 no longer
38 thanks to
39 over and over
40 win first place
41 turn down
42 present A with B
43 take a class

단어 TEST Step 3

1 excellent, 뛰어난
2 teammate, 팀 동료
3 baseman, (1, 2, 3) 루수
4 fail, 실패하다, ~하지 못하다
5 rudely, 무례하게
6 classical, (음악이) 클래식의

---

7 pain, 아픔, 고통
8 lend, 빌려주다
9 major, 주요한
10 overcome, 극복하다
11 bat, (공을) 치다
12 positive, 긍정적인
13 recognize, 인정하다, 알아보다
14 award, 상
15 calm, 침착한
16 support, 지지

대화문 TEST Step 1

p.05~06

Listen & Speak 1 A

1. find, math problem / too hard, I'm not good at math / Let, see, It's important that, to solve, use
2. looks great / finish yours / draw, How, good at drawing / takes, important, as often as you can / mean, keep practicing / right

Listen & Speak 1 B

1. hard to be, What / important, never give up / not forget
2. hard to, should / It's important that / will not forget

Listen & Speak 2 A

1. hard to do / matter / how to make / What do you mean by / mean, easy to do
2. have, want to win first place / crossed / What do you mean by / means, wish, good luck

Listen & Speak 2 B

1. are better than / What, mean by / mean, together, than working alone
2. Practice, perfect / mean by / mean, by doing, over and over

Conversation A

To achieve, failed, However, give up, took, classes, Finally, achieved, that, never give up

Conversation B

look, wrong / don't think, achieve / What do you mean by that / fail auditions, have to give up / actor / famous / failed more than / should keep trying, practice / It's important that you never give up

대화문 TEST Step 2

p.07~08

Listen & Speak 1 A

1. G: Hey, Minho. Did you find the answer to the math problem?
   B: No. It's too hard for me. I'm not good at math.
   G: Let me see. It's important that you use this math rule to solve the problem.
   B: Oh, I see. I'll use it.

2. G: Your poster looks great.

   B: Thanks, Kate. Did you finish yours?

   G: Not yet. I can't draw well. How can I become good at drawing?

   B: It takes time. It's important that you draw as often as you can.

   G: You mean I should keep practicing?

   B: That's right.

Listen & Speak 1 B

1. A: It's hard to be a good dancer. What should I do?

   B: It's important that you never give up.

   A: Okay. I will not forget that.

2. A: It's hard to write a good story. What should I do?

   B: It's important that you read many books.

   A: Okay. I will not forget that.

Listen & Speak 2 A

1. G: Oh, this is hard to do.

   B: What's the matter?

   G: Can you teach me how to make cookies?

   B: Sure. It's a walk in the park.

   G: What do you mean by that?

   B: I mean it's easy to do.

2. B: I have a singing contest tomorrow. I really want to win first place.

   G: I'll keep my fingers crossed for you.

   B: What do you mean by "keep my fingers crossed"?

   G: It means I wish you good luck.

   B: Thank you.

Listen & Speak 2 B

1. A: Two heads are better than one.

   B: What do you mean by "Two heads are better than one"?

   A: I mean working together is better than working alone.

2. A: Practice makes perfect.

   B: What do you mean by "Practice makes perfect"?

   A: I mean you learn something by doing it over and over.

Conversation A

M: To achieve my dream, I went to many auditions, but I often failed. However, I never gave up. I took acting and dancing classes. Finally, I achieved my goal. It's important that you never give up.

Conversation B

Hana: You look sad, Jiho. What's wrong?

Jiho: I don't think I can achieve my dream.

Amy: What do you mean by that?

Jiho: I want to be an actor, but I always fail auditions.

Maybe I have to give up.

Amy: Do you know this actor?

Jiho: Sure. He's a famous movie star.

Amy: He failed more than 100 auditions.

Jiho: Really? Maybe I should keep trying. I will practice more for my next audition.

Hana: That's right! It's important that you never give up.

본문 TEST Step 1   p.09~10

01 Breaks, Color Line   02 It, on April

03 went on, as, for

04 couldn't believe, eyes

05 first, American, player on

06 color line, broken

07 faced many difficulties

08 Although, talented, gentle, with

09 Every, turned, down because

10 bat, rudely, at

11 thought, himself, keep, focus

12 try, become, like

13 there, be more, league

14 put, energy into

15 With practice, batting, running

16 effort moved, teammates

17 one, up, tapped, on   18 Do, listen to

19 doing fine

20 support helped, to, harder

21 Finally, earned, respect, other

22 Thanks to, won, in

23 recognized, presented, with, same

24 other, asked, to join

25 uniform number

26 no longer, to honor

27 however, every, wears, wore   28 is called

본문 TEST Step 2   p.11~12

01 Breaks the Color Line

02 on April 15, 1947

03 African American, as, for

04 couldn't believe their eyes

05 the first African American player

06 the color line was broken

07 faced many difficulties

08 Although, talented player, to play with him

09 turned the team down

10 was at bat, rudely shouted at

11 thought to himself, keep calm, focus on

12 become, who people like

13 there will be more

14 put, into

15 With practice, at batting, base running

16 effort moved, teammates

17 shouted at, one of his teammates, up to, tapped him on the shoulder

18 Do not listen to   19 doing fine

20 helped, to play harder

21 earned the respect

22 Thanks to, won

23 recognized, presented, with, same year

24 other, asked, to join

25 uniform number

26 no longer wear, to honor him

27 Every, however, wears, wore   28 is called

19 너는 잘하고 있어."라고 그가 말했다.

20 그의 지지는 Robinson이 더 열심히 경기하는 데 도움이 됐다.

21 마침내, Robinson은 다른 선수들과 팬들의 존경을 받았다.

22 Robinson 덕분에 다저스는 1947년에 내셔널리그 챔피언십에서 우승하게 되었다.

23 리그에서는 Robinson의 탁월함을 인정했고, 같은 해에 그에게 신인상을 수여했다.

24 그 시즌 이후, 다른 팀들은 아프리카계 미국인 선수들에게 자신들의 팀에 합류할 것을 요청했다.

25 Robinson의 등 번호는 42번이었다.

26 메이저리그 팀의 야구 선수들은 그에 대한 존경을 보여 주기 위해 더 이상 42번을 달지 않는다.

27 하지만 매년 4월 15일, 모든 선수들은 Robinson이 달았던 번호를 단다.

28 이 날을 '재키 로빈슨 데이'라고 부른다.

1 Jackie Robinson 인종 차별을 깨다

2 1947년 4월 15일 뉴욕시에서였다.

3 아프리카계 미국인 Jackie Robinson은 브루클린 다저스의 2루수로 경기장에 나갔다.

4 사람들은 자신들의 눈을 의심했다.

5 그는 메이저리그 팀에서 경기한 최초의 아프리카계 미국인 선수였다.

6 그날 인종 차별이 깨졌다.

7 Robinson은 많은 어려움에 직면했다.

8 Robinson은 재능 있는 선수이고 온화한 사람이었지만 그의 팀원들은 그와 함께 경기하기를 원하지 않았다.

9 Robinson이 팀에 있었기 때문에 모든 호텔에서 그 팀을 거절했다.

10 그가 타석에 있을 때, 관중석에 있는 사람들이 그에게 무례하게 소리치기도 했다.

11 Robinson은 마음속으로 생각했다. '나는 평정심을 유지하고 야구에 집중해야 해.

12 나는 노력해서 사람들이 좋아하는 선수가 될 거야.

13 그러면 다음 시즌에는 아프리카계 미국인 선수가 리그에 더 많이 생길 거야.'

14 Robinson은 자신의 모든 시간과 에너지를 야구에 집중했다.

15 연습을 함으로써 그는 타격과 주루를 잘하게 되었다.

16 Robinson의 노력은 그의 팀원들을 감동시켰다.

17 사람들이 Robinson에게 소리쳤을 때, 그의 팀 동료 중 한 명이 Robinson에게 다가가 어깨를 두드렸다.

18 "그들 말을 듣지 마.

1 Jackie Robinson Breaks the Color Line

2 It was New York City on April 15, 1947.

3 Jackie Robinson, an African American, went on the field as second baseman for the Brooklyn Dodgers.

4 People couldn't believe their eyes.

5 He was the first African American player to play on a Major League team.

6 That day, the color line was broken.

7 Robinson faced many difficulties.

8 Although Robinson was a talented player and a gentle person, his teammates did not want to play with him.

9 Every hotel turned the team down because Robinson was on the team.

10 When he was at bat, people in the stands rudely shouted at him.

11 Robinson thought to himself, 'I need to keep calm and focus on baseball.

12 I will try and become a player who people like.

13 Then, next season, there will be more African American players in the league.'

14 Robinson put all his time and energy into baseball.

15 With practice, he became great at batting and base running.

16 Robinson's effort moved his teammates.

17 When people shouted at Robinson, one of his

teammates walked up to Robinson and tapped him on the shoulder.

18 "Do not listen to them.

19 You're doing fine," he said.

20 His support helped Robinson to play harder.

21 Finally, Robinson earned the respect of other players and fans.

22 Thanks to Robinson, the Dodgers won the National League Championship in 1947.

23 The league recognized Robinson's excellence and presented him with the Rookie of the Year Award in the same year.

24 After that season, other teams asked African American players to join them.

25 Robinson's uniform number was 42.

26 Baseball players in Major League teams no longer wear the number 42 to honor him.

27 Every year, however, on April 15, every player wears the number that Robinson wore.

28 The day is called "Jackie Robinson Day."

2. France was the first country which I visited.

3. Mary is the girl who I met in Paris.

4. The blue watch is the gift which I bought there for my brother.

Enjoy Writing B

1. How I Will Achieve My Dream

2. I want to be a designer.

3. There are three things that I need to do to achieve my dream.

4. I need to be healthy, be creative, and never give up.

5. Being healthy will help me keep going for my dream.

6. Being creative will help me do something different.

7. Plus, I will always tell myself never to give up because it will make me try harder.

Wrap Up 2

1. B: It's difficult to learn English.

2. G: Rome was not built in a day.

3. B: What do you mean by that?

4. G: I mean it takes time to achieve something.

5. B: I see .

구석구석지문 TEST Step 1 　　p.19

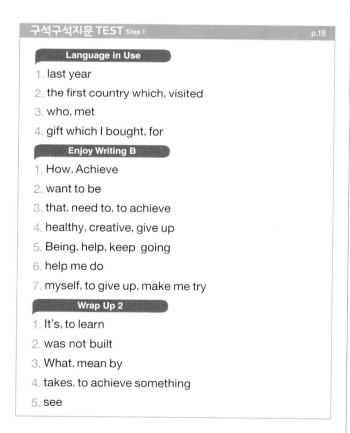

Language in Use

1. last year

2. the first country which, visited

3. who, met

4. gift which I bought, for

Enjoy Writing B

1. How, Achieve

2. want to be

3. that, need to, to achieve

4. healthy, creative, give up

5. Being, help, keep going

6. help me do

7. myself, to give up, make me try

Wrap Up 2

1. It's, to learn

2. was not built

3. What, mean by

4. takes, to achieve something

5. see

구석구석지문 TEST Step 2 　　p.20

Language in Use

1. I visited three countries last year.

9 decorate, 장식하다, 꾸미다　10 app, 애플리케이션
11 virtual, 가상의　12 station, 역, 정류장
13 advance, 발전　14 drone, (원격 조종의) 드론
15 law, 법칙, 법　16 charge, (지불, 대금 등을) 청구하다

단어 TEST Step 1　p.21

01 계산대	02 자동적으로	03 상태, 조건
04 가격	05 ~을 추천하다	06 장식하다, 꾸미다
07 약	08 재료	09 사회
10 구조하다	11 과학 기술, 생산 기술	
12 (치수·모양 등이) 꼭 맞다		13 발전
14 온도	15 경험	
16 (지불, 대금 등을) 청구하다		
17 화려한, 공들인, 고급의		18 낮추다
19 기술	20 구입(품)	21 거대한
22 나중에, 후에	23 가상의	24 차이, 차이점
25 심하게, 아주 많이	26 법칙, 법	27 ~ 이후로
28 중력	29 배달하다	30 (돈을) 지불하다
31 방법, 방식	32 작동하다	33 환자
34 진짜의	35 ~할 것을 잊다	36 공중에
37 ~을 돌보다	38 ~할 준비가 되다	39 입다, 쓰다, 신다
40 돌아다니다	41 일어나다, 개최되다	
42 미래에	43 ~하고 싶다	

단어 TEST Step 2　p.22

01 heavily	02 automatically	03 charge
04 librarian	05 condition	06 work
07 experience	08 save	09 advance
10 fit	11 gravity	12 huge
13 since	14 price	15 deliver
16 decorate	17 lower	18 rescue
19 skill	20 temperature	21 recommend
22 medicine	23 patient	24 difference
25 virtual	26 purchase	27 method
28 society	29 taste	30 material
31 offer	32 guess	33 pay
34 technology	35 take place	36 be ready for
37 put on	38 add up	39 take care of
40 don't have to 동사원형		41 move around
42 be worried about		43 in trouble

단어 TEST Step 3　p.23

1 medicine, 약　2 rescue, 구조하다
3 automatically, 자동적으로　4 patient, 환자
5 material, 재료　6 recommend, ~을 추천하다
7 method, 방법, 방식　8 deliver, 배달하다

대화문 TEST Step 1　p.24~25

Listen & Speak 1 A

1. forgot to turn off / need to return / turn, off / surprised that, off, with
2. Welcome to, like to visit / put, on / right, looks / isn't it / I'm surprised

Listen & Speak 1 B

1. there, surprises / surprised, walk
2. there anything, that surprises / I'm surprised that, itself automatically

Listen & Speak 2 A

1. help / looking for, show me one / Look at, for / Sounds / search for, by talking / will take
2. don't have to use, turn, on, off / tell, how to / on, out / on, simple

Listen & Speak 2 B

1. play, play . Sure
2. messy, clean
3. to go out, walk

Conversation A

work like, travel without, simple, by talking to, I'm surprised that, already living

Conversation B

are, books / Where can, gravity / librarian / looking for, gravity, recommend / fifty seven books / that you can recommend books / amazing / on, third floor

대화문 TEST Step 2　p.26~27

Listen & Speak 1 A

1. G: Oh, I forgot to turn off the heater before I left home.
   B: Really? Then do you need to return home?
   G: No. I can turn it off with my smartphone.
   B: Wow, I'm surprised that you can turn off the heater with your smartphone.
2. W: Welcome to VR World. Would you like to visit Niagara Falls?
   B: Sure.
   W: Okay, put this on.

B: All right. Wow, it looks so real.

W: It is huge, isn't it?

B: Yes, and I'm surprised that I feel water on my face.

Listen & Speak 1 B

1. A: Is there anything in these pictures that surprises you?

   B: Yes. I'm surprised that this drone can walk a dog.

2. A: Is there anything in these pictures that surprises you?

   B: Yes. I'm surprised that this car can drive itself automatically.

Listen & Speak 2 A

1. W: May I help you?

   B: Hi, I'm looking for a smart watch. Can you show me one?

   W: Sure. Look at this one. It can play music for you.

   B: Sounds cool.

   W: Also, you can search for anything just by talking to it.

   B: That's great. I will take it.

2. M: Welcome. This is our new smart light. You don't have to use your hands to turn it on and off.

   W: Really? Then can you tell me how to do it?

   M: Just say, "Light on!" or "Light out!"

   W: Light on or light out? That's very simple.

Listen & Speak 2 B

1. A: I want to play go. Can you play go with me, please?

   B: Sure.

2. A: My room is messy. Can you clean it, please?

   B: Sure.

3. A: The dog wants to go out. Can you walk the dog, please?

   B: Sure.

Conversation A

M: These days, many things can work like humans. Some cars can travel without a human driver. We can make smartphones do simple work only by talking to them. I'm surprised that we're already living in the future.

Conversation B

Amy: Wow, there are so many books in this library.

Hana: You're right. Where can we find books about gravity?

Terry: Hi, I'm Terry, the AI librarian. Can I help you?

Amy: Hi. We're looking for books about gravity. Can

you recommend one, please?

Terry: We have fifty seven books about gravity in this library. I think *The Law of Gravity* will be the best one for you.

Hana: I'm surprised that you can recommend books.

Amy: Right. That's amazing. Where is the book, Terry?

Terry: It's on the third floor. Come with me.

본문 TEST Step 1   p.28~29

01 Changing Society

02 Advances, caused, so far

03 future, make, changes

04 what, like, near

05 Shopping Center   06 much easier

07 There, lines, counters

08 enters, with, special, app

09 shop, takes, items

10 items, automatically added, virtual

11 puts, back, automatically removed

12 shopping, need, line, pay

13 adds up, charge, later   14 Isn't, fancy

15 Printed House, Clothes

16 lives, 3D printed

17 Building, cheaper, with, methods

18 looks fantastic, unique

19 produce, shapes, traditional, materials

20 also, clothes, by using

21 choose, fit, suit, tastes

22 fashion designer   23 in, Hospital

24 visiting, grandfather, hospital

25 AI nurse enters

26 moves around, checks, conditions

27 high temperature, medicine, lower

28 Have, thought, changes

29 take place, others, near

30 imagine other changes

31 Take, think about

본문 TEST Step 2   p.30~31

01 Changing

02 Advances, technology have caused, changes, so far

03 In the future, make more changes

04 Let's, may be like, near

05 Shopping Center

31

06 much easier   07 no lines, no counters

08 with, special shopping app

09 takes the items

10 are automatically added to, virtual

11 puts, back, is automatically removed from, list of purchases

12 shopping, does not need to, in line

13 adds up, prices, charge, later

14 Isn't, fancy   15 3D Printed, Clothes

16 lives, 3D printed

17 Building, faster and cheaper, with traditional methods

18 looks fantastic

19 house shapes, traditional building methods and materials

20 her clothes, by using

21 that fit, suit, tastes

22 fashion designer   23 in the Hospital

24 is visiting   25 An AI, enters

26 moves around, checks, conditions

27 high temperature, to lower his temperature

28 Have you ever thought

29 take place, others, in the near future

30 imagine other changes

31 Take some time to think

14 정말 멋지지 않은가?

15 수민이의 3D 프린터로 만든 집과 옷

16 수민이는 3D 프린터로 만든 집에 산다.

17 3D 프린터로 집을 짓는 것은 전통적인 방법으로 집을 짓는 것보다 더 빠르고 저렴하다.

18 수민이의 집은 독특한 디자인 때문에 멋져 보인다.

19 3D 프린터는 사람들이 전통 건축 방법과 재료들로 만들 수 없는 집 모양을 만들어 낼 수 있다.

20 수민이는 또한 집에서 3D 프린터를 사용해 옷을 만드는 것을 좋아한다.

21 그녀는 색깔과 재료를 고를 수 있고 자신의 몸과 취향에 맞는 옷을 디자인할 수 있다.

22 수민이는 이제 패션 디자이너이다!

23 병원에 있는 동민

24 동민이는 병원에 계시는 그의 할아버지를 방문하고 있다.

25 AI 간호사가 병실로 들어온다.

26 그것은 병실을 돌아다니고, 환자들의 상태를 확인한다.

27 AI 간호사가 동민이 할아버지가 열이 높다는 것을 알았을 때 그것은 그의 체온을 낮추기 위해 그에게 약을 준다.

28 여러분은 이러한 변화에 대해 생각해 본 적 있는가?

29 어떤 변화는 이미 일어나기 시작했고 반면 다른 것들은 가까운 미래에 일어날지도 모른다.

30 여러분은 다른 변화들을 상상할 수 있는가?

31 그것들에 대해 잠깐 생각해 보자.

1 변화하는 사회

2 과학과 기술의 발전은 지금까지 우리의 삶에 많은 변화를 초래해 왔다.

3 미래에 과학 기술은 더 많은 변화를 만들 것이다.

4 가까운 미래에 우리의 삶이 어떻게 될지 살펴보자.

5 쇼핑 센터에 있는 상호

6 쇼핑이 훨씬 쉽다.

7 줄도 없고 계산대도 없다.

8 상호는 특별한 쇼핑 앱이 있는 스마트폰을 가지고 가게로 들어간다.

9 가게에서 그는 그가 원하는 물건들을 집는다.

10 그 물건들은 자동으로 그의 스마트폰에 있는 가상 카드에 더해진다.

11 만약 상호가 물건을 되돌려 놓으면 그것은 자동으로 그의 구매 목록에서 제거된다.

12 쇼핑을 끝냈을 때 상호는 돈을 지불하기 위해 줄을 설 필요가 없다.

13 그의 가상 카드가 모든 가격을 더해서 나중에 그에게 청구할 것이다.

1 Changing Society

2 Advances in science and technology have caused many changes in our lives so far.

3 In the future, science and technology will make more changes.

4 Let's see what our lives may be like in the near future.

5 Sangho in the Shopping Center

6 Shopping is much easier.

7 There are no lines and no counters.

8 Sangho enters a shop with his smartphone which has a special shopping app.

9 In the shop, he takes the items he wants.

10 The items are automatically added to a virtual card on his smartphone.

11 If Sangho puts an item back, it is automatically removed from his list of purchases.

12 When he finishes shopping, Sangho does not need to wait in line to pay.

13 His virtual card adds up all the prices and will charge him later.

14 Isn't that fancy?

15 Sumin's 3D Printed House and Clothes

16 Sumin lives in a 3D printed house.

17 Building a 3D printed house is faster and cheaper than building a house with traditional methods.

18 Sumin's house looks fantastic because of its unique design.

19 A 3D printer can produce house shapes that people cannot make with traditional building methods and materials.

20 Sumin also likes to make her clothes at home by using a 3D printer.

21 She can choose colors and materials and can design clothes that fit her body and suit her tastes.

22 Sumin is now a fashion designer!

23 Dongmin in the Hospital

24 Dongmin is visiting his grandfather in the hospital.

25 An AI nurse enters the room.

26 It moves around the room and checks the patients' conditions.

27 When the AI nurse finds that Dongmin's grandfather has a high temperature, it gives him some medicine to lower his temperature.

28 Have you ever thought about these changes?

29 Some changes have already started to take place while others may start in the near future.

30 Can you imagine other changes?

31 Take some time to think about them.

Enjoy Writing B

1. in, Years

2. Have, thought, how schools may change

3. may learn

4. Cleaning, may help

5. There may be, in every school

6. may go, two or three times

Project

1. Have, imagined, in the future

2. may, in their daily lives

3. may be traffic lights

4. A lot of, may be created, in lots of ways

Wrap Up 1

1. Are, ready for

2. worried about getting lost, good at finding

3. Don't, There are, apps you can use

4. show me one

5. shows you a map, pictures of streets

6. thanks

Enjoy Writing B

1. Schools in 20 Years

2. Have you ever thought of how schools may change over the next 20 years?

3. Students may learn drone design.

4. Cleaning drones may help students at school.

5. There may be an AI teachers' room in every school.

6. Students may go to school only two or three times a week.

Project

1. Have you ever imagined life in the future?

2. People may use personal drones in their daily lives.

3. So there may be traffic lights for drones in the sky.

4. A lot of AI helpers may be created soon and they may help humans in lots of ways.

Wrap Up 1

1. G: Are you ready for your trip to London?

2. B: Yes, but I'm worried about getting lost. I'm not good at finding places.

3. G: Don't worry. There are many good smartphone apps you can use.

4. B: Can you show me one?

5. G: Sure. Use this one. It shows you a map of the city and pictures of streets.

6. B: Oh, thanks.

Lesson **S**

단어 TEST Step 1   p.40

01 단 하나의, 단일의 02 휴식, (학교의) 쉬는 시간

03 (가볍게) 톡톡 두드리다, 치다   04 의자

05 생산자, 제작자   06 주인, 소유주

07 (무엇을 할) 차례, 순번

08 (부정문, 의문문에서) 아직

09 수를 세다, 계산하다

10 (음식, 음료 등을) 주문하다   11 연세가 드신

12 손자   13 (음식을) 씹다   14 만일 ~라면

15 ~도, ~조차   16 (자금 등을) 모으다

17 식사   18 손님, 고객   19 소설

20 침실   21 참가자, 선수, 배우 22 계산대

23 대접하다, 다루다 24 (우묵한) 그릇, 통 25 ~해야 한다

26 막 ~하려는 참이다

27 A에게 B를 대접하다

28 빨리 ~하고 싶다, ~하는 것이 기다려지다

29 들어올리다, 집다, ~을 (차에) 태우러 가다

30 혼잣말을 하다   31 (목적어)가 ~하는 것을 돕다

32 ~을 생각해 내다

단어 TEST Step 2   p.41

01 bedroom   02 counter   03 producer

04 chew   05 tap   06 turn

07 yet   08 order   09 player

10 chair   11 treat   12 elderly

13 count   14 bowl   15 raise

16 owner   17 break   18 grandson

19 if   20 meal   21 customer

22 novel   23 even   24 single

25 think up   26 have to 동사원형

27 pick up   28 treat A(사람)을 to B(사물)

29 help+목적어+동사원형

30 can't wait to 동사원형   31 be about to

32 say to oneself

단어 TEST Step 3   p.42

1 owner, 주인   2 single, 단 하나의   3 grandson, 손자

4 bedroom, 침실   5 novel, 소설   6 customer, 손님, 고객

7 treat, 대접하다   8 chew, (음식을) 씹다   9 meal, 식사

10 counter, 계산대   11 think up, ~을 생각해 내다

12 chair, 의자

본문 TEST Step 1   p.43~44

01 100th Customer   02 elderly, walked into

03 with her grandson   04 Quietly, asked, owner

05 How much, bowl   06 answered with, smile

07 poor, pay, bowls

08 ordered, single, grandson

09 sure, hungry, as, ate   10 No, hungry

11 Don't worry

12 picked up, chewed on

13 eat, feeling, over   14 thought up, free meal

15 about, pay, waved, need

16 pay if, 100th customer

17 woman, thanked, left

18 month later, saw, outside

19 was gathering stones

20 What, doing, asked

21 counting, number, who enter

22 Today is, grandma's

23 treat, to, bowl, himself

24 looked down   25 number, was, even

26 had, to help, gather   27 went back into, called

28 bring everyone, works with

29 There, needs, help

30 to arrive at   31 arrived, heard, turn

32 welcomed, served, free bowl

33 sure, hungry, asked

34 chewed loudly, with, smile

35 Don't worry, me

본문 TEST Step 2   p.45~46

01 100th Customer   02 elderly, walked into

03 with her grandson

04 Quietly, asked, the owner

05 How much, a bowl of   06 with a smile

07 too poor to pay

08 single, for her grandson 09 Are you sure, ate

10 No, not hungry   11 Don't worry about

12 chewed on, happily

13 watched, eat, came over

14 thought up, to give the boy a free meal

15 was about to pay, waved

16 pay, the 100th customer 17 thanked Mr. Kang

18 A month later, saw, outside

19 was gathering stones

20 What, doing   21 counting, who

22 Today is   23 treat, said to himself

24 looked down

34 정답 및 해설

25 the number, was, even fifty

26 to help

27 went back into, called

28 bring everyone who works with

29 who needs your help

30 began to arrive at　　31 It's our turn

32 welcomed them, served, a free bowl of Gukbap

33 Are you sure

34 chewed loudly, with a smile

35 Don't worry

본문 TEST Step 3　　　　　　　　　　p.47~48

1 백 번째 손님

2 어느 날 한 할머니가 식당으로 걸어 들어왔다.

3 그녀는 손자와 함께 있었다.

4 그녀는 조용히 식당 주인인 강 씨에게 물었다.

5 "국밥 한 그릇이 얼마인가요?"

6 "4,000원입니다, 할머니." 강 씨는 미소 지으며 답했다.

7 그녀는 너무 가난해서 두 그릇 값을 지불할 수 없었다.

8 그녀는 손자를 위해 한 그릇을 주문했다.

9 "정말 배고프지 않으세요, 할머니?" 남자아이는 따뜻한 국물을 먹으며 물었다.

10 "응, 난 배고프지 않단다.

11 내 걱정하지 마라."

12 그녀는 행복하게 김치를 집어서 먹었다.

13 강 씨는 그들이 먹는 것을 지켜보았고, 따뜻한 감정이 밀려왔다.

14 그는 남자아이에게 무료로 식사를 주기 위해 계획을 생각해 냈다.

15 할머니가 돈을 내려고 할 때, 강 씨는 손을 흔들며 말했다. "필요 없습니다, 할머니.

16 저희 식당에서는 그 날의 백 번째 손님이 되면 돈을 내지 않아도 됩니다."

17 할머니와 손자는 강 씨에게 감사해 하며 떠났다.

18 한 달 후, 강 씨는 식당 밖 거리에서 그 남자아이를 보았다.

19 그 남자아이는 돌멩이를 모으고 있었다.

20 "너 뭐 하고 있니?" 강 씨가 물었다.

21 "저는 아저씨 식당에 들어가는 손님들의 수를 세고 있어요.

22 오늘이 우리 할머니 생신이거든요."

23 '저 아이는 백 번째 손님이 되어서 할머니께 공짜 국밥 한 그릇을 대접하고 싶어 하는구나.' 강 씨는 혼잣말을 했다.

24 강 씨는 아래를 내려다보았다.

25 그는 돌멩이의 개수가 아직 오십 개도 안 되는 것을 볼 수 있었다.

26 그는 남자아이가 돌멩이 백 개를 모으는 것을 돕기 위해 무언가를 해야 했다.

27 강 씨는 식당으로 되돌아가 그의 친구들에게 전화했다.

28 "지금 내 식당으로 오고, 자네와 함께 일하는 모든 사람들을 데려와 주게.

29 자네 도움이 필요한 남자아이가 있어."

30 사람들이 식당에 도착하기 시작했다.

31 아흔아홉 번째 손님이 도착했을 때 강 씨는 남자아이가 "우리 차례예요, 할머니."라고 말하는 것을 들었다.

32 강 씨는 그들을 반기며 할머니께 공짜 국밥 한 그릇을 제공했다.

33 "너 정말 배고프지 않니?" 할머니가 남자아이에게 물었다.

34 남자아이는 큰 소리로 김치를 씹고 미소 지으며 말했다. "네, 전 배고프지 않아요, 할머니.

35 제 걱정 마세요. 생신 축하드려요!"

본문 TEST Step 4 · Step 5　　　　　　　p.49~52

1 The 100th Customer

2 One day, an elderly woman walked into a restaurant.

3 She was with her grandson.

4 Quietly, the woman asked Mr. Kang, the owner of the restaurant.

5 "How much is a bowl of Gukbap?"

6 "It's 4,000 won, ma'am," Mr. Kang answered with a smile.

7 She was too poor to pay for two bowls.

8 She ordered a single bowl for her grandson.

9 "Are you sure you are not hungry, Grandma?" the boy asked, as he ate the hot soup.

10 "No, I'm not hungry.

11 Don't worry about me."

12 She picked up some Gimchi and chewed on it happily.

13 Mr. Kang watched them eat, and a warm feeling came over him.

14 He thought up a plan to give the boy a free meal.

15 When the woman was about to pay, Mr. Kang waved his hands and said, "No need, ma'am.

16 In my restaurant, you don't pay if you're the 100th customer of the day."

17 The woman and her grandson thanked Mr. Kang and left.

18 A month later, Mr. Kang saw the boy in the street outside the restaurant.

19 The boy was gathering stones.

20 "What are you doing?" asked Mr. Kang.

21 "I'm counting the number of customers who enter your restaurant.

22 Today is my grandma's birthday."

23 'He wants to be the 100th customer and treat his grandmother to a bowl of Gukbap!' Mr. Kang said to himself.

24 Mr. Kang looked down.

25 He could see that the number of stones was not yet even fifty.

26 He had to do something to help the boy gather 100 stones.

27 Mr. Kang went back into the restaurant and called his friends.

28 "Come to my restaurant now and bring everyone who works with you.

29 There is a boy who needs your help."

30 People began to arrive at the restaurant.

31 When the 99th customer arrived, Mr. Kang heard the boy say, "It's our turn, Grandma."

32 Mr. Kang welcomed them and served the woman a free bowl of Gukbap.

33 "Are you sure you're not hungry?" the woman asked the boy.

34 The boy chewed loudly on some Gimchi and said with a smile, "No, I'm not hungry, Grandma.

35 Don't worry about me. Happy birthday!"

적중100
영어 기출 문제집

정답 및 해설

시사 | 박준언